To Bob For Happy Running Adventures, Love Helen x

First published 2018 by Soap Box Books
www.soapboxbooks.co.uk
Copyright © 2018 Helen Hall

All rights reserved. No part of this publication may be reproduced, stored in or introduced into a retrieval system, or transmitted, in any form, or by any means (electronic, mechanical, photocopying, recording or otherwise) without the prior written permission of the author. Any person who does any unauthorised act in relation to this publication may be liable to criminal prosecution and civil claims for damages.

ISBN: 978-1-907261-09-1

Printed by Book Empire

Book Design and Illustrations by Doozer Design

Studio Photography/Videography by Dave Newton of Photopositive

Title conceived at BoB School's Brand DNA workshop with Linzi Boyd and Darren Shirlaw

Grateful acknowledgement goes to Penguin Books for their permission to reprint the short excerpt from Norman Doidge's book "The Brain's Way of Healing" on page 40. Text copyright © Norman Doidge, 2015, 2016.

PRAISE FOR 'EVEN WITH YOUR SHOES ON'

Helen, you might have expected me to give you some constructive feedback on how to improve certain aspects of the book, but I would honestly struggle to do so. I think this is an outstanding piece of work. And now that I have seen and read it, I am surprised how fast you managed to write it. That shows deep knowledge and passion for the subject, which is what will attract many people to read the book, when combined with tangible improvements in their running, performances and well-being.

The reaction that surprised me the most was from the kids when we played with the QR links. What attracted their attention was the graphic titles, like "Is there poo on my shoe?" They then completely got into watching the videos and doing the exercises. This is such a great addition to the book. The visual teaching is essential and accessible in such an easy way.

Sebastien Motte, Account Director at Huawei Technologies

Helen Hall is the reason I enjoy running down hills ... and usually overtake people whilst doing so! In *Even With Your Shoes On* Helen reminds us that our bodies were designed to move and run, but that many of us have forgotten how. She breaks efficient and natural running down into the bare essentials, and explains her rationale as she builds it back up in a series of steps that are intuitive and easy to follow. As you put the steps into practice you will have - as I did, working with Helen - so many wonderful "aha" moments, as it all begins to click ...

Cat St Clair, Distance Trail Runner

I'm so impressed and honoured to be part of the new movement that this book is sure to generate.

It brings a whole new approach to improving running form, combining clear guidance on improving technique with an array of practical exercises, backed up by years of practical experience and theory.

YOU HAVE BRAINS IN YOUR HEAD.
YOU HAVE FEET IN YOUR SHOES.
YOU CAN STEER YOURSELF
ANY DIRECTION YOU CHOOSE.
YOU'RE ON YOUR OWN.
AND YOU KNOW WHAT YOU KNOW.
AND YOU ARE THE GUY WHO'LL DECIDE WHERE TO GO.

DR SEUSS, OH, THE PLACES YOU'LL GO!

Efficiency of running form, efficiency of walking form, efficacy of the training programme ... and WujWum spark plugs. See you when your body and soul are ready for their next adventure ... with or without your shoes.

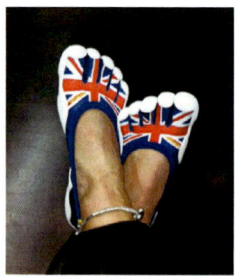

Helen

WHAT'S NEXT?

I'll leave you now, reluctantly. There's so much more to share, but if I don't let you get on with it you won't be ready to continue your running journey with me.

As an efficient runner, full of the joy that great running brings, you might want to discover ways of efficiently training for the kinds of endurance events that might previously have seemed impossible. So, having followed the trail creating your first running pyramid using this book, in due course there'll be another pyramid for you to build; another book.

My running friends have been working hard at SHMERF Club (Saturday Hill Madness Efficient Running Fun) - with their weekly subs split evenly between the charities of William's Fund, Beat and Young Minds Trust **http://www.williamsfund.co.uk/ https://www.beateatingdisorders.org.uk/ https://youngminds.org.uk/**. It's a win-win-win-win. I get to test my coaching concepts thoroughly before recording them in print, they get a feel-good glow through their efforts and donations, the charities get much-needed dosh and those that do the work will be ready for a huge adventure.

Really big. 400 kilometres of big over 8 days with terrain so difficult to cross and navigate that making the cut-offs is a real concern. A team of us are going to be heading out to run Britain's toughest trail, to explore a part of the world so remote that the term 'wilderness' truly still applies.

And why? I think writer and runner, Kristin Armstrong, summed it up beautifully when she said: *"There is something magical about running; after a certain distance, it transcends the body. Then a bit further it transcends the mind. A bit further yet, and what you have before you, laid bare, is the soul."*

None of the team are even close to being ready, and that's OK because the goal is 2020. Having said that, preparation has started. It's a big project and I'll be applying all the pending content of the next book; developing running for epic endurance challenges. Yes, you need muscular strength, of course you need durability and many are familiar with the aspect of ultra events being 'more mental than physical', but the key to success is *WujWuming spark plugs incorporated into fabulously fruitful training sessions*.

- *The Big Book of Endurance Training and Racing* by Dr Philip Maffetone
- *Like The Wind: it's why we run - a quarterly magazine, a collection of stories by runners, for runners*, beautifully illustrated and created by Simon Freeman and Julie Freeman Kummer
- *Primal body, Primal Mind* by Nora Gedgaudasl
- *Death by Food Pyramid* by Denise Minger
- *The Art and Science of Low Carbohydrate Performance* by Jeff Volek PhD and Stephen Phinney MD
- *Grain Brain: The Surprising Truth about Wheat, Carbs and Sugar - Your Brain's Silent Killers* by Dr David Perlmutter
- *Explain Pain* by David Butler and Lorimer Moseley
- *Painful Yarns: metaphors & stories to help understand the biology of pain* by Dr Lorimer Moseley
- *The Other Brain: The Scientific and Medical Breakthroughs that will Heal Our Brains and Revolutionize Our Health* by R Douglas Fields, PhD
- *The Brain That Changes Itself: Stories of Personal Triumph from the Frontiers of Brain Science* by Norman Doidge
- *The Brain's Way of Healing: Stories of Remarkable Recoveries and Discoveries* by Norman Doidge
- *Being Human: Life Lessons from the Frontiers of Science (on Audible)* by Professor Robert Sapolsky
- *Stalking The Wild Pendulum: on the Mechanics of Consciousness* by Itzhak Bentov
- *The Biology of Belief: Unleashing the Power of Consciousness, Matter & Miracles* by Bruce H Lipton, PhD
- *The Breakthrough Experience* by Dr John F Demartini
- *The Seven Spiritual Laws of Success* by Deepak Chopra
- *The Celestine Prophecy* by James Redfield
- *The Alchemist: A Fable About Following Your Dream* by Paula Coelho
- *Abundance Now* by Lisa Nichols
- *The Seven Paths: Changing One's Way of Walking in the World* by the ANASAZI Foundation
- *Rising Strong* by Brene Brown
- *Unravelling: Letting Go - Getting Well* by Philip M Greenfield

Appendix 3:

 Just A Few References + My Bookshelf - those well-used, dog-eared books that have most influenced my understanding and thought processes:

- Ways of learning: see Fleming, N., and Mills, C., 1992, *Not Another Inventory, Rather a Catalyst for Reflection*, Published in: *To Improve the Academy*, Vol. 11, Page 137.
- About sitting too long: **http://fitness.mercola.com/sites/fitness/archive/2015/05/08/sitting-too-long.aspx).**
- Dart, R.A. "*Voluntary Musculature In The Human Body - The Double-Spiral Arrangement*", The British Journal of Physical Medicine. Dec 1950 Vol 13 No 12.
- *What The Foot? A game changing philosophy of human movement eliminating pain and maximising human potential* by Gary Ward
- *Atlas of Human Anatomy* by Frank Netter, MD
- *Anatomy Trains: Myofascial Meridians for Manual & Movement Therapists* by Thomas W Myers
- *Manual of Structural Kinesiology* by RT Floyd
- *Multidisciplinary Approaches to Breathing Pattern Disorders* by Leon Chaitow, Dinah Bradley and Christopher Gilbert
- *Muscles and Meridians: the manipulation of shape* by Phillip Beach
- *Healthy Intelligent Training: The Proven Principles of Arthur Lydiard* by Keith Livingstone
- *Born To Walk: Myofascial Efficiency and the Body in Movement* by James Earls
- *The Story of the Human Body: Evolution, Health & Disease* by Professor Daniel Lieberman
- *Eat, Move and Be Healthy!* by Paul Chek
- *Movement that Matters* by Paul Chek
- *Alignment Matters* by Katy Bowman
- *Move Your DNA* by Katy Bowman
- *Move Without Pain* by Martha Peterson
- *Born To Run: The hidden tribe, the ultra-runners and the greatest race the world has never seen* by Christopher McDougall
- *Running With The Kenyans: Discovering the secrets of the fastest people on earth* by Adharanand Finn
- *Feet in the Clouds: A Tale of Fell-Running and Obsession* by Richard Askwith
- *Once A Runner* by John L Parker, Jr
- *Slow Burn: Burn Fat Faster by Exercising Slower* by Stu Mittleman
- *Why We Run: A Natural History* by Bernd Heinrich

If the first thing you're thinking of doing when you walk towards your front door at the end of the day is kick your shoes off - not because of 'indoor' rules but because your feet want to be shot of them - consider changing those shoes. Your feet are talking to you, and you'll probably find life more enjoyable - certainly more comfortable - if you listen.

200 000 nerve endings.

Clever feet ... with a pretty clever body on top, ready to react to what happens 'down below'.

Just a few thoughts ...

If either consideration of footwear choice - or the impact of footwear on feet - is new science to you, you might want to check out a few images on the internet:

1: Chinese Lotus Feet are universally abhorred, causing extreme deformity:
https://www.theguardian.com/artanddesign/gallery/2015/jun/15/unbound-chinas-last-lotus-feet-in-pictures

2: This link takes you to many images of feet, both ones found habitually inside shoes (shoe-shaped ... and considered 'normal'!) and the now-famous images of habitually bare feet of native populations in the Philippines and Central Africa, taken from a study performed well over 100 years ago and published in 1905 in the American Journal of Orthopedic Surgery. Note that the widest part of the constantly bare foot is NOT where the toes meet the foot bones as we would normally measure it, but from the tip of the big toe to the tip of the little toe; a line can be drawn that runs through the heel, ball and big toe with the toes spreading naturally to fan out and provide a wide, stable base for standing, walking and running.
https://goo.gl/images/K13U4w

When I fitted footwear on a daily basis, it was not uncommon for me to listen to someone telling themselves that the smaller shoe felt better, because it was 'snugger', when the truth was they felt the next size up made their feet 'look big'. I know this, because I heard them say that too. Bums, noses and feet! Isn't it interesting that 'smaller' so often gets to be considered as 'better' in the context of only *certain* body parts?

Look at your own feet, and those of your family and friends. Look at your shoes. Look at your socks. Recent studies have shown that even the fabric around the feet of a baby in an all-in-one suit can interfere with the normal development of the foot structure. Studies in Finland have shown that toe socks worn by children can improve their balance and co-ordination. Instead of being herded into the tubular shape of sock-ends, the toes are freed to enable more function.

Footwear: of course it's about personal choice, but informed choice is surely better than just choosing what 'looks good', or even more scary, what looks 'normal'.

FOOTWEAR OPTIONS

In terms of 'technical', barefoot is right up there ... 200,000 nerve endings, 34 muscles, 26 bones, 33 joints and 19 ligaments. Your feet are home to more than 25% of the bones in your body. I know I've already said that, but it's so awe-inspiring it deserves to be mentioned again. Most folk I meet have no idea there's so much going on down there.

If some kind of protective thick skin is preferred then it seems to me that if we consider **all 4** criteria listed below we might perhaps interfere with our innate brilliance less:

- **Maximum of 5mm** lift from the ball of the foot to the heel in order to minimise the counterbalance effect.

These days, most manufacturers put the heel to toe differential in their shoe technical specifications. And be cautious of labels; 'racing flats' are rarely zero differential and many are +5mm differential. Just to give you an idea of what the numbers mean:
  - A 22mm rise from the ball of the foot to the heel represents a 14.7% incline to the foot.
  - An 18mm differential inflicts a 12% incline on the foot.
  - 14mm of rise from toe box to heel is a 9.3% incline on which your foot rests.
  - A 12mm differential equates to a 8% gradient. Ever cycled up an 8% hill? It's steep!
  - A 10mm differential = 6.7% gradient.

- **Minimal cushioning** to give adequate and timely afferent feedback through the sensory nerve endings, and minimise impact forces through self-protective running form.

- **Light-weight** to reduce wasted effort in carrying heavy feet.

- **Space** for the foot to spread both lengthways (your foot gets longer in pronation) and widthways (your foot gets wider in pronation):
  - Those long foot bones have muscles between them that want to be used.
  - The bones want to move.
  - Everything wants to move to help you move!
  - A 'snug-fit' rather defeats the object of a 33-jointed appendage, no? Talking of which, stop pulling those laces tight!!

making it hit the chest wall. Elastic recoil has much more energy – with no effort! Adding insult to injury, a continually foreshortened Achilles tendon is one that will ultimately pull on the muscle controlling it, stressing that too.

But is there anything else glaringly obvious that would help us make an informed decision, devoid of marketing hype?

Our arches maybe?

Let's look at this from purely an engineering perspective. The structure of an arch spreads the load efficiently, enabling it to be supported by the least amount of effort and material. King of tunnels, bridges and viaducts, *Isambard Kingdom Brunel*, established it beyond doubt back in the early 1800s. An arch shape always has a keystone to make it innately strong; so strong in fact, that an arch is considered the strongest engineering structural shape.

Support an arch at its peak and you weaken it. A larger expanse won't have a support in its arch ... it will have more arches. For viaduct, read human foot!

Your foot has 3 arches - there to carry your bodyweight plus gravity, absorb shock and assist forward propulsion through elastic recoil of the muscles that help create them. With 3 arches, we have 3 keystones: the talus bone forms the apex of the medial longitudinal arch; the cuboid is the lynch pin for the lateral longitudinal arch; and the beautiful pyramid-shaped middle cuneiform holds the key to the transverse arch. Mess with any of these bones and biomechanics - from the very moment your bodyweight loads your foot inside your shoe - is changed.

I've got no reason to believe we're not 'Born To Run'. We seem to have an innate ability, and many have a passion, to run. Could that not represent our ancient heritage and residual capacities as endurance predators? Is the communal chase part of our biological make-up? You might have come across this now famous quote:

> "EVERY MORNING IN AFRICA, AN ANTELOPE WAKES UP. IT KNOWS IT MUST OUTRUN THE FASTEST LION, OR IT WILL BE KILLED. EVERY MORNING IN AFRICA, A LION WAKES UP. IT KNOWS IT MUST RUN FASTER THAN THE FASTEST ANTELOPE, OR IT WILL STARVE. IT DOESN'T MATTER WHETHER YOU'RE A LION OR AN ANTELOPE – WHEN THE SUN COMES UP, YOU'D BETTER BE RUNNING".

But what should we wear to run efficiently in?

We've discovered that wearing a 'traditional' shoe affects standing and both the walking and running gaits. At McGill University, Montreal, studies in 1998 by Robbins and Waked on gymnasts showed thicker, cushioned landing mats increased landing forces. They showed that if the foot has more material to plough through (during which time the foot – and the body above – are in a state of instability), it would push harder and faster to find stability. Further studies have repeatedly demonstrated a soft, cushioned shoe leads to increased impact forces and increased length of time spent finding the ground.

Bright minds have also shown that a shoe or trainer lifting the heel higher than 5mm above the level of the forefoot generates a compensation at the pelvis ... for every action, there is a reaction. In addition:

- The lift of the heel foreshortens the Achilles tendon ....
- And limits elastic recoil ...
- Limiting access to free energy ....

Mike Trees, former elite triathlete and duathlete and masters 10,000m world champion, showed me this lovely way of demonstrating the nature of elastic recoil. Place your hand on your chest; pull the middle finger back and let go; notice the satisfactory 'thump' as it hits the rib cage. Now try and repeat the noise just by levering the middle finger back and then

Appendix 2:
Good Footwear Options & Why You Might Choose Minimalist Footwear

Whilst I've deliberately steered clear of the old - but still continuing - heated debate regarding traditional cushioned trainers versus simulated barefoot or minimalist footwear, in the story of how to find *your* best running efficiency, touching on it here might be helpful for some. And given I'm 'known' as a barefoot runner, to not bring the subject up could almost be viewed as avoiding the 'elephant in the room' ... unless of course you noticed the irony in the title!

And in truth - away from the argy-bargy - what you put on your feet arguably does count as part of your running efficiency. So, almost as a mini Part 3, I'm going to leave you with a few thoughts.

One could be forgiven for assuming the human structure to be 'fit for purpose' by default and evolution. There is no proof to suspect otherwise, is there? And with 200,000 nerve endings, 34 muscles, 26 bones, 33 joints and 19 ligaments, you could easily declare the human foot a biomechanical masterpiece. So do we need to do anything to help our precious appendages?

Benno M Nigg, credited with the invention of orthotics, and author of more than 290 publications in scientific journals, has recently withdrawn some of that research, saying orthoses don't work after all; their efficacy at symptomatic relief is no more than chance, and they don't solve the problem causing the pain. He has recently published a study showing that of the 20 intrinsic and 14 extrinsic foot muscles, only 2 are working to their capacity in 'regular shoes'.

The founders of *Superfeet*, doctors Brown and Smith are acknowledged by their peers to be pioneers of cutting edge technology in the craft and science of podiatry. They began their careers over 45 years ago, and after many years of prescribing traditional orthotics reconsidered their direction. Few of their patients were cured. Most were still wearing the orthotic that was meant to solve the problem. Without the orthotic, many were still in pain. Brown and Smith thought 'outside the box' and came up with the then-revolutionary idea of simply holding the heel bone upright, offering the opportunity for foot strengthening rather than foot support. Now known as rear foot control, or 'sub-talar neutral', many have copied their work, although arch supports are still prevalent.

Scan to watch

Massaging The Calf Muscles

Muscles AND Wake Up Fluid Flow!
- Your first 'run' should be very short. No more than a mile! You may be glad you've taken this advice the next morning, when the tightness in your calf muscles can make it tricky to get your heel down on the floor when you first get out of bed!
- If you CAN walk normally the next day from the minute you get out of bed, there is a chance you hadn't shifted your first contact off the heel bone!! On your next run, try more downhill trotting and uphill walking (Level 1).
- Post-run: more pronation/supination WujWum drills and some more self-massage in lieu of stretching.
- Do not repeat your calf-conditioning mile again until you can 'roll' or massage your calves without wincing.

- Once you can put your heels straight down on the floor when initially rising the morning after a run, you're ready to increase the mileage (TTF 3). On that day, you could run your mile 'block' twice!

Repeat the above sequence for distances of 2, 3 then 4 miles.

This will probably take somewhere between 4 and 6 weeks. But these are guidelines only – you should act on what you FEEL rather than blindly follow a programme.

For some, when the distance is upped from 3 to 4 miles, there is no DOMS the next day, or the day after. Happy calves! Increasing your mileage from here is then down to your usual training parameters.

If you do suffer DOMS when you increase from 3 to 4 miles, it simply means your calves need more conditioning time. Stay at 4 miles for a few more runs before you try and add any more distance – perhaps even adding only a ½ mile. There are no rules – everyone is different, and you'll know when your calves are ready to do more work repetitively.

Many age-group athletes simply 'use' their bodies and if uninjured, one can only ponder on their amazing luck. *Minimise* your potential for injury by *caring* for those areas of your body doing the hard work, not just during this transition, but as a matter of habit. Rest isn't enough. WujWum daily and allow the 66 joints in your feet to *move* regularly and if necessary, get hands on!

distances we're asking our feet to cover, and we'd be forced to listen out of self-preservation! A protective, man-made, thick skin is a wonderful thing, but don't let it lull you into a false sense of distance or speed ability at the beginning of your 'natural' running journey.

During transitions, I always suggest avoiding the 'standard' calf stretches with the 10-30 second long holds; these tend to pull the muscle from one end to another linearly, and for too long, which is not how our muscles lengthen naturally. Instead opt for movements that eccentrically load calves in three dimensions - where there are no holds and the movement has a more natural 3D twist - as mentioned earlier, any and all of the WujWums would work well, especially the Feet and Sagittal WujWums. Also, 'rolling' or self-massaging your calves before and after your transition runs gives them a little extra love. Intuitive stretching - much like a yawning stretch when you get out of bed in the morning - is an instinctive part of your everyday life based on your sensory feedback loop, and is fine to do any time. If you time one, it rarely lasts longer than 3 seconds!

Just being *kinder* to yourself, especially your running tools - your legs - helps the transition. Generally speaking, your calves are what need most attention, as they're smaller than the thigh muscles, are more weight bearing and are getting a new eccentric workout to boot. Eccentric muscle loading (when the working muscle stretches under load) is the activity most responsible for Delayed Onset Muscle Soreness, or DOMS – you know, the one that feels bad the next day, even worse the day after and sometimes not easing until the 3rd or 4th day. There's no eccentric loading of the calves when the heel bone has first contact, so it's the change of action of the calf muscle that can cause them to complain initially. You aren't asking the calves to do anything more than what they are capable of doing – you just probably haven't asked them to do it repetitively until now.

Choose on-road running routes with fairly even surfaces to give you the best opportunity to focus on what you're sensing internally; off-road trails are great fun but your attention will be diverted to the job of staying balanced and on your feet.

My Suggested Protocol:
- Pre-run: apart from WujWuming the lower leg with pronation/supination movements, prepare your calves with some form of gentle massage – using other body parts (eg, your opposite knee cap stroking down the calf muscle), a rolling pin or a foam roller. This short video clip describes how. It's helpful at this stage to Wake Up Joints, Wake Up

Appendix 1:

Mastering the *Transition*:

- **of shifting first contact forward from the heel bone to the 'sweet spot'**
- **when switching to minimalist footwear from 'more shoe'**

For maximum comfort, the over-riding principle during the transition from a rearward/heel bone first ground contact point to one fractionally further forward, is simply to be kind to the area making the biggest changes: your lower legs.

Looking after the calf muscles with very gentle Feet, Sagittal, Frontal and Transverse WujWums, used as irrigation tools to pump nutrition towards as well as draw metabolic debris away, plus gentle self-massage, are all helpful practices. But what they'd be most grateful for is a massive reduction in running volume. What folk forget is the repetition of 'bodyweight + gravity' loads these smaller muscles are now performing in a different way to what they're accustomed to. Even a distance as short as a mile could be around 1000 repetitions on *each leg*. You wouldn't dream of doing that kind of volume for a new exercise in a gym; running shouldn't be that much different!

For those who don't cover high mileage, this may not feel so restrictive. But if you regularly run, for example 10 kilometres or 6 miles, try to adjust your concept of running for at least the next four weeks. It lowers frustration levels if you see this activity for what it is – calf conditioning – rather than your exercise fix. Do more of some other sport to avoid lowering fitness levels as you go through the process.

If you're new to minimalist footwear, precede running in them and the calf-conditioning journey with at least a fortnight of merely 'being' in your minimalist/barefoot shoes as often as you can. It also helps to take your shoes and socks off whenever possible. If you're stuck with having to wear restrictive, work-type footwear for most of every day, extend this 'non-running' period. You need time (that word again!) to wake up those muscles in the foot and lower leg that are practically dormant when moving 'shod' in traditional footwear. Some research has suggested that only 2 out of 34 muscles in each lower leg are working to their capacity when wearing stable shoes. An easy way of putting it all into perspective is to think about being 'skin fit'. In the initial stages, could you run the distance you're attempting with *nothing* on your feet? If we just removed our shoes altogether, the fragility of our skin would limit the

From before we're even born, we're wired for change. We pass through great epochs of change as we grow from infant, through childhood and into our adult life, with those stages both expected and easily recognised. Less noticeable and also perhaps less considered, is that once 'grown', we're still changing constantly. While you're learning the skills of running efficiently, your body is changing, your brain is changing and the changing of everything charges the whole with energy. Playing in and with your entire pyramid will *keep* change coming. Change is Flow is Energy is Life. You've got all you need now to start your next Epoch of Change.

And I'll still be with you, every light-hearted, fully-loaded, non-soggy step of the way ...

> "WE SHALL NOT CEASE FROM EXPLORATION
> AND THE END OF ALL OUR EXPLORING
> WILL BE TO ARRIVE AT WHERE WE STARTED
> AND KNOW THE PLACE FOR THE FIRST TIME."
> **T S ELIOT, 'LITTLE GIDDING'**

conditioned, flat sprints (green, Level 5) can be added to your weekly schedule, being careful to monitor the way your body is absorbing the work load with judicious use of MAFA (Level 6), about every four weeks and probably no further apart than eight weeks. The longer you leave objectively monitoring your body's progress, the more risks you're taking with your energy stores and ability to repair and heal. You don't need to 'run blind' anymore - you have all the tools now to make great decisions based on instinct and fact.

The top is platinum, because it's special. Magical even, especially the first time. Platinum is my 'Om' - *"it takes us to the next level and we can try and make it grand and big but it really is simply evolution. There is not really a choice anymore. We have signed up for the ride and now we have to take it all the way"* - Melissie Jolly. Dom's 'fairy dust' effect on the runner of the front cover was perfectly serendipitous. Cruise Intervals is the crowning glory of all the patience and effort you've put in to reach it. Return to it, but not too often. Let it keep its magic.

I haven't mentioned volume increases, have I? Miles to cover each week, training hours to tick off. It's not a mistake! I can't write a training plan for you without knowing you, your past history and your aspirations, and especially not when I'm deprived of the critical information regarding the myriad of daily drains on your Energy Bucket. You, however, *do* have all that. In fact, you have a running commentary on it. This book - along with development of your running efficiency - provides a training *paradigm* to help and guide, to develop self-understanding, self-awareness and self-confidence. Use the TTF table to help you navigate your volume increases safely, and the MAFA to check-in to make sure you're still on track. *"One of the facets of Mastery is self-reliance"* - Diana Cooper (and thank you to my soul sister, Clair Taylor-Powell, for sharing that with me at the perfect time).

And although *'You' Is All You Need*, you don't have to do it alone. PFM Coaches and Anatomy in Motion practitioners are here to help you should you either need or want a lending hand. *Helpful* is in all our natures.

"DO ALL THE GOOD YOU CAN, BY ALL THE MEANS YOU CAN, IN ALL THE WAYS YOU CAN, IN ALL THE PLACES YOU CAN, AT ALL THE TIMES YOU CAN, TO ALL THE PEOPLE YOU CAN, AS LONG AS EVER YOU CAN"
JOHN WESLEY

Far from just 'staying at the top', which could be a touch anti-climactic, now you can live in your pyramid, change the furniture around, go up and down the stairs, open some windows, look at the view from each and *every* level. Enjoy the space you've created and see where it takes you; you might surprise yourself ...

As James remarked recently, having just returned from successfully completing the Ultra-Trail du Mont-Blanc CCC event:

"I worked out this morning that my first ever event was the 2013 London Duathlon - almost exactly 4 years ago. At that point I couldn't run 10km without pain and discomfort. 4 years later and I've just completed over 100km plus a few lumps and bumps and done it only one third of the way down the pack - including all those youngsters! If that's not further evidence of the legitimacy of what you're writing about then I don't know what is."

▲ ▲ ▲

You might have noticed that my little illustrations summarise what we've covered, so you can easily refer back to what you'd like to improve upon.

The green foundations are the ground work, where the magic *begins*; the hangout for 'growth' and a place to store all your basics with unrestricted access. Many a time in coaching I've taken a runner 'back' to principles. Far from it being 'beneath them', they were amazed at how life seemed to have sucked the shapes they thought they were making into something 'more effortful'. As Chris Sritharan shared with us from Martial Arts Grandmaster Bobby Taboada: *"Basic Basic Basic, don't get sick of the basic ... and when you have the basic you go forward further ... easy".*

The middle blue section represents 'speaking the truth' and embodies the 'no short-cuts policy' in your commitment to refine and strengthen both the Principles and your Body. Your TTF is your truth. You either can do the session because your TTF indicates it's as safe as it can be, or you have to make the choice to do something less intense. When fit and well and with spare reserves in your Energy Bucket, a positive application of these levels is to approach one each week. Not 'one of each' each week; just 'one blue each week'. When you're really well-

Your Pyramid - your magnificent, stable, monumental structure - for Efficient Running is built. And it's *your* masterpiece. You followed the directions along the trail, and made it all the way to the top, listening to the wisdom innate in your body and senses.

THE END

THE TOP

"IT IS GOOD TO HAVE AN END TO JOURNEY TOWARD; BUT IT IS THE JOURNEY THAT MATTERS, IN THE END."
URSULA K LE GUIN, AMERICAN AUTHOR

What an amazing journey; following you along the trail trodden by others, sharing with you everything I can to help make the adventure safe, lively, worthwhile and ultimately, joyful.

Your body is incredible; and the fun you can have whilst doing something that many consider to be dull and boring! *Dull and boring*? Can you ever imagine being bored whilst running again? There's too much to think about, to feel for, to check-in with, to master, to hone and refine, to help put at ease, to imbue with free energy, to open and give space to, to create more speed for no more effort with, or even to generate more speed for *less* effort, to ... *ENJOY* ...

To be *present* in your body as you run is to be free from everything else. It can't be boring. Therefore it can only be *anything else but!!!*

The time it takes, and the time it takes to recover *from*, would preclude Cruise Intervals being a daily run, but I believe it should become a regular component of your overall running routine. Although it's longer than a MAF Analysis, it seems to hit the 'fun' button more readily; yes, the rhythmical variation of effort levels tends to feel more manageable than a sustained effort, but when focus is held, the satisfaction that comes with the 'reveal' never dims. It's just plain exciting to see what your body can do when mastery is in play, and that potential is in us all. I bet you can't wait to try it; if your gut says you can, and 90 minutes of running is in you, what are you waiting for?

... and no peeking at the numbers until you're done ... sense your way to the wonder that comes with playing the game well ...

> "EVERYTHING IS ENERGY AND THAT'S ALL THERE IS TO IT. MATCH THE FREQUENCY OF THE REALITY YOU WANT AND YOU CANNOT HELP BUT GET THAT REALITY. IT CAN BE NO OTHER WAY. THIS IS NOT PHILOSOPHY. THIS IS PHYSICS."
> **ALBERT EINSTEIN**

fails? This longer session hones pacing skills, practising the use of all of the invaluable senses: what you can see and hear and vocalise (if you're not nose-breathing) as well as feel internally. Cruise Intervals is an opportunity to excel in sensory-labelling and broaden your description vocabulary!

5. And finally, if cadence and non-sogginess are the tomato and cucumber on your cheese and ham 'wrap', and the hill drills form the dollop of mayo, sprinkling of omega 3 seeds and artful drizzle of balsamic glaze that make the whole too good to resist ... to finish it all off, we need to raise a glass of chilled, bubbly Prosecco to toast the sweet, penny-dropping moment when you realised Cruise Intervals revealed:

THE LESS YOU TRY
THE MORE YOU RELAX
THE MORE YOU LET YOUR BODY RUN YOU
THE LESS YOU INTERFERE WITH YOUR BODY'S INNATE ABILITY TO
RUN EFFICIENTLY ...
THE FASTER YOU GO!!

MORE SPEED FOR LESS EFFORT.

CHEERS!

Many runners, once over the shock of the numbers, think that the point of the exercise is "Why Bother Trying Harder?" If a similar speed can be generated with the sense of much less effort, then just stick to 'much less effort'. It's a fair point, but not quite the 'rationale' for the session. Actually, there are a handful of tangible payoffs that make incorporating this into your training schedule regularly 'good practice'. Let's take a quick look at them:

1. The *concept* of training runs at 10km race pace (or that which you could sustain for up to an hour and sometimes referred to as a 'tempo' session) - *'Power On'* effort levels - is sound; quite apart from the expansion of the boundaries of aerobic movement, training at higher levels of intensity improves speed and speed endurance. The harsh reality though is that of the runners that perform a tempo training session, many struggle because they haven't yet got the muscular endurance and/or the mental concentration to hold *efficiencies* in running form. The upshot of the struggle is a total absence of joy, and even injury. The *'Power Off'* recovery laps mean that building up more training at higher levels of intensity can be done without losing form, minimising injury risk. You can 'keep going' because you're not injured and because you still have the physical and mental capacity to. *And* you get to keep the joy.

2. The varied pacing helps to prevent the stride length (read: joint actions) from becoming overly repetitive, which can generate stiffness in the body prematurely. This is one of several factors contributing to the empirical evidence that many can run further when playing off-road; no two steps are the same when the terrain is natural rather than uniformly man-made, and so the emphasis on areas of working soft tissue continually changes. The periodic and rhythmical switch in pacing also stimulates the refocusing of brain activity that might have drifted off, away from efficiency of movement and towards 'to-do' lists or other such humdrum neuronal hustle and bustle.

3. The change in pace from 'somewhat strong' to 'uber-easy' is the very thing that relaxes you to the point you're able to tap into the fluent form inherent in our architecture. We seem to respond well to some effort first, enabling a tangible 'letting go' after.

4. *Pacing Practice Makes Perfect* (not that we're seeking Perfect of course, but Pacing Practice Makes Progress doesn't quite hit the mark, does it?). Many of you run against the clock; your gadget tells you your pace and if questioned, you describe the effort in single-syllable adjectives like "tough", "hard" or "nice". But what happens if your gadget

THE BIG REVEAL

So what happens?

It seems a shame to let the cat out of the bag before your first Cruise Interval session, but such is the limitation of reaching more runners through the more impersonal medium of a book. Whilst it's great fun to watch the faces of the runners I coach as I reveal the lap time differences, I'm going to have to let go of the 'surprise' and offer you everything on a plate!

Here it is. Drum roll please ...

IF THE NOSE-BREATHING GEARS ARE NAILED,
THE TIMES OF THE 'POWER ON' LAPS REMAIN ROUGHLY THE SAME,
SLOWING A BIT AND FEELING TOUGHER AS YOU TIRE -
JUST AS DURING THE MAFA SESSION.

ON THE OTHER HAND, THE 'POWER OFF' LAPS FEEL
EASIER AND EASIER BY COMPARISON ...
... AND GET FASTER AND FASTER!!

AS MORE AND MORE LAPS ARE COMPLETED, THE TIME
DIFFERENCE BETWEEN 'POWER ON' AND 'POWER OFF' REDUCES,
TO THE EXTENT THAT IT BECOMES NEGLIGIBLE WHEN THE EFFORT
INVOLVED IS FACTORED IN (I ONCE COACHED THIS FOR 8 MILES WITH
THE VERY STRONG, VERY GLAMOROUS FIONA, AND BY THE END SHE
WAS ONLY A FEW SECONDS SLOWER THAN HER 'EFFORT' LAP WHEN
SHE WASN'T TRYING AT ALL!!!)

Off, 3 x Power On) but you need to have the endurance to maintain form for that distance (depending on how long your 'lap' is of course).

Your last 'Power Off' marks the end of the running section of this final length of trail, and given the distance you've covered, I'd suggest your cool-down walk be at *least* 5 minutes, and more like 10. A useful rule of thumb is that the further you run, the further you walk to calm systems down, rhythmically moving the limbs that have worked so hard on your behalf. Walking is the beginning of your recovery.

- *hard against the waistband on the inhale*
- *this is as hard as you can run whilst still breathing with your mouth closed*
- *feels like the effort of 10km race pace*
- *10° of Non-Soggy*
- *world becomes smaller, and tunnel-like, with limited peripheral awareness*
- *breathing louder than all external sound*
- *couldn't hold a conversation even if you wanted to; can only manage staccato words between strong, but not raggedy, breath patterns.*

Each lap is timed. GPS devices can be used but must NOT be looked at for the duration of the main set. This is critical. You are not running 'against the clock'. You are running to a perceived effort level and the times are simply being recorded for your post-session analysis. Checking the times will mess with your head. If effort levels are well-adhered to, the results are mind-boggling for most runners newly exposed to it. Scrap that - the results will doubtless ALWAYS be astonishing. No matter how many times you perform this session, you'll probably always be wondrously impressed with the (seemingly) counter-intuitive results.

This is a form and endurance-building pacing session. And SO MUCH MORE. Possibly the most jaw-dropping running gig in existence.

Stay focused on noticing form, thinking form, feeling form and keep a lid on the laps where the effort levels are meant to be Power Off. The most common tendency is for runners to lean towards 'comfortable' (NB 2) rather than 'uber comfortable'. You need to recover properly between laps, in order for the very strong breathing of Power On to remain sustainable for multiple laps.

You will almost certainly feel as if you're hardly moving when you relax into 'Power Off', because the context is that of being *relative to* the prior effort level. Build your confidence in the truth from your always-there-friend Sensory Awareness and seek to use *all* the parameters that tell you which gear you're in, to help you stick to the game plan.

The more laps you can manage, the more data is available for analysis (and tales of derring-do!) - 5 laps will give you 3 x Power Off and 2 x Power On, which is realistically the least you can have and still have some wow-factor with the result. Better, is 7 laps (4 x Power

CRUISE INTERVALS

Fully prepared, we come to the **Main Set** of the session, which is a take on a reported favourite work-out of Simon Lessing, a South African born British triathlete who won 5 ITU world titles between 1992 and 1998. Nothing new about interval training - we used it at Levels 5, 7, 8 and 9 - but this is a bit different.

In keeping with the spirit of Leonardo da Vinci's famous quote:

"SIMPLICITY IS THE ULTIMATE SOPHISTICATION",

we define **Cruise Intervals** as long, repeatable laps (1-1.5km) alternating between nose-breathing (NB) gears 1 and 3, for as long as is necessary. Mr Lessing apparently enjoyed regular 20km stints at this, but I'd suggest starting with half of that. 10kms of Cruise Intervals is plenty initially, especially given the long and thorough warm-up suggested.

For even more simplicity, we now dub NB 1 as **"Power Off"** and NB 3 as **"Power On"**. Always start and finish with Power Off (and don't increase your speed on the final lap just because it's 'the last one'! Stick to the perceived effort and wait to be amazed).

NB 1. Uber-easy. **Power Off:**
- *tongue is relaxed*
- *legs can go on all day*
- *world feels panoramic*
- *external sounds of birds, traffic, wind are louder than the breath sounds*
- *60% effort*
- *form-focused*
- *1° of Non-Soggy*
- *mitochondria-multiplying territory*
- *can natter if you wanted to.*

NB 3. Somewhat Strong But Not Uncomfortable. **Power On:**
- *tongue is pushing hard against the soft palate, and the diaphragm is pushing the belly*

- Frontal WujWum.
- "Is There Poo On My Shoe?" from Level 2.
- "Waking up the Nerve Chassis". Turns out, jumping up and down on the spot is quite hard to do with feet together too.
- "Hammie Crab Load" and/or
- "The Pentopus", both from Level 7.

● Too much or too little rotation (most commonly, too much upper body twisting paired with too little movement of any kind in the pelvis!)? Try:
  - "Codpiece and Nipples - Differentiated" from Level 5.
  - Fine-tuning the use of *The Lemni*. The human being is more 'spirals' than twists, more 'rolls' than returns like an old typewriter, so hands that are following the 'roll of the ship' ROLL gently, rather than slide sideways. The pelvis, the rib-cage and *The Lemni* all create the rolling shape of the figure-of-8-on-its-side. It may feel like too much movement to you, but use your somatic sense - even if it feels goofy, does it also feel fluid, free, loose and relaxed? If it's not contrived but is just happening because you've given it permission to, embrace this 'crazy amount' of movement - and just see what happens.

For all trouble-shooting, it often helps to ask a friend to film you - just a few seconds on a mobile phone is all you need. What you see is rarely what you *feel*, and eyes are fantastic confirmers that 'the-right-for-you-goofy' often looks calm, balanced and effortless.

- YOUR tracking width is wherever you access the full breadth of each foot with every step, where your feet and lower legs feel relaxed and are able to adaptively weight-bear accordingly to the surface they are running upon.

- YOUR supreme balance of upper and lower body rotations is where the pelvis is able to trail in company with the extending leg, with the upper body rotating counter to the pelvis *just enough* to create opposition and a tightening in the obliques, but not so much that it drags the pelvis out of its backward rotation prematurely.

- YOUR perfect range of cadence *today, on this route* is the one that allows you to fully-load the tissues to access the stretch of elastic tissue without losing any of the recoil potential by over-staying your ground contact.

- YOUR non-sogginess in the uber-easy beginnings of your trot, is 1° more of knee behind you before it switches direction than when you were soggy. Soggy is slower and harder; the thought *of one degree more than 'that' of knee behind you* is faster and easier.

- Nothing is still and no one movement, in any plane, over-rides another.

Trouble-shooting goes a long way to improving your understanding of how your body functions. Most runners have a few nemeses, strong 'isms' often connected to the environment they spend most time in. To be able to notice these same form issues or common themes emerging in your running is great progress, and you now have several tricks up your sleeve to take a crack at some self-help:

- Still forward-leaning? Try:
  - Sagittal WujWum, making sure you're up against a wall to remind yourself of where vertically aligned really is.
  - "Waking up the Nerve Chassis" from Level 5. Jumping up and down on the spot is very hard to do with a forward lean; what difference(s) do you notice when jiggling (apart from the jiggling!) versus your habitual alignment?
  - Maybe your anterior musculature is so tight, it's pulling you into a forward lean, in which case "Oh! Mr Darcy ..." also from Level 5, is another good one for separating the base of the sternum from the pubic bone.
- Still narrow-tracking? Try:

FRONTAL WujWum: your 'Goldilocks' Tracking Width; gets your weight shifting from left to right and gifts you your lateral hip muscles, whole breadth of forefeet, greater base of support and more relaxed running. This has been the butter on your bread since Level 2.

TRANSVERSE WujWum: actions the DNA-driven rotations that enable the human race to be the most efficient, most enduring runners on the planet. With pelvic rotation possible, you can maximise the potential for hip extension; the honey on your butter in various forms since Level 3.

WujWumed, briskly walked and ready to run, the warm-up run section will always be full of form thoughts. Whilst I reiterate that I'm neither coaching a 'method' nor stating a 'right or wrong' way to run, I am most certainly saying that each person has a his or her *"Absolutely Right"* way, and if you want to run as efficiently as possible, then search and you shall find:

- Topping and Tailing: YOUR upright is wherever your cervical spine (neck) is able to rotate to its fullest extent AND your ankles have least tension, so allowing fluid movement rather than locking them into a shape. It's also where your abdominal wall automatically fires to retain the viscera *without* holding your belly in (which would interfere with your breathing pattern and is, therefore, bonkers).

So for this final length of the trail, a check-list might be handy:

- **FEET WujWum:** *preferably* bare-footed (don't you think I've been good? This is the only time I've requested it!); 'Turning the Talus', slowly and deliberately, generating a rotation of the whole body *only* from the space between the ankles; maintaining tripod contact with the ground (inside heel of one foot, outside heel of the other, both bases of big toes and little toes), so one foot pronates and the other supinates.

By now, you might be noticing that your feet seem to be changing shape; where there was no movement, there is some; where toes were clawed, they're straighter; where arches were high and locked, they seem a bit more relaxed; where arches were flat and unresponsive, they've woken up a bit.
Where there is *no change* in a locked/lifted/bent/floppy area after all this input, is fabulous information; perhaps it's a strategy to protect another area of your body? Help yourself by finding out with expert help from the Anatomy in Motion guys ...

SAGITTAL WujWum: finding vertical to fire up abs and glutes (the power-houses) and locate relaxed ankles and neck. You should be very familiar with this by now; after all, you've been using it since Level 1 ... haven't you?

CHECKPOINT TEN NOTICEBOARD

▲ ▲ ▲

TERRAIN: FENCE OR WALL OPTIONAL, FLATTISH GROUND (A SLIGHT GRADIENT CAN BE HELPFUL), A MILE/KM 'BLOCK' OPTIONAL
RUNNER STATUS: TTF 8 OR ABOVE, FOCUSED, EMBRACING RUNNING MASTERY
KIT LIST: LAYERS, COMFORTABLE FOOTWEAR, TISSUES, YOUR LEMNI

Focus is at the core of this session. If you don't need to cross a road, or worry about roots and rabbit holes, it helps. Many folk use the same 'block' for their MAF Analysis and this session - their Cruise Intervals - and I think that's a good idea, especially when it's new to you. In time, you might find you enjoy *'power on, power off'* in a straight line on your longer runs, taking in ever-changing scenery. You need your *Lemni*, probably some tissues and if I'm forced into giving a number, TTF 8 should be an absolute minimum.

You've got 30-40 minutes of warm-up before the main set to revisit all the Basic Principles - a brush-stroke if you will of everything you've internalised from Levels 1-5.

Whilst there are no rules as to whether you WujWum before the pre-run brisk walk or after, you'll get better results with the Feet WujWum if shoeless and sockless. So my recommendation is to always do that bit before heading outside. The rest of the WujWum sequence is entirely up to you. Before or after the brisk walk - your body might have its own preference, or it might not care about the order, only that you perform them!

And have fun as you run as you wait, and look forward to the day when you wake *knowing* you're ready. If you took Route A to cover *Principles*, you might arrive here around five months from the start of your adventure; if you took the scenic Route B, it might take twelve. There are too many variables to be able to predict, and whatever it is, it's *right for you*. What I *can* say is I've *never* coached this - either in a group or individually - without each **ready runner** having an incredible moment of 'WOW!' (one could say 'enlightenment') as times are revealed for each lap, at alternating levels of effort, backing up the whole premise of how the body seems to enjoy itself the most when it's interfered with the least! It's worth sticking around for.

feeling like the right time. If you can be patient enough to wait until you feel as if you've absorbed all the internal information and the progressive training loads from each level up til now, and that you're ready for more, then reward at the end is guaranteed. I've been very careful with 'absolutes' all along the trail, and if I had come across even one *vague* result - which I haven't - I would have caveated that statement. It's about being ready for the cherry on top of the icing on the top - the Benben stone. 'Being Ready' for this session isn't so much about TTF numbers, but rather an ability to run being able to stay relaxed and mindful of efficient form for 90 minutes duration as a minimum. That said, given it's a long session you certainly can't do this if you have any kind of niggle or injury.

This is the most extended, sustained running session I coach (workshops are longer, but movement tends to be more of the 'stop-start' variety which maintains focus more easily). Rhythmical movement that goes on for long enough is tiring on body and brain, and if you continue into fatigue with 'press-on-itis syndrome', your internal antenna will get unplugged without you even realising it; you'll be thinking that you're doing 'something', whilst actually doing something completely different. *Flagging* is a Red Flag!! Great Practice makes for Great Progress; rubbish practice is time wasted. Ah - so there ARE junk miles after all. Be ready, *really ready*, for this showstopper.

So, for the third time of asking - phrased slightly differently to make sure I've resonated with everyone - "don't hurry to the top!". Entertain yourself by mastering all the levels, seeking better answers from the continual scanning of your body as you run. Back-up all the Principles and Details that have been covered thus far with lots of Great Practice. Reinforce pacing paradigms through the perceived efforts of breath, pacing being a skill you'll continue to hone long after you've repeated this session a dozen or more times.

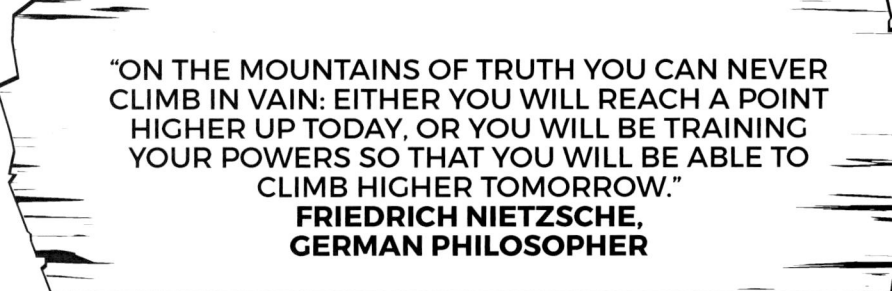

"ON THE MOUNTAINS OF TRUTH YOU CAN NEVER CLIMB IN VAIN: EITHER YOU WILL REACH A POINT HIGHER UP TODAY, OR YOU WILL BE TRAINING YOUR POWERS SO THAT YOU WILL BE ABLE TO CLIMB HIGHER TOMORROW."
FRIEDRICH NIETZSCHE, GERMAN PHILOSOPHER

10: CRUISE INTERVALS

A lot of runners hate interval training and dread the expected pain. It really doesn't have to be this way; here you'll discover how to train out of your comfort zone, comfortably.

 The final intention marker relays the simplest message of them all ... that less is so often more ...

It's such a well-used phrase, and this - the capstone of our pyramid - intends to show how it relates not just to running per se, but the joy of running. We're going to use the combination of the power of the mind, perceived effort expertise, running skills and running strength already developed ... whilst continuing to develop said mind power, perceived effort expertise, running skills and strength. A rather neat package, don't you think?

The capstone or pyramidion is intrinsic in ancient Egyptian mythology, and formed the summit of each pyramid; *"known as a Benbenet, it associated the pyramid as a whole with the sacred Benben stone, which was believed to have the power to enlighten the person who was in its surroundings and was capable of producing an awesome power."* - **landofpyramids.org**

My goodness, what a finale! Beginning the story of the final section of the trail is giving me goosebumps.

This level - the peak of your Pyramid - should be a greatly anticipated finale, rather than a premature washout. The 'right time' for it is a bit of a nebulous concept; it's more about it

LEVEL TEN
POWER ON, POWER OFF

LEVEL TEN CONTENTS

Checkpoint Ten 346
Cruise Intervals 351
The Big Reveal 354

DEPARTING LEVEL NINE ▲▲▲
RUNNER STATUS: TTF 8 AND RISING
✔ FLYING THE DOWNHILLS
✔ POWERING THE ASCENTS
✔ SKILLFULLY MASTERING RUN PLANNING
✔ WUJWUMING DAILY

- Alternate which leg you lead up the slope with.
- Start with small sideways strides - these muscles are often sources of repetitive injury, so are typically neither robust nor particularly functional, so wake them up kindly ... **Crabettes** if you will (with degrees of Non-Soggy once again not being relevant, as although we're heading up the slope, we're facing sideways).
- Create opposition between the pelvis and the ribcage - if the pelvis is pointing downslope, you need your ribs to be leading you upslope. *The Lemni* works a treat here, helping you co-ordinate everything with a rolling action of the ribcage. If you know your Strictly moves (which I don't), it's probably something like a rumba or a cha-cha-cha! Happy to stand corrected on this - dancing was never my strong point! Unless in rollers, at the hairdressers, with a glass of bubbles at the ready ...
- Initial Crabettes are short sideways-trotting strides, high reps, low intensity.
- Build over a handful of Grapevine encores into longer sideways-running strides, lower reps and higher intensities.

Intermix your **Sailfish** downhills and your **Crabs** uphill with a good number of gratifyingly simple, yet agreeable **Pats On Your Backs** to conclude an entertaining session that never fails to please.

With blood pumping to every nook and cranny of your happy running body, finish your session with the grandest finale - the last **Sailfish** on no more than the 10th descent (less if you know your body has had enough), using the entire slope if you feel comfortable enough to, and 'letting go' as much as you possibly can. This isn't the time for tension - that will just feel horrible and lumpy and impactful. You've been building skill, speed and confidence with each descent after each drill, so even though you'll feel as if your crazy-fast-leg-turn-over simply can't keep up with the speed your body is travelling at, it always does (self-preservation is a wondrous thing).

Have trust in your body, build confidence through the process, *haul ass* at the bottom and you'll finish wreathed in beaming smiles.

'Exhilarated' is the general outcome of Level 9. Expect nothing less. It is endlessly inspirational to watch runners discover skills and strengths they simply didn't know they had because the motor programme wasn't one they'd ever explored.

- Concurrently, the journey of the internally rotating rear arm continues, adding extension at the elbow to extension at the shoulder joint, with elevation of the scapula allowing maximal loading of the bicep.
- Step back with the lead leg, so remaining in a split stance posture but now with the opposite leg being the forward one.
- Arms unravel their twist and now reload in the opposite direction.
- The torso always rotates towards the lead leg.

A handful of repetitions to each side - taking less than 30 seconds - is generally enough to create a noticeable 'lightening of the load' of previously 'dead' arms; arms you had no idea were secretly being so heavy! Quick, easy and effective. And surprisingly useful for 'The Grapevine' ...

The Final Hill Drill: Crabs!

So, we've worked on quads (and abs), glutes (and abs), hammies (and abs), calves (and abs). Last, but by absolutely no means least, and arguably the most important (without these monkeys - pun *absolutely* intended - we'd still be chimps), the lateral hip muscles. The tensor fascia lata, or TFL, connects the outside hip to the outside knee via the iliotibial or IT band and along with the medial glute fibres helps us create that amazing three-dimensional figure-of-8-on-its-side, loose-on-its-hinges-see-saw, lemniscate motion of the pelvis. They work to contribute to our ability to land, manage flying body mass and launch off again *ON ONE LEG* smoothly, elegantly, efficiently and fluidly ... unlike chimps who have to waddle in the frontal plane (along with penguins and Frankenstein - who was clearly missing a sideways-facing pelvic bowl as well as a few bolts).

The word 'lateral' of course means we're referring to 'side-seams'. And of those, we have four: two on the outside, and two on the inside. So anytime we're loading the outside of one leg in gait (the abductors), we're loading the inside of the other (the adductors).

Crabs is all about The Grapevine - up a slope! You know the one: sideways step with the lead leg, other leg steps behind, sideways step with the lead leg again, other leg now steps in front ... repeat. Because this is a running book, you'll be trotting The Grapevine rather than walking it, although many benefit from walking the first ascent whilst they organise their wayward limbs.

Uphill Drill 2:
Give Yourself A Pat On The Back: *vimeo.com/244976006*

After all that lower leg (and abdominal - did you notice?!) exertion, time to switch things 'upwards' and focus on the main muscles of the upper arms - the biceps and triceps. *Everything* needs to be 'awake' if the job of running is going to be a complete aggregate of global biomechanics. The effect of this lovely little drill is often quite surprising …

- Split stance, one leg in front of the other.
- Contra-lateral (opposite) arm to front leg swings forward and externally rotates; ipsi-lateral (same side) arm swings backward and internally rotates.
- The journey of the externally rotating forward arm continues, adding flexion at the elbow to flexion at the shoulder joint (lifting the elbow as high as possible whilst pulling the shoulder blade down encourages this) until the hand falls behind, as if to 'pat yourself on the back'; the tricep is now fully eccentrically-loaded.

- The weight-bearing leg is being externally rotated by the dropped pelvis rotating towards it, spotlighting the 2 points of contact of base of big toe and base of little toe. This inverts the heel (sucking it in) and '**P**itchforks' all the met-heads into the ground:
  - ankle, knee and hip extension couple with posterior pelvic tilt (bum in)
  - thoracic & lumbar spinal flexion (hunchback)
  - cervical extension (head falling backwards above caving chest and general 'banana' spine).
  - Make sure all the elements are there - the tendency being to lift the lead knee instead of the lead hip; keep the lead knee 'heavy' and below the hip in the "Propulsive" position.

- The full P-P-P movement is demanding! Just a few on each leg are enough to illicit grunts of exertion from most (James won't mind me saying he had quite a few during filming, as to hold this position for the camera is extremely challenging!).

Psychedelica - and his little sister, Psychedelicette!

- It's all about 'Big Air'! You're basically ascending the hill in a series of single-legged, explosive hops. Degrees of Non-Soggy aren't relevant because the goal is UP rather than forward.
- The greater the vertical oscillation the shorter the distance travelled over the ground for the same effort.
- The goal therefore is minimum ground covered for maximum Big Air gained over your familiar 2 rolling + 20 explosive strides.
- Now bearing in mind all the common running injuries mentioned since Level 1 - so many of them being at or below the knee - judicious 'Psychedelicetting' is required. B-u-i-l-d your plyometric-prowess, rather than 'go for broke' right from the get-go ... or that might just be exactly where you end up.
- Adding *The Lemni* at any point makes this drill even harder as it removes any upward leverage from the arms.
- Walk up any unused sections of the slope to make sure there's enough distance to enjoy each of your **Sailfish** descents.
- A handful of Psychedelicettes growing into Psychedelica's - interposed with a couple of P-P-Ps to each leg - is generally enough to start with. You often don't know the full extent of the tax to the lower leg tissue until the following morning when you get out of bed!

'let go of' the soft tissue under your sole? Is there internal rotation of the shinbone? This is a 3D load, not a 2D stretch.

- Weight-bearing **P**ronation:
  - ankle & knee flexion couples with hip flexion
  - anterior pelvic tilt (bum out)
  - thoracic & lumbar spinal extension (chest rises and tilts backwards)
  - cervical flexion (chin drops to lifting chest).
  - Make sure all the elements are there before reversing the foot mechanics - the tendency is for folk to lean forwards too much, making it tricky to keep the heel on the floor.

- Focusing on the movement of the pelvis, drive the free hip 'forward and up' from its 'back & down' previous position; the pelvis literally lifts the weight-bearing leg onto its toes and into full extension from the hip down.

- The goal is for the dynamic shift of the pelvis to translate the foot action from pronation into supination - so creating the '**P**ropulsion' element.

their brothers draped around the thigh bone - after all, hefty lower legs would be arduous to have to pick up and carry across the ground with every stride. They *are* the most weight-bearing muscle groups though, so they still need to be strong and of good quality tissue. We don't want to *build* them, we want to put lithe life into them. We're looking to wake up the 34 muscles in the lower leg compartment, all able to stretch under load and gift free energy in the form of elastic recoil; to drive blood to them and give them great 'catapult potential'. In my experience, it's this 'potential' that's missing, as these supposedly springy, resilient workers get used, abused and generally forgotten until they hurt … or until that magnificent beast of a tendon - the Achilles - which often bears the brunt of all the misuse, brings runners to a grinding halt. The inflamed Achilles tendon often isn't the 'cause' of anything, but the *result*.

By now you know the form: a preparatory movement to open the joints' range of motion, creating reactive length to the soft tissue on all sides, followed by a drill in the form of something decidedly 'fishy'. For calves, we need to fully dorsiflex and plantarflex the ankles with the 'PPP' drill, and then we use the power of plyometrics to mimic the 'big air' of the bouncing Psychedelica fishes (yes, they really do exist - I did my research):

Uphill Drill 1:
"P-P-P" Pronation - Propulsion - Pitchfork:
vimeo.com/245616155

- Hanging onto something for balance, stand on one leg (the goal is the full movement of the drill, rather than the challenge of not falling over).
- Keeping 'tripod' contact with the ground (heel, base of big toe, base of little toe), drive the free hip backwards and down, allowing your body to fold into a curtsy-type posture. The loaded hip is now in a lifted and forward position.
- Allow the forward weight-bearing knee to bend as much as it's comfortable to, and to travel medially (but don't push it there) and flex at the ankle as deeply as it will allow.
- Because of the medial travel of the knee and the internal rotation of both the femur and the tibia, the pressure should be on the inside of the heel (whilst maintaining contact across the full breadth of the foot). You are now in full weight-bearing ankle dorsiflexion and your calves should be OK about it. If calves are grumbling, have you softened and

- Every descent as you build your confidence is the same:
  - Fly - stop - fly again [- stop - fly again if the slope is long enough or you're treading cautiously] - stop at the bottom.
- Stay relaxed - brake with your glutes and stop whenever you feel tension growing; let yourself travel freely again when you're ready.
- You'll know you've 'got it' when you don't brake until you've reached the bottom, and your face is plastered with a grin from ear-to-ear.

That's it!! Well - that's the beginning of 'it'. And it just gets better with each descent you 'let happen to you'. The more you convince yourself through indisputable *evidence* that you're able to halt whenever you want to, the more assured you'll be in 'letting go', allowing gravity to do more and more of the work.

The progression in Sailfish is in gradually increasing the distance of the free-fall, gathering more speed in the process, and in turn snowballing the skill required to come to a controlled halt. Repetition builds the 'stopping-certainty' that generates the most elegant, relaxed downhill running - apparently the kind that gets you gigs at running clubs!

It's also the least effortful way I know to generate huge quad strength - every single downhill stride strongly eccentrically-loads them. You're actually working them VERY HARD but you just don't realise it at the time, because it feels like gravity is doing everything and you're entirely focused on keeping your legs under you! 'Wobbly legs' before you've even reached the shower is the give-away, so take things steadily ...

BOUNCING UP

Leaving talk of descents for the moment (you'll be executing them after each ascent, of course), the final weight-bearing muscle group left to 'hone' are the lower legs. In common with most mammals, our shin and calf muscles are designed to be long, but slimmer than

Of course, the reality is we *haul alternate asses*! We use the Power of the Glutes to stop within a *few paces*. Please note the 'within a few'. If you stop literally on the spot (if that was even possible), parts of your skeleton would still be travelling forwards under the effect of momentum, with others now stationary; that's not going to end well - somewhere. Start fairly easy, and build your ability to both have Hammie-Hamster feet as well as *Hauling Asses*.

FLYING DOWN

How to **Sailfish:**

Let's begin at the top of your hill venue.

Similar to the "Waking Up The Nerve Chassis" of Level 5, we're going to prepare our central nervous system and ankles by "**Shaking Legs**". This is *exactly* as it sounds, and precisely as it looks when you see the athletes on the start-line on the TV - flicking the ankles and toes to generate a shimmy-shake all the way up the flesh of the legs to the hips. A few of those each side and the central nervous system will be wide awake and ready for the imminent super-fast turn-over of legs:

- Start running easily down the hill.
- As soon as you notice gravity start to 'take you', let it, whilst thinking 'quick feet', 'pitter-patter', 'hammie-hamster' or anything else evocative that springs to mind.
- As soon as you feel 'Whoa - I'm losing control', fire up your glutes alternately and come to a controlled halt over a few paces.
- Did that take less time than you expected it to?
- Once you've regained your composure, continue running down the hill. When you feel the pull of gravity, let yourself go until you feel you need to slow things down again. Immediately, **haul ass** and fire up those glutes with a couple of alternating squeezes over the next couple of strides. Get familiar with how much control you really DO have; the hill can only 'take you' if you want it to.

STOPPING

I started then as I'll start now - with the stop! More critical than anything else when 'descending at speed' is the ability to stop - and quickly. Downhill running is not about effort - after all, it doesn't require power to cover ground in the same direction as the earth's strong gravitational pull. The skill is in co-ordinating relaxed, high-cadence movement with the absolute faith that you have the ability to safely 'stop on a sixpence'.

Most runners when stopping quickly will throw out their lead heel, and BAM! (ouch).

Our entire body plus gravity (probably a weight equal to twice your body weight) is hitting the ground on one point of one bone when we do that. Shoes will mitigate the immediate sense of impact, but cannot fully dissipate it - that aftershock travels up the bones, away from the epicentre, stopping at the next joint (the knee) if there's a kink in it, or continuing up to the hip, which will have a kink in it if you've just struck the ground ahead of you with your heel! So, huge loads through your knees or hips with first contact on the heel, or huge loads spread across all the joints in the foot with a 'sweet spot' first contact? By now, I hope you're feeling confident in intuitively making sound, safe, comfortable, non-injurious movement choices.

Buttocks, runners. Always. They're ingenious. We're ingenious. Whether we're heading forward into the wide, blue yonder ... or stopping ... give the buttocks the job and they get it done. Don't just believe me - let's test it:

> Try to walk with both buttocks squeezed tightly together - as if stopping a rather urgent poo-call. It's not happening, is it? Full contraction of those peaches have you stopped dead in your tracks (with no chance for accidents!).

If we want forward motion, we harness the power of the glutes by loading them in hip flexion in the expectation we'll receive a free contraction from elastic recoil in return.

Conversely, if we want to stop, we can **Haul Ass** (for perfect scene-setting, this needs to be delivered in an Irish accent, as this brilliant phrase comes to you courtesy of my running friend Gearoid ...)

One of my personal running highlights was being approached by Cat St Clair from Clapham Chasers - a London running club of some repute - after being spotted descending a steep slope on an ultra event in the Cotswolds (boy, there are some *really sharp* descents in that stunning neck of the woods!). Cat is a fabulous runner, ranking in the top 1% of females at parkrun events and, at the other end of the racing spectrum, winning the female category at ultra distance events; I was truly honoured to be asked by her to come and show them "how to do it!" On the tube, travelling to teach runners I viewed as 'better than me' how to run downhill, was when I knew that 'this' (helping folk explore beneficial ways of using their bodies) was what I was destined to do, my unique gift. The warm-hearted and generous Cat will forever be in my daily gratitudes.

 I'm day-dreaming again ... of the moment we all realise that together, we've lightly nudged the indeterminate, hazy 'warm-up' phrase aside; that we've stopped boxing up body parts in singles and groups; that no matter the activity about to be started - even just 'living the day' - we've adopted the straightforward 'waking up of joints to wake up muscles', in globally-integrated 3D. That we're all WujWuming daily. I can vouch for it, as can my clients - both running and not. All those who've passed through the *Anatomy in Motion* doors will stand with me. Gary Ward will be proud. Let's Do It. WujWum. Nothing else makes as much sense ...

▲ ▲ ▲

Sailfish is the *Carlsberg* of running fun. It's essentially a free-fall descent; either not braking at all (until when you need to, of course) or braking minimally. The key is to relax everything whilst your cadence ramps up to 'nineteen-to-the-dozen'. The feeling is akin to being a hamster spinning inside its wheel - which of course you're familiar with. Isn't everyone?

That's it.

It has to be kept simple because with everything happening at speed, you'll struggle to think about anything else. The only concept you're introducing here is 'quick, quick, quick feet' - probably the quickest feet you've had in all your life!

Anatomy Dog-Leg: the 'theory' (if you can theorise an uncomplicated premise) is that a long stride would have the foot landing much lower than the piece of ground it left. So unless your pelvis can manage an ENORMOUS drop (see-saw action), the foot would "crash-land" rather than "touchdown", creating a lumpy, impactful and therefore uncomfortable ride down the slope - with increased potential for joint distress.

The concept is so simple that once experienced, most wonder why they didn't run 'like that' before. Not that I'm suggesting you should run 'like anything' of course; I'm simply offering another safe way to experiment with using gravity to your advantage. It's common to both watch runners *walk* the downhills - generally because running them hurts their knees (see anatomy dog-leg above) - and to see a braking action with first contact on their heel bones ... even the pros ... scoot to minute 55 of my favourite clip again (that great Great North Run!) and watch Mo and Haile shift 'first contact' backwards along the only down slope in the event. There is no change in Bekele's form as he slides past effortlessly, embracing the gift of gravity. I never get tired of watching Bekele run ... so effortless.

CHECKPOINT NINE NOICEBOARD

TERRAIN: 50-100M OF MEDIUM GRADIENT SLOPE
RUNNER STATUS: TTF 8 OR ABOVE
KIT LIST: LAYERS, COMFORTABLE FOOTWEAR, YOUR LEMNI, YOUR NERVE

Plan a route with a decent length of slope available to career down; somewhere between 50-100m long would be ideal. If it stretches out further you'll start by using only a part of it, but as soon as you feel ready, you'll be revelling in its entire length. Make sure your slope is of medium gradient; steep is VERY challenging on ankles new to this kind of thing, so progress to steep, but perhaps avoid starting there.

The Lemni will of course feature, as will your minimum TTF 8 mentioned at the beginning of Level 7 as being a pre-requisite for all the hill power sessions.

As per Levels 7 and 8, we pick up the session notes at the point of fully WujWumed, basic form tuned into, cadences explored, nose-breathing effort-levels and non-sogginess refined, and around 30 minutes in. But unlike the previous two sessions, degrees of Non-Soggy no longer feature once you're into the main set: the only 'pelvic feature' that's helpful to think about on the downhills is that it should be relaxed, free to move wherever it needs to.

We reach Level 9 of the pyramid with this wisdom firmly planted in the trail's fertile ground. After this session, the roots will spread as you discover for yourself the challenges of profiteering from the speed a decline freely delivers ... probably more speed than you'd have ever expected.

This session is possibly the most fun you can have whilst vertical.

I've tried for five minutes to rephrase that eloquently and succinctly, and I've given up; your filter is none of my business! I stand by my initial, innocently-typed sentence - the grins, the endorphins, the high, the thrill, the squeals of delight - never, ever failing to produce all of those ... meh, it IS the most fun you can have whilst vertical.

AND it's challenging!!

It throws down the gauntlet to all the physical and neurological connections that are going to have to sizzle to keep you on your feet. So to this BIG downhill, we're rounding up the power drills with the smaller, but no less important muscles of the lower leg. They are statistically more vulnerable, but not by their nature; the lower leg injury stats simply reflect how badly - and regularly - folk are beating them up! As Providence would have it, "Savvy" is now your middle name.

experience. So - as usual - don't just accept what I'm saying if you don't know it to be true for yourself; go and test it!

Let's look at a run programme rescheduling hypothesis:

What if you had planned Detail 9 for today, but woke up feeling yesterday's run in your legs? Yup - you've got it - you'd change your plan. That was your answer, wasn't it? For whatever reason (and it's generally the all-encompassing 'life' stuff), your TTF had dropped, so instead, you'd use your new insight to replace the scheduled run with an appropriate one prior to Level 7 in the pyramid, and help your body heal, gently influencing it through productive movement rather than focusing on trying to get back to where you'd expected to be.

Remember that word 'try'? In the context of your athleticism, you've reframed this into 'something less effortful'; and anyway, you can't speed things up, so there's no point in trying! Just let your body get on with what it needs to do, without you interfering and asking it to do things it's not ready to. In the long run, you'll get to where you want to be quicker. Always. There are no short cuts, but there are most certainly ways to get there as quickly and as efficiently as is humanly possible - by listening to your body guiding you. Your ability to train isn't governed by the sum total of your running so far, but by the sum total of **life**.

My intention is to help you keep your run schedule *moving* by making it a rule of thumb to avoid combining BIG uphill drills with BIG downhill ones. If over-enthusiasm wins, your legs will inform you of how they feel about it probably later that day, and the next and sometimes, even a handful more after that. Even when racing, use this insight to assist your pacing. It's no good racing up *and* down the hills right from the beginning if it's a long and lumpy event; you might get a fast start, but you're more likely than not to get a disappointingly slow finish.

gravity its 'full pull'. Fit and well, having progressed attentively and intelligently through all the previous sessions over however long a period that needed to be, we're going to "release the leash".

 **Here, you reap the rewards of following a well-beaten path to the beat of your drum, whilst honing skills to customise your running programme.**

With our Intention Marker staring us in the face, let's start enhancing both your run training *and* your all-important programme planning with a bit of clear thinking.

The trail so far has taken us along a journey of connectivity within our structures, where feeling for what networks with what in terms of joints and soft tissue has been explored, with new associations discovered at every level. *'If something moves, everything moves'* seems an overstatement, but actually, whilst we can try to isolate body parts, in gait of any speed, the joy of movement is in the *integration*. And if you're using your body explosively, *everything* gets charged to help out; where each previous downhill focused on kindly taxing the quads, *the quads were still working on the uphill*, you simply noticed it more where the targeted work was directed.

You might have exemplified this for yourself if you found you fatigued earlier when performing Flounders than you did with Salmons. Yes, the drill itself is more explosively effortful, demanding that you dump all your momentum and rely only on eruptive power to drive you up the hill. But the quads are being fired up in *both* directions of the slope, and so the quicker weariness is likely to also come from the double-whammy of loading.

If you feel comfortable embracing that thought-process, then can you see that if you overtax the quads during a hill power session by *strongly* challenging them both on the up <u>and</u> the down, you'll probably find your reps peter out sooner rather than later? And when your quads are trashed, it's just plain difficult to run. Period. So many times at events, I'm passed on the uphill (I'm efficient remember, not fast) by runners leaning in, driving themselves up against gravity using their toes, knees, elbows and determination, only for me to pass them back once the gradient becomes kinder because my legs still work and their quads are in pieces. It's not rocket science, it's just a modicum of understanding, reinforced by repetitive

DETAIL 9: HILL DRILLS 3 SAILFISH, CRABS AND PSYCHEDELICA

Do you love running up hills, but hate going down because your knees hurt? Maybe you're one of many I listen to, afraid of embracing the assistance of the downward slope? Let's have fun with our friend Gravity.

Up until now, you've held back on every downhill, controlled your momentum and not allowed the hill to gift you speed, conceding only to the bonus of reduced effort levels. You've been doing this willingly because you discovered for yourself, back along the trail, that down slopes are a goodie bag of efficient form guidance, offering you invaluable structural alignment and internal sensory advice.

Whilst slicing off a good chunk of perceived effort, they also provided the opportunity to gently increase the workloads of the swathes of muscles tracking along the front of your body, particularly your quadriceps muscle group at the front of your thigh.

So co-operatively and concurrently, your flat and uphill running have been successfully conditioning everything that propels you forward from the back, and the downhills have been busy developing dynamic endurance in all the soft tissues that create counterbalance at the front.

Now, you're in a position to capitalise on the accumulated improved co-ordination and increased strength of your integrated, 3D movement patterns. By waiting and allowing *Time* its effect, your ankles will also be better prepared for the challenges inherent in allowing

LEVEL NINE
FLYING DOWN, BOUNCING UP

LEVEL NINE CONTENTS

Checkpoint Nine 327
Stopping 330
Flying Down 331
Bouncing Up 332
Checkpoint Nine Noticeboard:
    Summary and Departure 339

DEPARTING LEVEL EIGHT ▲▲▲
RUNNER STATUS: TTF 8 AND RISING
- ✔ INCREASING STAMINA AND RESILIENCE
- ✔ FEEDING NOURISHING MOVEMENT
- ✔ STIMULATING HEIGHTENED AWARENESS, AND SO
- ✔ READY FOR THE GIFT OF GRAVITY

LEVEL EIGHT SUMMARY + CLOCK IN/CLOCK OUT ▲

- ✓ WujWums, walking and running warm-up, to include 'Range of Cadence' and pacing detail.
- ✓ The Flounder Hill Drills:
  - 'Test' Flounder at 3/4 effort (with 15° of Non-Soggy being the goal).
  - 3 drills to highlight sagittal, frontal and transverse plane joint rotations challenging the glutes, quads and hamstrings and connecting those to the torso:
    - Bent Knee Hammie
    - Round The Clock You Go!
    - 3D-D3
  - 3 more Baby Flounders with recovery after each one provided by the stationary drills.
  - Add *The Lemni* and notice any global co-ordination changes with one last Baby Flounder.
  - Repeat each drill, followed by 4 grown-up Flounders incorporating *The Lemni* and adding the *thought* of 20° of Non-Soggy when that's possible.
  - Final ABARAFAP Flounder.
- ✓ 15 min recovery trot into a final walk, or just a walk back to base if you're that close.
- ✓ And REST!

On a practical level, if you're short of time, Hill Drills sessions are the perfect use of it - particularly if you happen to have the ideal hill within a 5 minute cool-down walk. Having warmed up thoroughly, and once you're familiar with the movements, you could perform up to 5 big power reps with enough rest in between provided by the drill execution time in a total of about 45 minutes, *including* cool-down. That's around half of your explosive strength potential honed in less than an hour, whilst having fun. Bish-bash-bosh; they don't call me the Queen of Efficiency for nothing.

You might find you recover more slowly from Flounders than Salmons. They're both power hill sets, but explosive single leg squats are more challenging than the fluid bounding actions that make use of the free energy from elastic recoil. If you notice this, avoid planning them into your schedule within 48 hours of any longer runs.

Things are really coming together now. And the wait for the Gift of Gravity is nearly over ...

Mama Flounder 6 after repeating Drill 1:
Bent Knee Hammie + The Lemni

Papa Flounder 7 after repeating Drill 2:
Round The Clock You Go! + The Lemni

Mama Flounder 8 after repeating Hang Onto Your Newton's Cradle! (Sagittal WujWum) + The Lemni

Papa Flounder 9 after repeating Drill 3: 3D-D3 + The Lemni

Mama & Papa Flounder 10:
Final Hill Rep: Just Thinking "As Big, As Robust, As *Floundering* As Possible" (ABARAFAP)

Common sense should always prevail during sessions that involve intensity. Ten powerful hill drills is something to work towards not necessarily achieve on your first attempt. If you feel your body wilting and your oomph starting to disappear halfway up the incline, then either revert to Baby Flounders or call it day. If you feel you have 'one more good one' left in you, make it an ABARAFAP one. As you regularly repeat the challenge of the power hill drills you'll find you'll be able to complete more of the ascents and before long you'll notice that the length of hill covered increases as your stride length increases. Simple yet objective measures of improvement.

Unlike the Salmons session, the final hill ascent of Flounders is often the toughest; accumulative huge efforts have taken their toll, so the run back to base will be blessed relief! Interestingly, many are so relaxed their form is often the most fluent, fluid and fabulous they've ever displayed. If this happens to you, it's a bit of an eye-opener, as you'll probably consider yourself doing little more than 'drifting' back. A prime example of you finally 'letting your body run you'.

Baby Flounder 4:
Is Ascent 4 of Baby Flounders accessing BIGGER and more GLOBALLY co-ordinated movements following Hang Onto Your Newton's Cradle and 3D-D3 for slings? These drills normally invoke so much tangible difference that the chatter of biofeedback from your body can seem almost audible! What did *you* feel?

Baby Flounders 5: Add *The Lemni*
Having gone global, there's nothing left to do but gather up all this bubbling, potential energy to drive it in the only direction you want it to go - UP THE HILL! Grab your *Lemni* and Flounder up one more time at 3/4 effort. You might actually *look* like a Flounder now!

From here on - provided you feel it's safe to do so - all the hill repetitions will be at *maximum effort* - full Flounders. *Mama & Papa Flounders!* You may or may not yet be able to transition to 20° of Non-Soggy, just know that the goal is to be able to think about degrees of Non-Soggy in due course. There is no 'running form' as such - Flounders are all about co-ordinating sequential single leg squats - although you do want to be mindful about staying upright and not trying to Flounder along a tightrope; the drill is hard enough as it is without adding even more balancing into the equation. The faff time around the stationary drills will provide the couple of minutes' rest between each ascent needed to ensure both good recovery and the management of the alactic energy system.

The Sagittal WujWum - is there no end to its usefulness?

Don't you just love it when nature's cleverness all 'comes together'?

Talking of which - grab a tree or a lamp-post at shoulder height or a partners opposite arm for **"3D-D3"** for slings: *vimeo.com/244976486*

- The same side leg as the gripping arm steps far back as your body bends forward (sagittal plane loading).
- Your rear leg crosses behind (dropping the pelvis, creating more load in the frontal plane).
- The free arm drives through the 'rabbit hole' created by the gripping arm and it's 'pillar' (breathing or otherwise); with this rotation t*owards*, you've added the final transverse plane loading of the POS.
- Maintaining the hand-hold, come to upright and step *forward* simultaneously rotating *away*.

- You've now extended, abducted and externally rotated the shoulder joint, lifting the sternum and loading the AOS.
- Step back, flex forwards, cross free leg behind and drive through the rabbit hole ...
- Step forward, extend upright, rotate away making sure that you step into different forward positions to load as many vectors of muscle fibre as you can within the sling of the AOS.

- What's happened to your legs?
- Have they externally rotated?
- Now then, where was that final attachment of the POS ...?
- Yup - that'll be lateral upper shin, which is internally rotating relative to the external rotation of the thigh ... tick - POS fully loaded.

Anatomy Dog-Leg: to avoid missing the icing on the cake: The Front Functional Line - or Anterior Oblique Sling, AOS - 'starts' on the upper arm too, but this one flows across the pectoralis major muscle to the 5/6th rib cartilage, along the lateral sheath of your rectus abdominis (6-pack muscle) and then across to the opposite adductor longus muscle via your pubic bone, 'ending' mid-thigh. We're sandwiched by Efficiency Apps, whose updates require no more than frequent use!

And what about the Anterior Oblique Sling?

- From the position of a fully loaded POS, release the tension.
- Now externally rotate the arms, driving outwards with the thumbs.
- Feel the shoulder blades get pulled together, towards the spine (retraction).
- They'll travel further in if you allow the chest to lift and open .
- Notice the head tip forwards ...
- ... and the tailbone untuck with the anterior tilt of the pelvis ...
- Taking that pubic bone further away.
- We're really loading those pectoralis and abdominal muscles now!
- Remind you of anything yet?
- If you don't recognise Sagittal Cog on the inhale and our Amazonian Warrior I'm going to have to rewrite the book!
- What's happened to your thighs?
- Have they been drawn together slightly?
- Now then, where was that final attachment of the AOS ... ?
- Ah yes - adductor longus ... and with the internal rotation of the thigh bone, that's getting a lovely load too.
- AOS fully loaded? You bet!

Well, we've got our own. We're the only upright mammal in possession of these amazing slings and we have them across our backs AND our fronts. They're our evolutionary tour de force – our strokes of genius to evade double-trouble locomotive problems: the inefficiencies of having to defy gravity AND the resultant loss of momentum. Not for us the sideways slither of a reptile, wasting time repetitively moving at 90 degrees to our destination, nor the up and down yo-yoing of a kangaroo or rabbit, with energy expended against the force of gravity and energy lost into the ground at impact ... no, as humans we have the tools to skillfully and efficiently effect forward motion with minimal loss of energy, through the transverse motions of the pelvic rotation and the torso counter-rotation, and without loss of momentum through the staggeringly efficient storage and release of energy in our not-very-stretchy-but-stretchy-enough slings. Fluid, flowing, forward motion.

Perpetual Forward Motion. We are AMAZING!

And just to recap – that natural torso counter-rotation to the movement of the pelvis is a series of muscle actions ... across your back AND your front. Every step folks is activity of the oblique abdominal muscles that wrap up your waist. Say you take the advised 10,000 steps per day ... that's 5000 contractions of your obliques on each side. Your activity tracker pedometer suddenly seems so much more ... meaningful, doesn't it? Steps, blah, blah, blah. Ab workout? Helloooo!

OK - back to business and the third drill. We have a Posterior Oblique Sling to 'wake up' and offer the soft tissue a bigger world in which to create energy. Here's a simple version:

vimeo.com/244975264

- Bi-lateral stance.
- Internally rotate the arms, driving inwards with the thumbs.
- Feel the shoulder blades get dragged around the rib-cage (protraction).
- They'll go further if you allow the chest to cave.
- Notice the head fall backwards ...
- ... and the tailbone tuck under ...
- Remind you of anything yet?

- Goodness me, if we haven't bumped into our old friend Sagittal Cog, Mr Hunchback on the exhale? Small world!

Anatomy Dog-Leg: Just as a reminder, the Posterior Oblique Sling 'starts' (if anything can be considered 'starting' or 'stopping' within the context of the human body) where the latissumus dorsi muscle attaches to the inner part of the upper arm, threading its way across the lower spine to the opposite glute, wrapping around the upper thigh to the vastus lateralis and 'ending' on the outside of the tibia (main shinbone).

Simplifying things, imagine it as a not-very-stretchy-but-really-quite-strong sheet of fabric – like a bandage - connecting the back of the armpit to the opposite hip (we'll leave the limbs out of the picture for the moment, just to gain some brain bandwidth). Now picture a matching pair forming a great big X across your back. Let's call this big X a pair of slings, which are elastic but NOT very stretchy.

So if one end is pulled, it will probably lift whatever it's attached to at the other, right? If you stand up, you can join in. You don't need to delve into anatomical hypotheses, just pull gently on the top of the sling by easing that shoulder forward, and notice that the opposite heel lifts a little via the opposite hip which lifted first. But if that hip lifted a little, then the other side of your pelvis must have been pushed down a little – just like a mini see-saw.

Wait! A downward hip rotation fires the buttocks ... and a buttock contraction is all part of hip extension, which pushes us forward into a stride. We started this line of discovery at the foundation level of this trail, with the depth of connectivity our amazing biomechanics has evolved to possess just continuing to be realised the further along the path we go.

And so to the christening of this drill: Sir Isaac Newton apparently 'lent' his name to the Newton Cradle steel ball desk pendulums ... you know the ones, where you pick up the outside ball and let it fall against the waiting row of steel balls; the impact travels through the row to the outside one, which kicks out, and on its return starts the process from the other side? On and on, seemingly forever, because there's so little loss of momentum and energy.

Drill 3:
Hang Onto Your Newton's Cradle! And so to **3D-D3**
By now, you'll probably have noticed that this particular level of the pyramid is quite tough terrain, with the focus so far having been on what's happening below the waist. Now, with this drill, let's go global.

As runners, we're interested in posture because as one of my tutors, Paul Chek says *"Posture is the foundation from which movement emerges"*; phrased slightly differently, he describes posture as *"... the position from which movement begins and ends"*. If we consider that movement begins with one posture and ends with another - which may or may not be the same (your backflip might have ended with you in a crumpled heap on the floor) - *what's the bit in between?*

Let's be radical and call it a 'series of postures' that in slow motion can be broken down, but in real-time motion happen so fast we only see - and feel - the fluid nature of the constantly changing postures. What generates those is the activity of co-operative, co-ordinating swathes of soft tissue following the dance of transitioning skeletal poses, driven by complex reflexive motor programme patterns stored in the brain.

It's all in our pre-programmed DNA of course, and has become more 'mainstream' with the amazing work in the dissection lab of Thomas W. Myers and described in his *"Anatomy Trains"*. His theories build on the concepts of others too numerous to mention, but the anatomist Raymond A. Dart seemed pretty in-tune with it all as far back as the 1950s. Gary Ward's Flow Motion Model™ is the first time the series of postures that create gait has been broken down and described in three-dimensional detail at each joint. Truly a visionary piece of work.

Anyway, this book isn't being written to prove anatomy and biomechanics, but to *use them*!

We have what is dubbed a Back Functional Line (functional lines always appear as a spiral and work like a helix) - otherwise known as the Posterior Oblique Sling, POS. It popped up at Level 5, around the time you were swooning in the manner of 'Oh! Mr Darcy'.

Anatomy Dog-Leg: Here's a useful formula:
pronation = VMO action = its job in gait!
Not allowing pronation through, for example, deliberate thought processes or restrictive footwear, restricts the ability of the VMOs to fire, leading to muscle weakening (read: atrophy!); you can do as many reps on the knee extension machine in the gym as you want to 'make' the tear-dropped shaped muscles so necessary for controlling knee movement, but you won't get to use them effectively as long as the pronation potential of your feet is disabled. The act of pronation is your free knee-gym membership. We don't need to be 'anti-pronation': pronation is 50% of the mechanics of 66 joints in your body!

(This is *much* harder than it looks, and James did an incredible job to hold the position for the camera shot with his face calmly belying the effort his neck sinews were showing. Especially after the 5th 'take'. Well done and thank you James - great training!).

And because we're runners moving on natural terrain when we can, our feet might land on something that causes our foot to rock outwards during the weight-bearing process. So we need to reproduce those more 'sport-related forces' to be ready for them:

- Free, straight leg taps around the clock, with pelvis rotated *away from free leg, and towards stance leg (foot no longer pronates).*
- 1 o'clock to 5 o'clock with the right leg.
- 11 o'clock to 7 o'clock with the left.
- Notice the vastus lateralis get fully-charged up with this subtle change.

<u>Baby Flounder 3:</u>
Is Ascent 3 of Baby Flounders accessing better/more explosive knee extension following Round The Clock You Go? Did the biofeedback change from the previous rep? What is your body telling you about its state of balance and explosive power? Now that the drill isn't so new, were you able to spare some brain space for thinking about 15° of Non-Soggy? How do you feel?

Drill 2: Round The Clock You Go!: vimeo.com/245615295

With Floundering being about strengthening via the explosive action of knee extension, we'd better 'wake-up' those muscles that are eccentrically-loaded (lengthened under load) in knee flexion. That way, they'll get the chance to step up and give us more response when they contract via the shortening of elastic recoil. The greater the knee flexion, the more the knee travels inwards via the eversion and internal rotation of the heel and talus bones i.e. p-r-o-n-a-t-i-o-n, and the more the vastus medialis oblique (VMO - the tear-drop shaped muscle just above the knee on the inside) and the vastus lateralis (along the outside of the thigh) will kick in to decelerate the inward knee travel.

In single leg stance with a bent knee:
- Free, straight leg taps around the clock, with pelvis rotated towards free leg; really reach with the tapping foot to charge the weight-bearing VMO with something interesting to do:
- 1 o'clock to 5 o'clock with the right leg.
- 11 o'clock to 7 o'clock with the left.

- The hip needs to flex faster than the knee to lengthen the proximal fibres, so keep the pelvis in anterior tilt ie keep your bum sticking out (this couples with spinal extension, so we'll be avoiding rounding backs for this drill).
- Reach forward and down with both arms.
- If you feel more quad than hamstring, you've posteriorly tilted the pelvis; in fact, let's try it. Lunge forward with your tailbone tucked under and feel the quads load strongly - this isn't what you're looking for - yet!
- The knee needs to be flexed, but if the lead foot is too close to you the distal fibres won't get the length you're aiming to gift them, so throw that foot out to get a decent stride and more bang for your buck.
- Repeat this dynamic lunge pattern, with arms moving through 10 o'clock to 2 o'clock and back again to access both the medial and the lateral fibres of the hamstrings at the bent knee.
- Swap lead leg and repeat.

Baby Flounder 2:
Is Ascent 2 of Baby Flounders accessing a longer stride following Bent Knee Hammie Load? What biofeedback did you receive from your internal antenna?

the centre of the body) of the *entire* hammie muscle group are shortening at the moment of ground contact, as they work to control knee extension; they flex the knee slightly to bring the foot more or less under it for a safe landing.

This is an example of what's happening continually all the way through the body, in that tension through the length of a single muscle (or muscle group) is not consistent; you could say that at that critical moment of touchdown, the muscle group is multi-tasking. And it's normal; it's in our DNA to be able to perform perfectly-timed combinations of the same muscle lengthening and shortening in different areas whilst under load. But we can only manage these musculoskeletal medleys 'healthily' (read: safely) if we don't repetitively bump into their maximum boundaries of motion. If we keep in mind that muscles react to the action of the joint:

'SAFETY IN MOVEMENT' IS WHERE THE PERIMETER WITHIN WHICH A JOINT CAN MOVE IS BIGGER THAN THAT OF ITS FAMILIAR RECITAL.

Put another way, if a joint starts to occupy a world that reflects an ever-decreasing echo of its potential, then one false move could have the soft tissue responding to the next joint action with a 'Yelp'!

Simplified further, a stride will be instinctively foreshortened by the central nervous system (our self-preservation mechanism) if its sense is that the lead knee can only extend out of its state of flexion "so far" before loading takes place at touchdown. All that glute power, snatched from glory before the foot even gets a chance to touchdown. Shame.

Shall we continue to broaden the horizons of an active knee? Particularly on behalf of our flexed-hip/extendING-but-still-flexed-knee running hero? **The-bent-knee-hammie-load:** *vimeo.com/245612404*

- The movement starts with a split stance lunge, one foot in front of the other, with the lead knee bending.

A *little* bit of anatomy first. Most folk think of the hamstrings starting on the ischial tuberosities (your sit bones) and ending in the tendons on either side of the knee joint. And this is true, but incomplete. The biceps femoris has two heads, a long one - attaching alongside the semitendinosus and the semimembranosus on the sit bone - and a short one - attaching along a good length of the back of the thigh bone, starting from about half way down it.

Anatomy Dog-Leg: This might be the perfect moment to grab your favourite anatomy book or app and get a visual of the hamstring muscle group whilst we work our way through this session. And whilst you're at it, sit yourself in an upright kind of chair, without nestling your back-side into the back of it, and lean slightly forwards, as if at a desk or eating from a table (but don't stay here long). The front edge of the chair seat digs into the mid-back of your thighs, just in the region of the start of one of your main hamstring players. Just sayin'!

Hamstring strains are common even in elite athletes, such as is seen when the footballer or the sprinter hauls him/herself to an abrupt stop, clutching the mid-back of their thighs whilst grimacing in agony.

Scan to watch
Slo-mo sprinters

Consider the lead leg, knee bent in early flight, then extending as the foot heads away from the body to open the stride out, but actually still FLEXED as the foot comes down to take the body's load (the embodiment of running - at whatever speed - is that the lead knee IS NOT STRAIGHT AT TOUCHDOWN (that's walking, right?). Scan the QR code to see a slo-mo clip of sprinters and observe the moment I'm referring to. Can you see that at touchdown, the proximal (closest to the centre of the body) part of the hamstrings are lengthened and therefore eccentrically loaded? They are busy controlling hip flexion (apart from the short head of the biceps femoris - it doesn't cross the hip joint so isn't part of hip movement). Simultaneously, the distal fibres (furthest from

Ascents 1-5 are "Baby Flounders" at 3/4 effort - so 'quite hard' but not 'all-out' - gradually exposing your joints to bigger ranges of motion and the soft tissue to greater intensities of reaction, minimising injury risk and enabling you to focus on the co-ordination of flailing body parts.

Ascents 6-10 are 'all-out' "Mama and Papa Flounders" - they still won't look pretty (that being the onomatopoeic nature of Floundering), but they should be more powerful as assorted limbs start to fire in some kind of order.

 Whilst in theory this would equate to 15° of Non-Soggy for the Baby and 20° for the Mama & Papa versions, the drill is so challenging, you might find it difficult to notice the difference between the two, especially at the beginning. Don't lose heart, and at least pay lip service to thinking about the two; in time, you'll find your awareness, strength and skills improve enough that your degrees of Non-Soggy become an integral part of your Floundering prowess.

Baby Flounder 1: The Control
Playing our game of comparisons, this is our start point. Ascent 1 is 'The Control' - no pre-drills, no *Lemni*, just your first attempt at this 'easier than it sounds' action, which is actually much harder than it looks! Unlike Salmons, this isn't a 'strong' version of what you've been practising since the beginning of the book. By adding 'sticky' time-on-ground, this is no longer even 'running'! This drill is all about chunking down the components of running and amplifying them. It looks a mess, but it's effective and it's fun. And its particular strength is highlighting individual mass-management weaknesses within runners. Flounder drills are intent on fulfilling their intention: *HOW balanced are you as you fly through the air landing on an itsy-bitsy part of one foot, spreading the load through 33 mobile joints and pausing there before launching off again?* How far do you travel up the slope with 2 strides to 'get you going', followed by 20 standing leaps?

Drill 1: The Bent Knee Hammie Load!
Ooooo - this is an interesting one! And all the more fun for not being stereotypical.

- To reinforce that hip extension should ALWAYS result in "2 points of contact in trail leg". *

- To create awareness that the big muscles of the upper body work in synergy with the big muscles of the lower body *when enabled to do so*. The movement information is already present in our make-up, but most runners just simply aren't aware of the connections.

- To create a strengthening shortening-lengthening cycle of the hip flexors via:
  - enough knee lift to maximise the stride's potential length (lifting your leg is weight-training in and of itself - it's heavy!).
  - momentarily holding the squat position.
  - the subsequent explosive extension.

- Yes, well done - you noticed the anomaly! Actively lifting the knee whilst running **is** a waste of effort and therefore inefficient, but our hip flexors need to be strong and of quality soft tissue if they're to be the fabulous catapult that they *can be*. We *pump* the muscle under non-efficient, self-limiting, powerful and explosive conditions to generate the functional strength we need for enduring, productive, efficient running form.

- To work powerfully hard whilst maintaining the basics of form (the goal remains to stay upright, with weight-shift), stopping before fatigue negatively affects form, to avoid risk of injury.

There's a lot here to benefit from, you just need to leave your self-consciousness at home, and be willing to laugh at the antics your befuddled and probably less-balanced-than-you-thought body is going to show you.

Begin at the top of your hill venue; all descents are the same as Levels 3 and 7 - with you controlling the pull of gravity. Once the power work in all the gross-mover muscle groups has had a chance to create a strengthening effect (Levels 7 and 8), we'll be ready to safely enjoy the thrill of taking the downhills *using* the benefits of gravity. Your patience will be rewarded!

---

remembering that's the sum total of pelvic rotation, pelvic drop, hip external rotation, hip extension, knee extension, ankle extension and foot supination.

recognisably opening their bodies by creating more joint space in preparation for bigger, easier, more fluid movement ....

Coming back from my reverie, let's head straight to the 'flesh on the fish bones' of Floundering, which you should be warmed up to and ready to start no more than 30 minutes into the session.

WHAT'S SO GOOD ABOUT FLOUNDERING?

It's a good question, especially with one of Dom's 'stickmen' depicting a clear image of 'Knees Up Mother Brown'; I can only advise that you don't knock it until you've tried it. Quite apart from the sheer fun you're going to have by getting into character and generating the inimitable style of a discombobulated, stop-start, lumbering 'Flounderer', the concepts behind the brilliant Flounder Drills are:

- To strongly challenge the hip flexors and quads, assisted by the hamstrings and posterior oblique sling (remember the fascial sling connecting the huge latissimus dorsi muscles to the opposite glutes from Level 5?) functionally and maximally. With Salmons focusing the power on the glutes and hamstrings, we can use Flounder drills to create muscular balance in the anterior thighs.

- To lurch up the slope in a series of leaps, strung together with pregnant pauses just long enough that momentum is lost - if it looks fluent, fluid and 'good', you're cheating!

- To powerfully translate the momentarily stationary single-leg **balanced** squat into as big a stride as possible through hip, knee and ankle extension.

- To travel as far up the ascent as possible using the familiar formula of 2 rolling + 20 explosive strides.

- To regain from the plantar-fascia some of what is lost through lack of momentum, by ensuring the *whole* of the lead foot is in contact with the ground before one *single* explosive push-off is instigated. A little bounce on toes before the 'spring' IS considered cheating, because it's MUCH easier! Think coiled cat ready to leap ...

PRINCIPLE 8: HILL DRILLS 2 MAMA & PAPA FLOUNDERS

You're as strong as your weakest link. You might have buns of steel, but they'll only punch their weight if muscles at the front of your body are made of equally sturdy stuff.

▲ **This is where you'll discover the art of running balance: building strength on both sides of your thighs and the skill of single-leg loading.**

Detail 8 is fondly known as 'Ronseal'; it does (and looks) exactly as it says on the tin! It actions another 'flavour' in the bag of power hill drills, offering a second example of how you can use hills as an outdoor gym to positively affect enduring running strength; the essence of it flows seamlessly from Level 7. Everything you needed for Salmons you need for Flounders, although a steeper slope than the one you used for Level 7 of your pyramid actually works to your advantage here. Please note that a shallow slope won't work very well at all. Don't forget your , and finally, be honest with yourself and do one of the other non-strength sessions if your TTF score is less than 8.

As mentioned before, the warm-up sections of Levels 7, 8 and 9 are all the same. So to avoid repetition and more printed pages than is necessary, I'll remind you of sagittal, frontal, transverse and feet WujWums and leave it at that. When I day-dream, it's of watching runners I've never met WujWuming on their door-steps, in the park, at the track,

LEVEL EIGHT
BALANCING FLOUNDERS

LEVEL EIGHT CONTENTS

What's so good about Floundering? 305
Checkpoint Eight Noticeboard:
    Checkpoint Eight Summary 320

> DEPARTING LEVEL SEVEN ▲▲▲
> **RUNNER STATUS:** TTF 8 AND RISING
> ✔ CONFIDENCE BUILDING BY PROVIDING INTENSITY
> ✔ MOTHER NATURE PROVIDING THE GYM
> ✔ IMPROVED JOINT SPACE PROVIDING THE POWER

LEVEL SEVEN CLOCK-IN/ CLOCK OUT ▲

Once you've reached the *whoopee!* action of Functional Strength Hill Drills, you can plan this session into your running programme once a week. Provided you stick to the strategy of strict limitation on strides/seconds, you can run the next day and even do this session the day prior to a longer run, subject to the focus of the long run being only high volume - not intensity - and you have the TTF to support the activity.

When both your body and brain have become more familiar with the drills and with internal sensing, you'll feel confident in launching into full Salmons after just a few Salmonettes; the 3/4 efforts are there to ensure your body is properly prepared for the full efforts. Just be careful not to do more than 10 hill reps at full power; longer big efforts means dipping your toes into type IIa muscle fibre work which means a longer recovery ... from 48 hours to a week, dependent entirely on 'you'.

> "FOR THE 99 PERCENT OF THE TIME WE'VE BEEN ON EARTH, WE WERE HUNTER AND GATHERERS, OUR LIVES DEPENDENT ON KNOWING THE FINE, SMALL DETAILS OF OUR WORLD. DEEP INSIDE, WE STILL HAVE A LONGING TO BE RECONNECTED WITH THE NATURE THAT SHAPED OUR IMAGINATION, OUR LANGUAGE, OUR SONG AND DANCE, OUR SENSE OF THE DIVINE."
> **JANINE M. BENYUS,**
> **AMERICAN SCIENCE WRITER**

As much as learning about how your body moves better, great running is about studying your recovery times too, paying attention to them, noticing them modify with the ever-changing balances within your energy bucket. Use your internal radar, and learn to trust it. 'You' really are all you need, and 'you' really are all you've got - what a great team - body and brain showing rapport and unity, just as they have for millennia.

LEVEL SEVEN SUMMARY CHECK LIST ▲

- ✔ WujWums, walking and running warm-up, to include 'Range of Cadence' and pacing sensing details.
- ✔ The Salmon Hill Drills:
    - 'Test' Salmonette at 3/4 effort, introducing 15° of Non-Soggy.
    - 4 drills to highlight sagittal, frontal and transverse plane joint rotations around the lower back, pelvis, hip and thigh, to improve hamstring activity:
        - Dive In
        - Hammie Stork
        - Hammie Crab
        - Pentopus

    with four 22 stride sprints (representing 9-10 seconds) after each one.
    - 6th Salmonette introducing *The Lemni*.
    - Following a repeat of each drill, 3 Salmons at full effort, introducing 20° of Non-Soggy and adding one of the thought-processes introduced in session 5:
        - energy rises through bones falling with gravity
        - 2 points of contact with trail leg
        - leave the pelvis behind youuuuuu ... (with the trail leg!).
    - 10th and final sprint uses 'ABARAFAP' (As Big, As Relaxed, As Flowing As Possible) as the primary thought to pull together the now-effective hip extension with an ever-present Big Toe in the presence of s-p-a-c-e.
- ✔ 15 recovery trot into a final walk, back to base.

- Repeat Drill 4: Pentopus; run **Salmon 9** adding *The Lemni* and the thought **"2 points of contact, trail leg"**.
- **Salmon 10** is your Final Hill Rep. Your Thought is **"As Big, As Relaxed, As Flowing As Possible"** - **ABARAFAP** - it sounds like a spell and it's often pretty magical.

The final hill ascent is often described as the 'easiest'. Despite accumulative efforts giving rise to natural fatigue, you'd probably finally stopped *trying* so much and were simply letting your body's newly-discovered joint rotations, stretch recoil catapults and DNA-driven co-ordination do all the work - often to surprisingly better effect. Not an uncommonly heard remark is "Where did the hill go?"

After all the short but very hard efforts, the easy run back to base will feel effortless by comparison, and very enjoyable because of it! And if Salmons or Pentopodes aren't the main topic of conversation the next time you're with your running mates, then A-Bara-Fap should surely feature!

Always remember to incorporate a final walk into your cool-down, especially important after you've used muscles with intensity. It's perfectly acceptable to stress your muscles and create metabolic waste products - in fact, to get stronger that's what you have to do - provided the stress is followed by helpful movement to pump the metabolites away without creating more. Next to the MAFA and *The Lemni*, walking is every runners' best friend and in my experience, not enough use any of those three tools.

With the exaggeration inherent in power drills, you might start noticing that as your trail, propelling foot supinates, the same side hand pronates (palm down) as it 'throws its weight' over to the opposite foot via the lemniscation of *The Lemni* ... once found, this little gem is ready for you to use whenever you want to; it's weight-shift on (legal) steroids. And it helped Mat to his destination (a marathon-a-day-for-7-days to cross the UK along Wainwright's Coast to Coast path):

"Thank you so much for your help, I never would have got past the first couple of days without improved form, all your great advice, and my Lemni!"

You'll find a moving sub 3-minute documentary of his and Katie's adventure on YouTube under "**c2c4BLC Our Journey**".

Here's Pip, enjoying his Lemni, on one of his enjoyable jaunts along the Thames.

If you notice yourself start to struggle to maintain the same forward momentum throughout the 20 big strides, then either continue according to the session plan but reduce your Salmons to Salmonettes or, if you feel you have energy for one last big one, skip to Salmon 10 and finish your session with an 'ABARAFAP'.

From Ascent 7, we start adding some brain power to the drills, using the same 'thoughts' as we covered at Level 5.

- Repeat Drill 1: Dive In; run **Salmon 7** adding *The Lemni* and the thought **"energy rises through bones falling with gravity ..."**
- Repeat Drill 2 or 3: Hammie Stork or Hammie Crab (use whichever you felt achieved the better result); run **Salmon 8** adding *The Lemni* and the thought **"Leave the pelvis behind youuuuu!"**

<u>Salmonette 6:</u> Adding The *Lemni*.

There are no further new drills to Level 7, but before you repeat them all once again, add *The Lemni* for the first time, and feel efficiency-reducing flailing arms disappear, co-ordination of upper and lower bodies spontaneously improve and listen to your internal commentary of 'ooo, more abs' and 'wow, more power' ... I'll be smiling contentedly. You're 'getting it'.

From here on, **provided you feel it's safe to**, all the hill repetitions will be at *maximum effort whilst holding form* - full Salmons, Full Monty, 20° of Non-Soggy.

 Please note: max effort, max non-soggy, max speed ... whilst holding form.
NOT 'lose all sense of self and welly yourself with full charge up the hill'.

Each drill creates the couple of minutes rest between each ascent required to ensure both good recovery and the management of the alactic energy system.

Get into character and play the game; no-one's looking:
- An Octopus has its tentacles wrapped around your trail ankle and is pulling it inexorably down into its lair; this both increases the pressure through the pitchforking met-heads and pulls on the pelvis - both down on that side and slightly backwards, increasing posterior tilt.
- *Can you feel your flexor chain being loaded through your abdominals and the hip flexors?*
- There's a momentary tug-of-war going on between your amazingly strong 'pitchforking' met-heads, coupled with their wonderfully 'flat-to-the-ground-and-not-flexing-or-clawing-at-all' extended toes - and the Octopus ... And suddenly you're free ...
- Your ankle is abruptly released and with the sudden freedom comes an upward swing of the pelvis; we're using the recoil from the propulsion of two points of contact in the trail leg to hike the hip. The Pentopus is born ... 'suckered' met-heads ... who knew?
- Don't be a party-pooper - get into the spirit of the drill, which is fun and use your imagination to get your Pentopus to beat the Octopus, generating recoil speed as your met-heads get unsuckered. Pelvis's should be Pinging into 'Free Hike' all over the place (James was having fun, he just looks serious because he was focusing to maintain the honesty of the recoil for the repeat 'takes' required to capture the recoil!).

Start with slow repetitions so you can feel what's going on, then speed things up to get some real 'swing from the spring'. It's common for this drill to highlight a missing link. You may well be able to position yourself into a split stance with the pelvis hiked with the forward foot and the pelvis dropped with the rearward foot *statically* ... but the natural, fluid movement in and out of the pelvic hike/drop can feel like a real struggle, with a *reactive recoil* almost impossible for some initially. Don't worry - this drill is simple and the movement is in your DNA - so applaud any little bit of progress you notice. You WILL get there if you *let* and don't *try*, with the benefits being rewarding in terms of free energy. Sooo worth the patience of giving birth to ...

Salmonette 5:
On the following ascent at 3/4 effort, 15° Non-Soggy, tune into the molten, free-flowing effect of a pelvis swinging lightly upwards, equipping the running gait with the powerful addition of an effortlessly flying leg, recoiling weightlessly, and worthy of notice.

PENTOPODES

Drill 4:
The Octopus fell in love with all 5 Met-Heads, giving birth to the Pentopus (pl. Pentopodes!): *vimeo.com/245614375*

We can approach the concept of improving elastic recoil (and so efficiency of movement) in several ways. We can explore the muscle tissue from one end to the other via all its muscle fibre vectors, *and* we can dig into the influence of ground reaction - *effectively* using the ground as a springboard. The ground - of course - isn't springy, but using our imaginations and positional changes taken from a couple of hundred or so nano-moments in the gait phase, we can gain access to some recoiling joint actions. Let's leave no stone unturned.

- Split stance with weight in the front, bent leg.
- Tripod contact front foot (heel and right across the forefoot), 2 points of contact trail foot - this (as you know well now) is from base of big toe to the base of little toe, and the only way you're going to access this is by rotating the pelvis towards the rear foot.
- Now we have an internally rotating lead femur and bent/open knee above a pronating foot and an externally rotating trail femur, leading through a straight/closed knee to a supinating foot with the heel inverted (sucked in and under) and all 5 met-heads pitched down into the ground.

> "LOADING THE FLEXOR CHAIN TO FLOW ME FORWARDS."
> **GARY WARD, AUTHOR, EDUCATOR AND SPEAKER ON THE SUBJECT OF HUMAN MOVEMENT AND ANATOMY**

Drill 3:
Hammie Crab Load (Hamstring Side-Step Load): *vimeo.com/245651484*

This is a progression of the previous drill, where you simply step sideways, as if along the base-line of a tennis court, instead of stepping back. Important cues are:
- You are loading the hamstring group you're leaving behind! The stepping-sideways leg bends, and the 'left-behind' leg stays straight, with the foot planted and maintaining tripod contact (ie, it does NOT tilt onto its inside edge).
- Keep your arms reaching straight forward initially, and you'll feel it in the medial 'semi-sisters' muscles.
- Then lateral side-step by lateral side-step, gradually reach further and further down and around towards the static foot, aiming eventually to slide down the shin bone, towards the 'upright' ankle; the more lateral the reach the more noticeable the load on the biceps femoris.
- Repeat to the other leg.

Salmonette 4: repeat the Salmonette 3/4 effort, 15° hill drill: drill-run & sense-compare. What did you notice this time? Did your ground marker need to change?

- Finally, a rotation towards the outside of the straight leg will increase the eccentric load to the hamstring group, which you might feel as a seemingly central pull down the belly of the muscle. This - the linea aspera of the femur - is where (amongst others) the short head of biceps femoris attaches.
- A gentle 'slide down the shin bone towards the outside of the lead foot' will help you increase the load without straining - with practice, touching the ground is achievable, which for many runners is a novelty!
- Building the drill from smaller to bigger movements, changing the tilt of the pelvis, adding some rotation and finally sliding down the shin bone will probably have taken 6-10 repetitions.

Before repeating to the other leg, check out the difference you've already made in your body by taking a few steps within your drill area. It's common for folk to stumble slightly as the foot on the side they've just worked 'bumps' into the ground fractionally earlier than expected. Giving a hamstring group a 'bigger world' to play in, 'lets the leg out from the pelvis'; creating the effect of a longer leg. Now, how many of you have been told you've got one leg shorter than the other ...?
- OK - now you can even your legs up by repeating the process to the other side.
- Don't stay too long doing this drill - having warmed-up thoroughly, you don't want to cool back down again!

Salmonette 3:
Repeat your 22-stride bounding hill ascent at 3/4 effort, 15° of Non-Soggy, internally sensing for any changes, but also looking out for the distance covered this time. In my experience, 100% of runners report some or all of the previous descriptions: freer, looser, easier, travelled further (i.e. bigger strides for no more effort), no quads/knees and more glutes.

Waking up muscles with great dynamic 3D loads primes them for increased output in motion, without increasing perceived effort levels.

meantime we simply become increasingly aware of what the pelvis is doing relative to the heels and the forefoot, to avoid making knees grumpy; to that end, we are always, ALWAYS hankering after those **2 points of contact (base of big toe, base of little toe)** in the trail foot when running.

And so to the drill hammie-stork-load:
vimeo.com/244976165

- Pivoting on the front heel, step back onto a bent leg, keeping front leg straight, ankle in dorsiflexion (toes up) and pelvis in anterior tilt (stick your bum out); reach forward.
- Start small, repeat a couple of times, creating a bigger movement each time, 'waking up' the hamstrings kindly and avoiding overcooking it by reaching too far, too fast, too early ...
- Adding more of the long line of fascia that creates the 'Superficial Back Line' (reference *Anatomy Trains*, Thomas Myers) will enhance the load we've started, so let's allow some spinal flexion. Add more reach towards the ground by easing off on the 'sticking out bum', and allow some posterior tilt of the pelvis. When I'm coaching, the ensuing appreciative grunts indicate that folk have 'found' more soft tissue load along the all-important extensor chain.

- Look 'ahead' from wherever your forward flexion has taken you (more opposition, this time between cervical and thoracic/lumbar spine). Remember, Hunchback needs to see where he's going!

- With weight on the outside of the left heel, stay mindful of maintaining full forefoot contact with the ground - from the base of the big toe all the way through to the base of the little toe (toes remain relaxed - no scrunching!); here's the super-important opposition in the foot creating:
  - Full re-supination - you'll use this to optimise the propulsive phase of gait.
  - Full knee extension as the larger external rotation of the femur, articulating with the smaller external rotation of the tibia, creates a 'screw-in' of the knee joint, generating a continuation of the rigid lever of the foot in supination.

- Repeat to right foot and repeat whole process at least once, and twice if there's time (so a maximum of 3 repetitions of each rotation, alternating directions).

Salmonette 2:
Now repeat the 22-stride Salmonette hill ascent at 3/4 effort, 15° of Non-Soggy, focusing on feeling for any changes (ignore your ground marker). Be surprised if you don't feel freer, looser or that the whole Salmonette seems easier than before. You might find you notice you have bigger strides for no more effort and that you get a sense of less quads or knees and - huzzah - more glutes.

If you sense any (or all) of those, what you've created is more power output from the same body, without trying harder in terms of effort, but simply by paying attention to the details of joint movement, and offering them more space to rotate optimally in all three dimensions. And doesn't it feel good?

Drill 2: Hammie Stork Load
(Hamstring Step-Back Straight Leg Load):
Whilst understanding knee mechanics might not necessarily have been a priority for you, they are **your** knees, and knees seem to bear the brunt of an awful lot of grief considering they are the biggest joints in the body, and have a relatively uncomplicated two-plane axis of rotation! So, the relevant anatomy is dog-legged for you to peruse at your leisure, and in the

- Keeping a tripod contact with the left foot - heel, base of big toe and base of little toe - rotate your left femur by turning towards it. There's a sense of it rotating outwards, then reaching its limit whilst the pelvis continues swizzling on the top of it.

- Can you feel that you've created a really sturdy leg? You've closed the knee joint effectively by loading the (often forgotten) soft tissue at the back of it *and* through the rotation of your leg on top of a foot with good tripod contact.

- We need opposition *E-V-E-R-Y-W-H-E-R-E*, so now that the pelvis is rotated left, we need to bring the torso right; with relaxed arms falling naturally, rotate torso to 'nipples at 12 o'clock' as you bend over, reversing the lumbar curve, letting it fall backwards to 6 o'clock, rounding your back and relaxing into the space between your feet. If you push your way down, you'll create tension which will restrict you. R-e-l-a-x down ... you'll get more ... and easier flexion!

- You'll find it even more manageable if you complement your spine with your arms: a flexed spine pushes the shoulder blades apart, internally rotating the arms. If you help that along, it can feel as if you're 'diving' into the space between your feet.

- Lift right hip by tipping onto right toes keeping your right knee straight; allow your toes to turn inwards (right heel stays high).

- Tuck your tail between your legs (pelvis tilts backwards a touch) and think about your left leg being straight enough for the back of your knee to be 'loading' the soft tissue there. You're not pushing your knee back. You're not locking your knee-cap using your quads. If you tuck your tailbone too far, your knee will bend, so watch out for that.

Anatomy Dog-Leg: The hamstrings, attaching from the ischial tuberosities (sit bones) of the pelvis to the inside and outside of the top of the shin-bones (medially on the tibia and laterally on the fibula) are generally categorised into posterior pelvic tilters, hip extenders and huge knee flexors.

When viewed from the other side of the coin, they help **decelerate** the anterior tilt of the pelvis, hip flexion and the straightening of your knee both as your leg swings ahead of you as well as the knee extension that comes with 'leaving the stride behind'.

So the hamstrings are significant at both the non-weight-bearing end of the gait cycle as well as the propulsive moment.

Due to where they attach either side of the knee area, we can see that the medial 'semi-sisters' (the semitendinosus and semimembranosus) together help decelerate the external rotation of the knee, and the laterally attached biceps femoris works to control the internal rotation of the knee.

Great knee mechanics involve the head of the femur in the hip socket harmonising with what the base of the tibia and fibula are doing at the ankle joint - and vice versa - in concert with the other 32 joints in the foot.

- over rotation of upper body (probably due to lack of pelvic rotation and bonkers arms)
- 'dishing' of lower legs & feet and/or knock-knees (connected to lack of pelvic rotation)
- high knees (big hip flexor work compensating for lack of pelvic movement).

You might have one or two, but hopefully by now, not all of them!

Sensing any of the above is all part of the game, of your learning process and the journey of discovering exactly where your personal inefficiencies reside. These apparent regressions are NOT a reflection of poor learning, or that you're a slow learner, but more a sign that as soon as you 'up the anti', folk unconsciously tap into the basal ganglia of 'habit' to glean some efficiency out of the required extra effort; after all, it IS *mentally* more efficient to not bother thinking and just "get on with it" when the going gets tough!

Credit for all the following joint mechanics drills goes to Gary Ward, and his FMM™.

Drill 1:

Dive In (Transverse Cog with Flexion) dive-in: *vimeo.com/245613829*

It's common to see athletes achieving lumbar flexion as a forward bend from a bi-lateral stance (feet abeam each other), and both legs doing the same thing. And whilst it's really important that our spines can both flex and extend, as runners we are constantly managing fluid movement whilst flying through the air and landing on one foot, with the other leg doing something different. So here's a neat way of achieving just that, whilst remaining focused on the job in hand, which is finding *more power* from the same body, by creating *more space*:

- *Starting* in bi-lateral stance, outside ankles in line with outside hips, feet facing forwards (remember, if the start point is with the feet turned out, you're not going to generate much more in the way of rotation, because you're already halfway there).

- Weight shift towards your left foot, staying on axis, and ensuring your hip doesn't sag outside your ankle.

- To remember that the longer the stride behind you (hip extension), the greater the swing-through potential. An awareness of the forward shinbone is critical as if the knee doesn't lift *just enough*, the stride will get unnecessarily foreshortened by a foot that bumps into the slope prematurely. You're not consciously picking the forward foot up, but you're certainly not letting it dangle in the way either.
- To work powerfully hard whilst maintaining The Principles of efficient form, stopping before fatigue negatively affects movement patterns and increases injury-risk.
- To stick to the conservative formula of 20 'power' strides following a rolling 2-stride start, to safely keep each hill rep within a type IIB fibre working zone of around 10 seconds.
- To map progress of 'more speed for no more effort' you can throw down ground markers or just use landmarks.

Salmonette 1: The Control
Using **gravity to help run against gravity.**

You'll remember from your time passing through Level 3 that there's no 'fighting gravity'! It's simply not productive.

Run up the hill strongly for 22 strides (rolling 2 + 20 'big ones'), dropping your hip into each step, *thinking* 15° of Non-Soggy, imagining you're either Jess or Usain, holding your $\mathcal{L}_{emni}$ in one hand, or leaving it to one side and chucking down your marker at the 22nd footfall. It's a game of comparisons, so you need a start point and ascent 1 is simply 'The Control'. The aim is to notice 'something' within yourself; if you're with a running partner, they might be able to help with something they notice.

Common 'shout-outs' include:
- narrow tracking
- flailing arms or bonkers elbows
- leaning into the hill
- reporting a strong awareness of knees and/or 'quads, just above the knee' (from forward lean)
- heels touching when the slope is steep enough that they shouldn't (over-taxing calves/Achilles')
- overly turned-out feet (where the leg is being rotated as a substitution for a pelvis that isn't rotating)

Ascents 7-10 are 'all-out' "Salmons" once integration between brain and body has occurred. Naturally enough, in full flight the Full Monty of hip extension flows into play with the thought of 20° of *'knee behind you before it switches direction'*. It's the biggest *'shape'* you can make.

I'm going to repeat that. **It's the biggest shape you can make.** 'Shape' not 'strain'!

Sometimes, it's helpful to reach out and ask others to help you get the message across. In the name of our dear friend Eeyore, if you're still all flailing limbs at Ascent 6, stick to Salmonettes throughout. Discombobulated efforts with intensity is a time-out in the pending box. Focus on co-ordinating body parts with less intensity first; your time will come ...

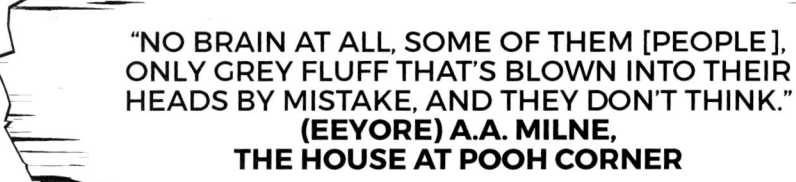

"NO BRAIN AT ALL, SOME OF THEM [PEOPLE], ONLY GREY FLUFF THAT'S BLOWN INTO THEIR HEADS BY MISTAKE, AND THEY DON'T THINK."
(EEYORE) A.A. MILNE,
THE HOUSE AT POOH CORNER

In the style of a Flying Salmon, the principles of Salmon Drills are:
- To bound up the slope smoothly and gracefully (imagine Jessica Ennis, Usain Bolt or a gazelle in full 'bounding' flight).
- To use power to generate as big a stride as possible.
- To travel as far up the ascent as possible using the formula of 2 rolling + 20 explosive strides.
- To be powerfully efficient *along* the rising ground, wasting as little energy as possible with excess vertical motion.
- To focus on "2 points of contact in trail leg".*
- To maintain upright posture and a relaxed upper body, avoiding the tension associated with leaning into the hill.

---

which will be the sum total of pelvic rotation, pelvic drop, hip external rotation, hip extension, knee extension, ankle extension and foot supination - and cause for celebration when your body gathers that lot together for you!

SALMONETTES AND SALMONS

Ascents 1-6 are "Salmonettes" at 3/4 effort - so 'quite hard' but not 'all-out'. This is important both to minimise injury risk by gradually increasing the range of motion of the joints and connected soft tissue, and to enable you to focus on co-ordinating new movement patterns. Think of the 'ettes' as 15° of *'knee behind you before it switches direction'*.

 Dog-Leg: And whilst we're here, the amount of hip extension doesn't necessarily equate to speed or effort:

- You can have a huge walking stride with maximum hip extension, but you're not going to win the 100m sprint with it.
- You could spend longer on the ground with each step, and that would feel harder than if you kept the flow going.
- You could have maximum rotation at the hip joint when running, but by choosing to not drive down into the ground with power, you'll not run at maximum speed.

The distinctions are important and become more relevant the more running you do, especially within the realms of ultra distances. There's another book coming dedicated to the ways you can 'spark plug' your body when taking part in big endurance adventures, but for now just explore the variables until they sit happily with you.

Remember that maximum hip extension results from the sum of the femur (thigh bone) disappearing behind you, the tilt of the pelvis and the rotation of the pelvis towards the rear foot. Given we're not going to be getting our goniometers out and we're *thinking* about numbers in the context of *relativity to other body parts*, 15° as a 'nearly there but there's still room for more' and 20° as 'this is all you've got' has worked consistently well during coaching. With the *thought* of 15° of Non-Soggy, getting a sense of the obliques being torqued through the rotation of the torso counter to the pelvis becomes stronger. You might have noticed this at lesser degrees of hip extension, but if you didn't you almost certainly will now.

Around 30-40 minutes into your session, you should find yourself at your hill venue, and preferably at the top; if your route brings you to the bottom get to the top as efficiently as possible, without raising your heart rate too much. You should find yourself taking lots of short, high cadence strides - and if you're not, you're using too much effort. Save it for what's coming ...

All descents on this hill power session are the same - YOU control the pull of gravity, just as at Level 3. We'll develop downhills at Level 9 (probably my *absolute* favourite session, and Cat's too), with the strengthening effects of sessions 7 & 8 already embedded.

- In the early days of shifting to 'better' movement patterns, once the brain is happy that you're in a cyclical, repetitive movement, it'll efficiently allow you to meander off with your thoughts to your shopping list, your chores for the day, the row you've just had with your partner ... but because your modulated running 'shape' isn't yet engrained as a habit, your brain will helpfully offer you one it had in a back drawer somewhere that did a similar job *because that's what it's designed to do - helping you be that 'higher' mammal able to plan and forecast and think about stuff whilst moving.*

- It's probably easier in the long run to recognise that this will happen; the attempt to never 'drift off' whilst you're running would seem to be futile. Forewarned is forearmed - if you connect your old habits to a *feeling*, and connect the feeling to depictive words - you'll recognise it sooner rather than later. Over a period of time, and with intelligent, questioning, introspective running practice encouraging the wiring together of new motor neuronal connections, you'll eventually 'lose' the old motor programme and 'use' the new one, even when you're not thinking about it. This process is the part of neuroplasticity that excites me most because it gives hope to all frustrated and in-pain runners who think their running days are history.

Things can change. We can change. Our brains can change just as much as our bodies. You have more control than you realise. You simply need to use your brain <u>with</u> your body!

> **"THE MIND <u>IS</u> THE ATHLETE; THE BODY IS SIMPLY THE MEANS IT USES TO RUN FASTER OR LONGER, JUMP HIGHER, SHOOT STRAIGHTER, KICK BETTER, SWIM HARDER, HIT FURTHER, OR BOX BETTER. HOPPIE'S DICTUM TO ME, "FIRST WITH THE HEAD AND THEN WITH THE HEART", WAS MORE THAN SIMPLY MIXING BRAINS WITH GUTS. IT MEANT THINKING WELL BEYOND THE POWERS OF NORMAL CONCENTRATION AND THEN DARING YOUR COURAGE TO FOLLOW YOUR THOUGHTS."**
> **BRYCE COURTENAY, AUSTRALIAN-SOUTH AFRICAN NOVELIST**

more efficiency? It's inefficient to focus on the detail of sniffing out your ROC if your toes are still clawing to stop you face-planting!

Use your metronome app to help you 'find' the cadences you feel most efficient at. Commit to shine in your ability to know what internal signals alert you to the NB gear you're in, and therefore how long it's sustainable for. Relax, as you think, as you feel, as you find words that intuitively express what you're sensing - whether it's what you're searching for or not. Words that evocatively capture your old negatives as well as your shiny new positives will help the brain-body connect that you've slipped back into a former habit, before you've done so many repetitions that you've re-wired an old motor programme you no longer need.

> "KNOWLEDGE LEAVES NO ROOM FOR CHANCES."
> **LEW WALLACE, BEN HUR**

This is an interesting concept and I get asked about it a lot because it seems in opposition to what I've been suggesting so far. It comes up enough times in conversation that, rather than box it as 'an aside', I'll flow through it here:
- The question is roughly that of 'if I create space that my body will then naturally move into, why would I then go back to moving in my old, restricted way'. I don't know enough about neuroscience to give you an exact answer, but I believe it's to do with the ability to multi-task. Part of your brain specialises in storing habitual motor programmes, enabling you to continue what you're actively doing whilst thinking about something else ... and whilst you can add more habitual motor programmes, the old ones never disappear. They remain in your basal ganglia - strongly linked to the brainstem - seemingly logged forever ... although I'm not sure anyone can say that for sure. We simply don't know everything, and we certainly don't know what we haven't yet discovered; it's that *Donald Rumsfeld* again! But it's important to recognise if we're to continue the pursuit of greater understanding. What *is* established is that we have a 'use it or lose it' brain, just as much as we have a 'use it or lose it' body, so the more you use a 'catchphrase' thought that summons an action, the more that action gets embedded with the thought, and vice versa. *Neurones that fire together, wire together.*

'gradual' won't give the effect you need, and steep is too challenging - you'll get fatigued too quickly. And you'll need your *Lemni*. Haven't got one yet? Shame on you! Here's the link: **http://www.helen-hall.co.uk**

Get WujWum'ing. **Sagittal-wujwum, frontal-wujwum, transverse-wujwum** always, and never *ever* forgetting your precious **foot-wujwum**. Use the video links until you can hear me in your head. Maximally joint-mobile following your WujWum moves in all planes, off you go for your walking warm-up.

You need a good 30 minutes of warm-up, moving from walking into NB 1 with 1° of Non-Soggy and then NB 2 and 5° of Non-Soggy. When you feel comfortable doing so, open out your stride for a few minutes at 10° of Non-Soggy to ensure you're ready for big hill drills. Ideally, this would all be done on flattish surfaces allowing you to focus on controlling the effort level whilst you think about where your knee reaches before it switches direction, so factor that into your venue choice.

As you run, scan yourself with the Principles in mind as well as the new Detail you started discovering in your pyramid's previous layer. Do you feel relaxed; Vertical without strain? Is your Weight Shifting effectively from one side to the other? Is your upper body relaxed enough not to interfere in the Pelvic Rotation that will gift you more glutes, and therefore

CHECKPOINT SEVEN NOTICEBOARD

▲ ▲ ▲

TERRAIN: AROUND 50M OF MEDIUM GRADIENT SLOPE
RUNNER STATUS: TTF 8 OR ABOVE
KIT LIST: LAYERS, COMFORTABLE FOOTWEAR, YOUR LEMNI, OPTIONAL GROUND MARKERS, THE POWER OF YOUR IMAGINATION

Given there is more risk of injury with big and intense movements rather than with volume of smaller repetitions (unless of course the quality of movement is unconsciously incompetent!), a higher ratio of power hill drills to flat sprints generates a safety net as the incline naturally reduces stride length. Nevertheless, with the red flag of 'intensity' waving in our faces, to be able to enjoy these fun sessions make sure you have a *TTF of at least 8*. If you haven't got there yet, spend more time being kind to your healing tissues by fully oxygenating them and building their endurance with copious amounts of nose-breathing walking and running ... *really* running ... nothing soggy, please.

 TTF 8 You notice the restriction only when active on rough terrain.

To get started you need a route that takes in a decent slope - around 50 metres in length would be perfect. I get a lot of runners telling me that the only hills they have around them are too long. Erm, just use around 50 metres of it then. Medium gradient would be ideal;

Under his influence, Levels 7, 8 and 9 harness the prevailing resistance of gravity to strengthen running muscle fibres, with the emphasis on exploration and play. I like to think we can have fun with our running, especially when effort levels go up. Sport can be tough, but I don't believe it should be punishment. On tour in the States, aged 86, Arthur Lydiard said *"My athletes didn't have to deal with pain! We enjoyed ourselves!"*. My plan is that we will too.

An all-too-common training mistake is to over-use the 'that feels nicely hard and I feel as if I've done something' effort level. Critical for building an effective training programme is the implementation of ALL the effort gears, remembering the intensities at either end of the spectrum of Perceived Effort: the uber-easy, subsistence hunting trot of NB 1, with the 1° of Non-Soggy to set it apart from jogging*, and the uber-hard and self-limiting power gear of "The Sabre-Toothed Tiger is Behind You" sprint, which naturally will require the maximum amount of 20° of Non-Soggy.

---

*There are - of course - no absolutes. There ARE times when thinking about any degree of non-soggy is inappropriate. It's all about context. If the surface you're on is slippy - crystal frost, ice and surface mud - or extremely uneven, the place you want your loaded foot is right underneath you, with any 'drive from behind' in those conditions more likely to see you face down on the ground rather than running over it. There is 'form' and there is survival. The latter always wins, folks. There are no medals for a fabulous hip extension when your face is in the mud.

The 'Detail' in the three hill drill sessions comes via the supplementation of golden nuggets of **hill power** to the Principles of **hill form** already covered. Each session focuses on a different part of the powerful thigh and buttock muscle groups using a variety of static and dynamic drills, so whilst each of these sessions begins and ends in the same way, the 'meat' on the bones is completely different. Here's running fun you can really get your teeth into!

bit, "warming up" he called it. Eventually, even he couldn't bear the suspense he was putting himself through, and off he went. *Halfway* up the pool - the furthest he'd swum - he stood up, arms aloft, fists clenched and roared **"I Am The Black Fish!"** And got out. He was so astonished with what he'd achieved, he had to stop in case it was a one-off. Less than a year later he swam 2.4 miles in Lanzarote and even before getting on his bike, he knew he was an Ironman. I've got a lump in my throat remembering it all. So, The BlackFish were born and with the name came the attitude: *You Can* and in the words of Ironman *Anything is Possible*.

The upshot of it all - and the relevance to you - is that all the power drills I teach have to hit the 'empowering' button and have fishy names, and to make them easier to remember, the names are evocative to the action.

The Hill Drills in the following three lessons are not *all* mine. I took advice from one of the most successful coaches of all time, the late Arthur Lydiard, and have coached his proven principles (as used by Olympic 400m, 800m, 1500m and 5000m champions, and beautifully explained in the great text by Keith Livingstone, *Healthy Intelligent Training*) for quite a few years now, simply adding biomechanical flavour in the specifics of execution and artistic relish in their moniker:

- His *Hill Bounding*, with the emphasis on rear leg extension, are PFM's "Salmons"; they 'fly' upstream in a series of long, elegant, streamlined leaps.
- Steep *Hill Running's* headline is slow forward momentum with exaggerated knee lift; our "Flounders" lurch up the slope, eliminating any momentum and driving the focus into the load of the glutes and the explosive extension of knees and hips.
- The original *Hill Springing*, demanding fully-mobile ankles to generate 'big air', is now tagged "Psychedelica" after the crazy, non-swimming fish that bounces like a ball along the sea floor, discovered in 2008.

My sense is that Mr Lydiard was a bit of a genius. He had an instinctive understanding of the nature of muscle fibres long before they were 'discovered' and given the labels they have today. I follow his insistence that all the power drills be time-efficient, functional to running, develop great strength in the prime-movers, be short and sharp, require proper recovery between reps so they don't tap into the fatigue-inducing, anaerobic energy systems and can therefore (with conditioning over *Time*) be performed several times a week in addition to a weekly longer run.

POWERED BY BLACKFISH

Time for a little story so you can really embrace the theme and get more out of the games. Our community triathlon team, active since 2008, has appeared in force at various events, from team sprint relays to the full Ironman distance, as well as at a variety of running endurance events (the more bonkers the better). We have a stand-out, wicked team kit (huge thanks to our old friend Robin Davies for the original design) and we're called The BlackFish. Credit for our brilliant name has to go to my husband, Brian (that's him, *not* in team kit; RB is with him, and siblings Kevin and Sarah are below left).

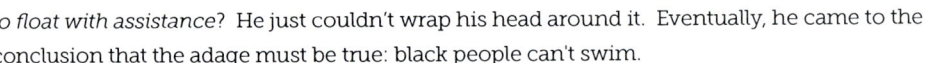

He had signed up for his first triathlon, and in keeping with his nature, had chosen the biggest and hardest one as an introduction: Ironman Lanzarote. The fact he couldn't really swim turned out to be a bit of an obstacle. Actually, that's an understatement; he didn't swim, he just sank. He watched endless videos and YouTube clips, had lessons for one 'method', more lessons for another, with every swim coach reassuring him that *everyone* could swim - Jamaican heritage or not - he just didn't have the right technique. He continued to prove them wrong and just sank to the bottom of the pool - even with the buoyancy help of a float between his thighs. He had always excelled at all sports, and the frustrations at not being able to conquer this one were huge; *to not even be able to float with assistance*? He just couldn't wrap his head around it. Eventually, he came to the conclusion that the adage must be true: black people can't swim.

Then he met the brilliant and visionary Trace Baumann, who just happened to be global director of Total Immersion swimming. Within a few minutes of his first session in her endless pool, she'd hopped in with him, repositioned his hips and ... he swam. As soon as he arrived home, off we went to the pool so he could show me his new skill before he 'lost it'. He was nervous; unusually 'jittery'. He got in and faffed around for a

PRINCIPLE 7: HILL DRILLS 1
SALMONS AND PENTOPODES

It's all very well knowing you need to get stronger, but what if you hate gyms? Say hello to strength training without strip lighting. This is all about discovering the fun of using hills as an outdoor gym to continue to positively affect running form-efficiency, as well as develop functional strength to either run faster, or go further. And naturally enough, we're going to do this with the help of our swimming cousins.

 This is where you'll notice that power for hills becomes available with the legal advantage of WujWums.

LEVEL SEVEN
SALMONS & PENTOPODES

LEVEL SEVEN CONTENTS

Powered by BlackFish.. 277
Checkpoint Seven... 280
Salmonettes & Salmons 285
Pentopodes.. 295
Checkpoint Seven Noticeboards:
    Checkpoint Seven Summary 300
    Leaving Level Seven 301

> "ONLY SPREAD A FERN-FROND OVER A MAN'S HEAD AND WORLDLY CARES ARE CAST OUT, AND FREEDOM AND BEAUTY AND PEACE COME IN."
> **JOHN MUIR**

Your 'block' will be there when your body is ready again. Your MAFA is there to self-monitor and assist, to be your running buddy, to examine the current situation without judging it or you and certainly not to become the dreaded opponent. Levels 1 through to 6 give you information enabling you to customise your movement patterns, with Detail 6 giving you the added bonus of understanding how to - and perhaps *why you should* - customise your movement schedule. You can have a training plan, but it needs to take into account *all of you* and be flexible to changing energy costs. If you keep that in mind, you'll nurture your running body back to a place of progress, enabling you to continue developing strength and endurance.

DEPARTING LEVEL SIX ▲▲▲
RUNNER STATUS: TTF 6 AND RISING
✔ RANGE OF CADENCE
✔ DEGREES OF NON-SOGGINESS
✔ NOSE-BREATHING GEARS
✔ LEVEL OF ENERGY BUCKET
✔ RUNNING MASTERY HAS BEGUN ...

▲ ▲ ▲

YOUR ENERGY BUCKET

Imagine all of your daily energy being stored in a bucket, with a tap at the bottom to release whatever needs to be used at the time. Now check all the places your body is expending its energy: work pressures, family and relationship pressures, digestive demands, liver challenges, the balancing act of controlling your core temperature (right up there on the survival list, not far away from breathing), staying awake for too many hours a day (you repair as you sleep, not whilst you watch the next box-set) and, of course, movement. If you're not sleeping sufficiently, is your bucket full again in the morning?

Daily deficits add up.

Sometimes, by the time you turn on the tap to engage in your favourite activity - which might of course be running - there's hardly anything left. But on that day you chose to do your planned Hill Drills anyway; "it was written on the schedule ..."

Maybe it's not such a surprise, after all, that your body didn't have the energy left to repair what had been challenged through the stress of training - however enjoyable it may have been at the time.

If your tank is low, stop for a while if that's what you feel you should do. But given we *are* movement, you might find you feel energised if you go for a short walk-to-uber-easy-run NB 1, 1° of Non-Soggy along quiet, tree-lined avenues or in the woods. No more than 30 minutes, door to door. The trees will share with you the oxygen they emit, and will gladly take up the carbon dioxide you need to rid your body of. Your great stacking and effortless movement will minimise energy use whilst driving blood to all areas maximising tissue oxygenation; your mental focus on motor control will pour calm over troubled minds. Nose-breathing, non-soggy running in the woods is my 'shed', my peace and quiet and my healer.

LEVEL SIX SUMMARY CHECK LIST + CLOCK IN/ CLOCK OUT ▲

Just when you thought your body had this running thing nailed, you discover that your feet don't load efficiently to your favourite motivational running tracks, you can't run in rhythm with your mate anymore and your 'easy' is categorically dripping precious energy down the drain. And yet … *you have so much more control than you ever realised* … and it's so much more satisfying than you ever imagined.

On the surface, Detail 6 is playing with numbers - steps per minute, degrees of Non-Soggy, nose-breathing pacing gears and watching your MAFA times change with your developing fitness and skills. Dig deeper, and more than a structured session plan with different elements, this is an exploratory, sensory experience where you lean into yourself and merge body with brain in focused harmony.

This layer is *so much bigger than it looks on paper*. It's where you learn about yourself, your mindset, and your willingness to do right by your body *because it's all you've go*t. Many people I work with know that when they train, they stress their body, and it's when they rest that fitness gains occur through recovery and repair … but they only pay lip service to it. This entire book is about looking inward to find all the answers you need - reading your body by sensing how it's moving, as opposed to reading it in a navel-gazing kind of way. At this pyramid level we become better versed in the multiple ways our bodies have of telling us how they feel about what we're putting them through.

"YOUR ATTITUDE, NOT YOUR APTITUDE, WILL DETERMINE YOUR ALTITUDE."
- ZIG ZIGLAR, AMERICAN AUTHOR AND 'ENCOURAGER'

Bodies seem to love fluid movement, and who doesn't love effortless? But maybe your body isn't ready for the weekly Hill Drills you've been asking it to do. *You* love the sense of accomplishment and the feeling of fully-opening yourself up, but those two consecutive matching results on your MAFA are an alert that despite the seemingly wonderful input it's receiving, your *body* isn't able for some reason to manifest it into any kind of physical improvement as an output. Your energy 'in' isn't resulting in the kind of energy 'out' you were hoping for. So if it didn't payoff in faster times, where did the energy go?

As your fitness and aerobic capacity improve, more laps will be able to be completed before fatigue sets in.

As your fitness and aerobic capacity improve, your laps will become faster for *no more effort*. See how nourishing that sounds? More enticing than heading out knowing you're going to have to beat yourself up?

By completing your first MAF Analysis sooner rather than later in your running journey - even if you can only manage one block - you'll be able to quantify the biggest returns for your 'efforts'. But it's not really 'effort' is it? Not in the way many are familiar with in the current world of exercise, driven in the main by: 'if it doesn't hurt, I haven't done anything'. *You're running at the limit of being able to keep your mouth closed, and it never gets 'harder' than this.* Going through the process regularly - say monthly - will help you become more intuitive with your pacing generally, as well as ingrain familiarity with all the gears you may not have known you had within you.

Monitoring your fitness improvements through the objectivity of faster times is of course encouraging, but sometimes recording data can show a *lack* of progress, most commonly associated with over-training. The path of run training can be a bumpy one and you learn about your body, its recovery times and its resilience through *all* of its feedback, the good and the seemingly bad. The latter shouldn't be viewed as a negative; if you're not yet able to sense the fact you're over-training, at least numbers - whether the same or slower - will sound the alarm for you.

Happily, the best solution doesn't tend to be to stop running, but to stop all *intensity* of running. Back-track to Level 4, combining it with your new Range of Cadence and Non-Soggy running play and spend some delicious time there, just staying comfortable whilst your body recovers.

If this is being done on a separate occasion to your first time on Level 6 (recommended; it's a LONG level), make sure you WujWum and get in a good 10 minute walking warm-up, starting as you mean to go on - with great form and with your mouth closed (walking being super-dooper-easy nose-breathing, Gear Zero!). Then enjoy a thorough 15-20 minute running warm-up, slowing creeping up through the gears and degrees of non-soggy to find that effort level which floats around the boundary of your ability to breath whilst keeping your mouth closed, all the while remaining focused on form.

Relax, drop the Non-Soggy to 5° and wait for your diaphragm and aerobic capacity to catch up with your leg strength. Being designed for the job, it won't be long before your primary respiratory muscles can manage at least one block - stay patient!

- Complete 1-5 'blocks', logging each lap time, stopping the MAFA and beginning your cool-down as soon as the lap times start to increase significantly. If you're able to complete the full 5 'blocks', your usual cool-down comes next.

So you've collected the data; what does it all mean?

When you start the MAFA fully warmed up, the first lap will be your fastest, and each lap thereafter (at the same NB gear) will be *slightly* slower, by a few seconds. This is right and proper! If the second lap is faster than the first, then you either need a longer warm-up next time or you hadn't quite found the right gear when you started the clock.

Once the lap time is longer than the previous one by more than say 20 seconds, the MAFA is over. You are fatiguing quickly now, and pushing to do more will create strain, which will disrupt your breathing ability, and lead to more frustration rather than its goals of measuring fitness levels and your running efficiency. Synchronously, the 'test' as a measuring tool will also help to improve fitness levels and sharpen your efficient running form through the intense *awareness* it demands.

The actual '**MAFA**' is very simple. You find a local 'block', roughly a kilometre in distance and no more than a mile long; by using a 'block' you minimise road-crossing interruptions and it can become an easy-to-repeat metric going forward.

Checkpoint 6 mentioned that an 'imperceptible gradient' would be an advantage; the loop I use when analysing both myself and my runners has an upward slope as part of the walking warm-up. No-one notices it's an incline until they have to run it. The discipline of running it whilst keeping your mouth closed is an extremely fast way of honing a 'response to terrain' in order to maintain a certain effort level. Delay acting on your internal signals, and that jaw is going to have to drop unless you reduce your pace significantly. By reacting quickly at the first signs of the incline, you can ease off a little - whilst always maintaining at least 1° of non-soggy - keep your mouth shut and despite the extra intensity of the work against gravity, have a net result of *maintaining the same effort level.*

On the other side of the block, the very gentle downward slope on the parallel road should see us all opening our stride out and letting gravity help us into an increased pace for *no more effort*. The important premise is to maintain the same effort level throughout (objectively measured through either a NB gear or through a heart rate limit) so a slope up should be run slower than the flat and a down slope should be faster than both. Variety both polishes your skills and adds interest to your runs!

The MAFA Run:

- Your running starts with uber-easy nose-breathing, which is NB 1 and 1° of Non-Soggy.
- As you warm, feel yourself naturally move into NB 2 and 5° of Non-Soggy.
- Towards the end of the running warm up, ease into the test NB 3 and 10° of Non-Soggy.

You should feel your diaphragm working hard, pushing down on the viscera, massaging it (another side benefit!) and forcing your belly to swell into your waistband.

You should JUST be able to keep your mouth closed. If you feel too 'stressed' staying here, then either you're pushing too hard (which defeats the objective of maintaining a 'somewhat strong but not uncomfortable' effort level) or your diaphragm simply isn't conditioned enough to do the breathing work without help from your accessory muscles which are pulling your shoulders up to your ears.

Neither is it affected by the heart rate monitors themselves, notorious in their ability to fail the moment you need to use the data for analysis and well-known for pushing out impossibly high numbers before you've even started sweating (hence the existence of yet more running accessories, like heart rate monitor electrode cream!!). They are seldom accurate with new batteries, and, my pet hate, they require snug strapping around the very apparatus you're aiming to expand whilst performing your aerobic activity - your ribcage and lungs.

There's burgeoning reliance on activity trackers these days, and whilst some have fairly good reviews regarding the accuracy of the wrist sensor, the heart rate information it displays is still dependent on the many variables mentioned above.

I searched high and low looking for cheaper, more reliable alternatives, and found the answer I was looking for right under my nose (sorry - I saw that one coming from so far away, my fingers were irresistibly drawn to typing the whole sentence out!).

The added bonus of both nose-breathing training and performing MAFAs - whether with your mouth closed or not - is in the inescapable truth that putting a ceiling on effort levels forces the vast majority of runners to *slow right down* ... thereby offering quality, focused training time to consolidate 3-dimensional sagittal, frontal and transverse plane movements in each stride, reinforcing new motor programmes (read: habits) whilst still having the capacity to be mindful of your new toys - 'Range of Cadence' and degrees of Non-Sogginess.

WE NAB THE WISE ADAGE:
FROM UNCONSCIOUS INCOMPETENCE ...
... THROUGH CONSCIOUS COMPETENCE ...
... TO ARRIVE AT UNCONSCIOUS COMPETENCE ... ALL IN GOOD TIME.

TASTY DETAIL 4:
COLLECTING DATA WITH A MAFA

An ideal way for you to embrace (read: be motivated to continue with) nose-breathing run training, is to perform what's generally known as a Maximum Aerobic Function (MAF) test. *RELAX.* You're only going to be running to an effort level that still enables your mouth to stay closed, so it *can't* hurt! It sounds technical (and hard), but you're simply replacing the more standard heart rate (HR) parameters by the boundaries of your ability to run whilst maintaining nose-breathing. After all, the very act of being able to breathe through your nose without dropping your jaw would appear - by definition - to be the absolute ultimate in aerobic activity!

Dog-Leg: The MAF test has become common practice as an objective measure of fitness in the last few years through the reputation of endurance authority Dr Phil Maffetone. As far as I know the MAF test isn't named after him; that's just chance. Or is it? He was the force for change regarding the test parameters with his formula '180 minus your age' replacing the original '220 minus your age', and he's become famous through it. His original yellow 'bible' "The Big Book of Endurance Training and Racing" is a wonderful reference if you're interested in the more complete picture of living, eating and exercising simply and sensibly.

And that word 'test'. It's not friendly is it? Nah. Let's use Maximum Aerobic Function Analysis. Our MAFA is *much more* neighbourly. We're helping our bodies, analysing them, figuring stuff out. Using the ability to breath through your nose as the defining criterion has the added benefit of the analysis parameters not being influenced by your previous night's sleep (or lack thereof), whatever digestion may or may not be going on, the air temperature, altitude, how hydrated you are (or not), or any of the other myriad of systems and influencers that affect heart rate.

Each 'gear' can be tried and tested along the length of road you've been working on whilst trialling the different cadences. You can embrace as much of Detail 6 as you want as one session; you can break it up into tasty snacks, or enjoy a feast. All the Detail levels require repetition; you need plenty of practice to savour and digest these relishes. Just don't forget to use your cool-down walk to return your heart rate to normal before you stand still.

What follows is a Level 6 progression. With our intention marker in mind, we still have *application* of rhythms, gears and non-sogginess to explore. Here we have an opportunity to incorporate form, cadence, non-soggy and nose-breathing gears in the form of a monthly 'analysis' for objective training and planning. It's a lot, so before you try it, make sure you have somatically pinned-down at least two of the characteristics at each effort level to 'hang your hat on', with one of them being the degree to which you're non-soggily running, of course.

- The world around you still feels panoramic but the sound of your breathing might be just as loud as the birds singing.
- You *think* about having five degrees of 'Non-Soggy'. Once again, it's not an action, it's a thought. You might not believe as you read this that you can distinguish between 1° and 5° of Non-Soggy, but in my experience, *everyone does*, with most surprising themselves. Of course, you can practise all the degrees of Non-Soggy running with mouth breathing (you'll find 15° and the maximum 20° *demand* an open mouth!), but when learning the skill of pacing, having as many parameters to tune into helps locate and refine each gear.

If only it had been three degrees and we could have had The Diana Ross of Great Running. Frustratingly - and amazingly - 3° didn't work; trailblazers ahead could sense it, but it didn't equate to nose-breathing gear 2!

Then there's the final shift into a gear which *only just* enables you to keep your mouth closed.

NB 3 is Somewhat Strong But Not Uncomfortable:
- Your tongue is pushing hard against your soft palate.
- Your busy diaphragm is pushing the belly hard against your waistband on the inhale.
- This is as hard as you can run whilst still breathing with your mouth closed.
- It feels similar to the effort of 10km race pace.
- With conditioning, you could keep this effort level going for *up to* an hour.
- Your world becomes smaller and tunnel-like, with limited peripheral awareness and your breathing is louder than all external sounds.
- Your thoughts of wanting ten degrees of *'knee behind you before it switches direction'* gift you 10° of 'Non-Soggy'. And many *love* it here. It feels strong and smooth. It's on the limits of your aerobic envelope which can be quite an exciting arena to run in when there are no expectations (it's the 'against the clock' pressure that tends to ruin the fun for many runners).

to give me the next step. Owning this understanding about your body gives you the miracle of new legs when your old ones have given up the ghost. When you're exhausted, you can just let the thought of having *one more degree* send you forward again. Trust your body, it's efficient by nature. Make it your mission to get out of its way.

> **"COME FORTH INTO THE LIGHT OF THINGS, LET NATURE BE YOUR TEACHER."**
> **WILLIAM WORDSWORTH**

And those grimacing runners out there hating every moment ... ? Soggy-soles ...

One last thing before the trail relish continues. The discovery that your slowest running speed could have been faster for less effort might have got you thinking that you wished you'd been offered your cucumber earlier. If you had worked with me in clinic so I understood your body and its joint mechanics, I might have introduced 'non-soggy' on our first run session. But it might not have been until our tenth. You need to *have* hip extension potential in order to be able to use it effectively. You need to have somatic awareness whilst in motion in order to think about *degrees* of bone movement, without the danger of over-cooking it. In person, non-soggy running is introduced at the Absolutely Right time. In this book, with the intent to be helpful, it's when I'm pretty sure you'll be able to absorb it. Never underestimate the power - or the indigestibility - of cucumber.

Back to your gears. I know you're itching to discover more after that whopper of a reveal ... moving up to nose-breathing gear two.

NB 2 is Comfortable:
- You become aware of your tongue gently pushing on the roof of your mouth.
- You get an undeniable sense of your belly rhythmically swelling gently against your waistband.
- With conditioning, you could run for several hours at this effort level; so for many this relates to 'half marathon' pacing.

TASTY DETAIL 3: DISCOVERING YOUR NON-SOGGY PACES

Non-Soggy is the organic Trail Mix of endurance running: it keeps you going (if you're low carb, we could dub it the Keto-Stride). Next time you're 'running tired', check in: are you 'running soggy'? When your body doesn't feel like it's working well, or you're at the stage in an event when you simply don't think you're ever going to get to the end, check in: are you 'running soggy'? Are you not only going slower than you could do, but making that slowness feel even harder than it needs to?

 Anatomy Dog-Leg: our fullest expression of hip extension is about 20°, comprising of:
- 10°-12° of thigh bone extension
- 3°-7° tilt of the pelvis
- 8°-12° rotation of the pelvis

It's not the numbers per se that are important, but the freedom for bones to move optimally, to offer hip extension through <u>combined</u> rotations.

The Ironman Shuffle is infamous amongst endurance triathletes. It looks exactly as it sounds, and it feels worse. I always made it my goal to look the same at the end of the 2.4 mile swim, 112 mile bike ride and 26.2 mile run, as at the beginning; Upright and Elegant. Too lazy to run inefficiently, I was always running non-soggily, even into the 14th hour of movement (I'm efficient, I never said I was fast; and I'm sick, a lot. So many stories to tell ...). At that time of day (it was often dark by the time I finished), I tended to attract appreciative applause and got noticed because I looked distinctly upright and fluidly moving when all around me were knackered, soggy shufflers. Little did the lovely spectators realise that *everyone else was working much harder than me*. Of course I was tired, but despite my fatigue, I refused to succumb to the trudge of soggy running as that would make everything *even worse*. Even if my muscles were mush, my bones weren't beaten. I would entertain myself by sending thoughts around my body, asking my bones to be where I needed them

Running - by everything I hold dear - means hip extension to me. 'Knee-under-body' *might* be a landing position, but it sure doesn't constitute an efficient stride, *regardless of the running speed*. It's 'something', but not running - maybe it's jogging? Or 'trit-trotting' if the cadence is reasonable; 'plodding' if it's not! Whatever you want to call it, it's relatively laborious for the speed it generates. It is not efficient; it is energetically *expensive*. Without the knee travelling back *just enough*, you can't expect any stretch recoil from the hip flexors and all the soft tissue stuff around them. Without the benefit of any elastic recoil, you have to drag your leg through the air ready for the next stride ... and man, it's *h-e-a-v-y!*

Of course reading this first, and 'knowing' the ending, might find you second-guessing yourself when you get out and explore; wondering about placebo effect, doing battle inside your head as you question your results, puzzling over whether they might be something to do with prior expectation. But I'd rank it up there as a pretty wonderful problem to have in the Grand Scheme of First World Problems. What I can offer here is encouragement to test for yourself, again and again until you're happy you *know*. I think the longest anyone has denied their findings when I'm with them is a couple of minutes.

"YOU CANNOT UNSEE AND UNFEEL EFFICIENCY AND ORGANISATION ONCE YOU EXPERIENCE IT IN YOUR BODY" - **CHRIS SRITHARAN**

Keep trotting and playing. *Nothing else changes ... only your astute awareness of how far your knee goes back ... remember, you remain at nose-breathing gear one throughout. No 'trying harder'.* 30 seconds Soggy, 30 seconds Non-Soggy, down the road One-Degree-Less, up the road One-Degree-More ... can you feel yourself slow down, speed up, decelerate, accelerate? It's pretty much an objective measurement; even without gadgets, we've all got a fairly good sense of how fast we're passing through the air.

What about the effort level? That's the bit that shocks everyone.

SOGGY ISN'T JUST SLOWER ... IT'S HARDER!
LESS SPEED FOR MORE EFFORT IS THE EPITOME OF INEFFICIENT.

1° NON-SOGGY ISN'T JUST FASTER ... IT'S EASIER!
MORE SPEED FOR LESS EFFORT IS SURELY THE ULTIMATE IN EFFICIENCY.

Runners often struggle for words to describe the 'easier'. They're often so blown-away by the moment, that analysing it is beyond them. Eventually words like 'smoother', 'more fluid', 'freer', 'swinging' and *'my front leg seemed to travel further without me doing anything'* drift out (I get really excited when I hear the last two).

Empirically, 100% of runners I've worked with can attest to this as their experience (for some I've used different words, but the majority grasped the 'soggy' metaphor instantly). But this isn't just observational science; it makes sense with theoretical science too.

Folk come to me wanting to improve their running resilience, root out their inefficiencies and get more speed for no more effort. What they don't expect to find lurking within them is more speed for *less* effort. Few realise that their 'really easy running' pace is often not 'proper' running at all, if hip extension is to be considered a necessary component of running.

it of course but trust yourself, you *can* feel it. Please don't look down - even if you don't fall over, you'll at the very least ruin your effortless balance. Note whatever seems most obvious about it, and particularly note what is or isn't happening at the front, side or back of the hips. Don't judge, just notice. If you notice 'nothing', then 'nothing' is your starter. No right or wrong.

Without *doing* - only *thinking* - keep trotting whilst you imagine your knee travelling back **one degree further**. I repeat - this is solely a thought-process; let your brain sort it out for you. You're not changing anything else, only the thought that you'd quite like one more degree of *'knee behind you before it switches direction'* ... "Non-Soggy Running".

WHOA!! WHAT HAPPENED THERE?!?!?!?!

I've had runners literally stop in amazement after just a couple of paces - which is a bit tricky if we happen to be in clinic on the medical-grade treadmill. No-one, but no-one (so far) expected what happens (every time) to have happened. It even makes some teary. Sometimes it makes me teary watching them. Proud, clucking Mother Coach that I am ...

> REMEMBER HARRIET FROM THE BEGINNING? "WELL I WAS DISAPPOINTINGLY VERY SOGGY, IT'S THE MOST RAINFALL CALIFORNIA HAS HAD IN 10 YEARS. IT'S BEEN MISERABLE (!) BUT MY RUNNING WAS NOT. I FLEW, MY GOD WHAT A DIFFERENCE!!!"
> THAT QUOTE FOLLOWED HER NEWLY-DISCOVERED NON-SOGGY EFFICIENCY.

So what *did* just happen? Because we're generally truly hopeless at trusting our instincts, we can repeat and repeat until there's no doubt. Go back to 'soggy'. You were happy there before, remember? Easy-peasy, can go on all day, birds are singing, tra-la-la 'running' (apostrophes deliberate, pending explanation); what happened when you went back to 'soggy'?

Let's paint a picture: you're trotting along uber-comfortably at whatever cadence feels most unhurried and yet least plodding. You feel effortlessly balanced with neck and ankles relaxed; there's space between your feet - just enough to access ground contact with the whole breadth of each foot and to feel as if you're swapping weight from your left foot to your right foot with your whole body responding, not just your easily-dangling legs. You're breathing in and out through your nose easily, the swell and shrink of your belly present, but barely noticeable against your waistband.

Important note if you have a deviated septum: all the NB Gear parameters still work, but your mouth will be slightly open through necessity, and that's Absolutely Right for you. An extra 'sensing tool' can be the use of your voice: NB 1, uber-easy, would equate to being able to hold a 'constant natter' with a running partner. You're not nattering of course, you're focusing, but you know what I'm saying! NB 2, comfortable, would be the ability to hold a polite conversation, one with pauses for the other person to speak. At NB 3, somewhat strong but not uncomfortable, you could speak but it would be in staccato, grabbed words; you can't string them together fluidly. Your breathing pattern, whilst strong, does not reach 'raggedy'. Gasping for breath isn't 'aerobic'.

Your pelvis is lemniscating and just like the sign of infinity, you get the feeling it could go on like this forever; you know your ribcage is too, because your *Lemni* is rolling beautifully between your cupped palms. You're trotting at NB 1, easy-peasy lemon-squeezy (my mantra for the Caesar's Camp 50 miler), running efficiently. *Or are you?*

We need a marker. For the purposes of comparison, let's call whatever you're feeling right now "Soggy Running" ... nose-breathing gear one, yes, but it's 'soggy'. The degree of 'soggy' refers to the furthest point behind you that your knee ends up, relative to the rest of your body's side view alignment. At 'this' effort, at 'this' pace you're at now, where you sense your knees' change of direction - from being anchored to the ground via the foot, to becoming part of a forward swinging airborne limb - we're going to call *that* place 'soggy'. You can't see

TASTY DETAIL 2: ARE YOU A SOGGY RUNNER?

Keeping things simple, I define three nose-breathing (NB) gears:

NB 1 is Uber-easy:
- Your tongue is relaxed.
- You feel as if your legs could go on all day - and with conditioning, they will!
- The world feels panoramic, with the external sounds of birds, traffic and wind being louder than the sound of your breath.
- It equates to about 60% effort.
- It lends itself to running whilst being form-focused.
- It is the magical 'mitochondria-multiplying' territory; mitochondria are the energy factories or power plants of cells, turning chemical energy into cellular action, with more present in tissues and organs that need a lot of energy ... like muscles. The more you have, the more efficient you are at transforming energy in cells to 'output'. We grow more when we need them, but there seems to be an optimum 'effort-level' this cellular multiplication occurs at; it's called "uber-easy" - that effort level poo-poo'd by many. Maybe there really IS no *such thing as junk miles then!!!*

... UNLESS YOU'RE NOT REALLY RUNNING THEM ...

I'm sat here typing with the biggest grin on my face almost unable to contain myself, because I know what's coming. I've got a feeling a lot of italics are going to get used with the excitement of it all - poor grammar I know, but sometimes prose just needs to be unrestrained to get the message across. Are you ready to add some cucumber and really get your teeth crunching on some relishingly great running?

> "WHENEVER YOU FIND YOURSELF ON THE SIDE OF THE MAJORITY, IT IS TIME TO PAUSE AND REFLECT"
> **MARK TWAIN**

Moving on now, you can either seamlessly incorporate the following whilst playing with your cadence preferences, or you can separate them. For ease of writing (and reading), we'll look at the two topics in sequence. (You might want to have your metronome in the background for quiet reinforcement of your feet's new heights of 'twinkle-toes' friskiness).

Whilst writing this, I googled *'bpm for running'* just for a bit of fun. On page one of Google several sites were headlining that 149/150 bpm was good for "an easier jog", it was touted a "slow jog" on another and "a 10 minute mile" on a fourth. Can you see the problem with this? Those numbers and those words simply don't belong in the same sentence for many folk! A 10 minute mile might be a 'slow jog' for elite athletes, but for many it's quite an achievement. Low 160s got a shout-out for general enjoyment running (so you've all been listening to *this* music then!!) and higher 160s worked for an "intense run". 171 was the highest cadence I could find on page one.

I believe the disappointing range suggested is simply a derivative of popular music - that's what's out there, and that's what we plug into when running. My favourite 'guaranteed to get me off my backside and jumping up and down' track is *Macklemore & Ryan Lewis - Can't Hold Us*. I can dance and prance, thoroughly enjoy it and be motivated by it ... but with a beat of 151 bpm, I *can't run to it* and yet it appears in a 'top 100 running songs of all time' list.

Another one is *She Said*, by Plan B. When it came over the hair salon's speakers where I was being preened before my wedding, I couldn't help myself. With rollers in my hair and a champagne glass in my hand, I was found strutting my stuff with energetic abandon. But at 149 bpm, I could neither walk, nor run well to it. Before I met Kirsty Hawkshaw and we made our own music with higher beat rhythms, I took to exploring cadences with my feet moving at double time to reggae beats; that felt comfortable and more efficient *for me*. The contemporary flamenco music of Gipsy Kings (anything from 200-210 bpm) is wonderful for tricky off-road terrain where your feet have to fly if you're to stay on them. Kirsty and I will have to get busy again for you all ...

A word of caution here: one of the very few downfalls of running in a group is 'pack cadence'. Who knows whether it's mirror neurones at work, or maybe synchronizing vibrations or sound; whatever it is, we fall into rhythm with each other pretty quickly. With the average cadence of runners I see around me daily - wherever I go - being 'slow', you're more likely than not to find your 'pack bpm' is *below 170*. So when you're in the preliminary stages of cadence trials, you'll discover more about yourself, more swiftly, if you play solo. Once you're no longer speculating, you can encourage your running mates to follow in your path-finding footsteps, read this book and then they might keep up with *you*!

the 10 minutes of warm-up walking and then another 20-30 minutes of running, gradually loosening up, to simultaneously experiment with cadence whilst feeling for all your Principles of form.

With practice and over *Time* you'll find the rhythms you enjoy running to the most. What's right for you will be a *Range of Cadence* - ROC - rather than a single number; a range of 5-15 bpm would be 'average' in my experience. I feel it just makes sense that your cadence *would* change, given the physiological variables mentioned earlier, and depending on how tired and how well hydrated you are, and the terrain you're running on (off-road, uphills and downhills all tend to increase cadence quite naturally).

Be clear on what your numbers are describing: your cadence range should be quick enough for feet to feel rhythmical and fluid and allow enough 'ground contact time' to load the elastic tissues effectively to achieve effortless weight shift. And although you're using an app to help you find your ROC, the on-going solution to your running cadence efficiency *still lies within you*, as once you've found a range, you can speak (or think) your cadence with a variety of mantras for some rhythmical help whilst you run. Apart from anything else, listening to the metronomic 'ticks' long term will probably drive you mad.

You're not attempting to nail your range on the first exploration! For a while, you'll simply be experimenting, broadening your horizons on what's possible, playing with quick feet, slow feet and every rhythm in between. How you feel about different tempos will be relative to what you're used to, and 'manic' today may well feel relaxed once you're further along the pyramid. You're on a journey *towards* increased efficiency and your rate of footfall is just one of the parameters you'll spend time 'tuning'.

For the record, my body seems to enjoy itself most between very high 180s and low 200s steps per minute. And many of the more adventurous runners I work with find themselves performing best at similar tempos too.

---

momentum into the ground. I'm very familiar with this cadence, as I run behind many who are blissfully unaware they're stuck at it!

- 'Having a **cup** of tea with each step' is running at **170 bpm.**
  It's an interesting cadence, one that many runners arrive with, telling me they've "already changed to a quick cadence". It's a *little* easier on me when I'm running behind them but I can still feel myself losing momentum into the ground.

- Shifting into 'having a **gulp** of tea with each step' at **180 bpm.**
  This is a rhythm that's rarely been previously explored by any runner I've worked with, but, ahhhhh, now everything begins to feel a little easier, a touch more fluid ...

- Let's trot (maybe) at **184 bpm.**
  Never 'believe me' (or anyone else for that matter). Always test for yourself. It certainly doesn't feel natural to me, so it's not on my bandwidth, but it might work for you ... maybe on a Tuesday, on a month without a 'y' in it, when you're feeling tired and a bit dehydrated? Just teasing!

- Stepping it up to 'having a **sip** of tea with each step' at **190 bpm.**
  If you're familiar with the Barefoot Audio coaching recordings, 190 bpm comes in at a lovely "on-the-ground, off-the-ground" verbal pace; if you say it rhythmically, as fast as you can reasonably speak it, it'll generate a guideline 190 bpm cadence. My body - and *many* of the folk I've run with - love this rhythm.

- Barefoot Audio's signature *"fly-fly-fly"* rhythm is '**missing** the tea altogether' at **200 bpm.**
  My ultra-distance running buddy (RB) Jason Smith told me he played his Barefoot Audio album on repeat for 9 hours at an event he ran without me. He said he didn't want to hear me say "fly-fly-fly" ever again, but it kept his feet moving and he made it to the end - injury-free! Well done, RB - you know you love me really!! This is probably around-and-about where I spend most time when running the more technical trails.

Monkey around and have fun. Playing with footfall rhythms is often enlightening, frequently debunking many preconceptions about 'right and wrong' when done in the context of accessing great joint mechanics with efficient tissue loading. You've got at least

In case it helps, I WujWum first; it feels better in my body and gives me the opportunity to notice what isn't moving as well as I'd like once I start walking. I can then revisit it before I start running and as I don't wear any kind of restrictive shoe, it's easy for me to WujWum without taking off whatever 'thick skin' I've put on that day. Not that you have to WujWum in bare feet, but I'm greedy. I like to feel everything!

- Steady walk at **120 beats** per minute (bpm).
  Hang out here for a while. This is a really relaxed cadence to get your 'swagger on'.

- A brisk walk at **130 bpm.**
  This might start to get quite tricky for some. I love walking around this bpm.

- Fast walking at **140 bpm.**
  This requires such a rapid turn-over that you need to check you're still loading each foot well. Stiffness or tension in the hips or groin in the effort of 'trying' to keep up with the beat is the most common result when first playing with this one. Stay relaxed, let the pelvis drop into the step and keep your feet relaxed ... around 140 bpm is a great area to get to know for conditioning the stretch recoil of the hip flexors in preparation for running.

- **150 bpm.**
  Urgh - I don't even know what this is! It seems too fast to walk but too slow to run, all at the same time. In fact I'd go as far as to suggest this is almost *impossible* to walk to with efficient tissue-loading weight shift, and horribly ploddy to run to - a *serious* amount of 'zero motion' happening here whilst on the ground! As far as gait of any speed is concerned, around 150 bpm is a very difficult rhythm to move fluidly to in my opinion.

- Moving into a run, but *'having a **mug** of tea with each step*' is **160 bpm.**
  At low efforts and therefore shorter strides this remains on the plodding side; it smooths out a little if your effort level increases, but I think this rhythm still loses quite a bit of

TTF 6 You notice the restriction only after a run. No pain, just discomfort.
TTF 7 You notice the restriction on the day following a run.

Whilst building resilience we need to move, but in such a way that won't knock our progress. As well as telling us whether our tissues *can* tolerate a particular session or not, TTF can also be used to select what would be most helpful on any given day, and to guide us towards productive choices when mixing running with other efforts. Let's say you're a cyclist *and* a runner, it's Friday and you'd planned a hard ride on Sunday. You really fancied returning to explore Level 3 again, but recall that last time you played with hills enthusiastically, it took four days for your legs to feel fully recovered. With Level 6 being about rhythm and pacing discoveries, it would be a better choice for today; volume without intensity. The more you use the TTF metrics to your advantage, the better you'll become at applying balance to your movement planning.

Back to the checkpoint noticeboard. You'll be exploring 'how long' you need to be in ground contact for each step and your phone is probably the easiest gadget to use, as many of us are never without one. Simply download one of the many free metronome apps to call out the beat for your experiment. Further on, you'll be using your breath to discover a few more of your gears, no doubt requiring some tissues (possibly lots of them); of course you'll have your *Lemni* with you and lastly, you need a flattish route. Don't worry if it's not pan-flat; an imperceptible gradient is an advantage on this session.

As you've progressed, more and more has been introduced into the warm-up on each session, and now all warm-ups have the same two elements: WujWums and a brisk walk, in whichever order works best for you. So rather than re-type the same warm-up details for Levels 6-10, just flick backwards if you need a quick reminder; that way I won't bore you with repetition, and on a carbon footprint level, there'll be fewer pages!

Time to play with your rhythms and muck about with 'cadence'. We'll begin right from the start of the walking warm-up and gradually increase the rate of your footfall:

CHECKPOINT SIX NOTICEBOARD

▲ ▲ ▲

TERRAIN: FENCE OR WALL OPTIONAL, FLATTISH GROUND (A SLIGHT GRADIENT CAN BE HELPFUL), A ROUTE ENCOMPASSING A MILE/KM 'BLOCK'
RUNNER STATUS: TTF 6 OR ABOVE
KIT LIST: LAYERS, COMFORTABLE FOOTWEAR, TISSUES, YOUR LEMNI, YOUR PHONE

Level 6 is the first flowing run to be explored along the trail; following warm-ups, all previous sessions have been 'sense-drill-compare'. Here, you'll put all the basic principles together into fluid, continuous motion, reinforcing what I consider to be the four cornerstones of effective and efficient running dynamics:

1   vertical
2   weight shifting into each foot
3   3D rotations more 'rolling' than 'twisting'
4   hip extension

The intensity of this session is medium, but the volume of repetition is high, so you need a *TTF of 6 as your minimum; TTF 7 if you plan to perform the analysis too.*

You'll notice that your minimum TTF here is lower than that of the fifth level, where you reached the end of the foundational principles. No, I'm not expecting you to have gone downhill, I'm simply reflecting the work demand on the soft tissue along this section. There are actually several ways to use the TTF metric.

Finally, jump with the natural pre-bend in the knees, without any pause, repeating several times rhythmically to allow fluid, flowing movement to occur and this time letting the heel 'kiss' the ground on each landing - what's the difference? Of course, you're now benefitting from the full elastic recoil of the bigger, stronger thigh muscles, the calf muscles, Achilles tendons AND the feet muscles. Your catapult has 'thwack' potential written all over it.

Anatomy Dog-Leg: And by the way, in 2011, Blazevich found that 17% of the force required in running comes from the recoil of the arches of the feet ... so if your 66 feet joints aren't fully mobile, it appears you can't possibly be as efficient as your potential allows.

The point of all the fascial information and the exploration is to, I hope, show beyond reasonable doubt that a runner's cadence should be an *individual and variable* thing, driven as it is by both physiology and mechanics. Recalling the 'parked' earlier sentence about the mother principle of cadence being the frontal plane action of 'weight shift' ... we're back to Goldilocks, with the number of steps per minute being driven by *how little time it's necessary to be on the ground for,* **whilst still fully-loading YOUR tissues**.

There are gadgets that monitor your cadence and present the colour-coded information on graphs, which would be interesting information if they were also able to correlate the figures with the amount of fascia being loaded at the time. 'Fast Feet' can be applauded if their moment on the ground enables them to relax, spread into a flexible adaptor for a few hundred milliseconds and then transform into a shorter, rigid lever for another few nano-moments. A 'Fast Feet' imperative is on very rough ground, often dubbed 'technical terrain', where your feet 'skipity-skip' in a light, dancing blur to keep you from face-planting. Whilst you're not fully loading your tissues, balance is a survival instinct, and when the challenge is on, efficiency goes right down the pecking order. The essence of the message is:

'BE ON THE GROUND ONLY AS LONG AS YOU ABSOLUTELY HAVE TO, NO MORE ... AND **EQUALLY,** NO LESS'.

With enough background to absorb what's next along the trail, let's get the kettle on ... it's a long traverse.

Anatomy Dog-Leg: A full lecture on the structure and function of all the myofascial layers is beyond the scope of this book, but educators who specialise in the subject have authored many titles going into great detail. A few I've found really helpful can be found in the reference section, with James Earls' 'Born To Walk' being a very readable introduction. Here, I'm drawing from Chapter 1: The "Walking System" and Chapter 2: The Mechanical Chain and include a few of his references, but am acutely aware I'm merely skimming the surface. My dog-eared copy is listed in the Appendix and I recommend it regularly to those who express an interest.

Put very, very briefly and simply, we have no gaps between structures, everything is connected to everything and all 'between structures stuff' is not filler but a key ingredient in communicating movement throughout the body, through the balance of compression and tension. It's the collagen and elastin fibres within this fascia and surrounding the muscles that help to create tension as muscles expand.

When muscles work they alternately get shorter and longer, and the communicating stuff surrounding them - the rest of the soft tissue - also repetitively gets stretched and then recoils to its resting length - like a spring - creating almost free energy.

Experiments have shown that *the stretch & recoil of the fascial system can be as much as 93% of the energy being returned to the system when walking (McNeill & Alexander 2002).*

The amount of energy returned with the stretch reflex and elastic recoil depends on the quality of the tissue - whether the ligaments are loose or tight, hydrated or dehydrated, young or old - and the 'transition phase' of the movement or its time at zero motion.

Then it gets messy (again!) because statements get muddled with opinions, and these may not be taking into account all of the variables. For instance, perhaps you've come across those who prescribe a "cadence per person" - implying that once established, it doesn't change? And of course there are those who simply feel as if they only have "one way of running", with this 'sense' of limitation seeming to encompass both their cadence and their speed. I've even had an article sent to me decreeing that "one cadence fits all" (184 bpm was the magic number, if you were wondering).

If we stick with "how we're made", and allow *the way we are* to have input into the story, we can proceed happily, unburdened by anything other than our structural anatomy and functional physiology.

The following dog-legs offer a basic run-down of how our soft tissue assists movement, and in summary, they tell us we have four energy-efficiency strategies at play under our skin. Given 'You is all you need' along this trail, we're particularly interested in anything we have direct control over. I'm not here to advise on nutrition, how you hydrate or slow down the ageing process, but I am here to get practical with you.

James Earls has a lovely way of bringing these concepts to life. Start with jumping on the spot without pre-bending your knees - how high can you go? How easy does it feel? Apart from being super-tricky, and for me nigh on impossible with that knee pre-bend being almost reflexive, I'm sure you can feel that you're only getting help from your ankle lever and toes.

Now bend your knees, wait a moment and then jump - how high can you go this time? How easy does it feel? It's not just easier, but more natural, isn't it? You added the power from the thigh muscles but the elastic recoil still got 'lost' through too long being spent on the ground before you left it. Your 'catapult' lost its 'ping'.

Next jump up and down rhythmically with a pre-bend, landing only on forefoot, without allowing heel contact - how high can you go now, and how easy does it feel? This time you've got some elastic recoil from the big thigh muscles, but keeping the heel high creates tension in the calf muscles, holds the arches stiffly and keeps the Achilles tendons short, losing the elastic recoil from all areas below the knee.

PRINCIPLE 6: CADENCE & NON-SOGGY PACING

Ever struggled to finish a race well? Is running out of steam prematurely a common occurrence for you? Pacing - in the context of spreading out effort rather than spilling it all out at once - is part art, part science and takes practice.

 This is where you'll unearth your range of running rhythms and gears and how to use them and discover that 'non-soggy' gives you more for less.

TASTY DETAIL 1: CADENCE

The 'mother' principle of cadence is the frontal plane action of 'weight shift' ... but let's just hold that thought whilst we explore some background.

Whilst the subject of 'running cadence' has grown in popularity in recent years leading to a fair amount of information being available, there are still many I come across who haven't heard of cadence being applied to running dynamics. It is still far from 'standard' running speak and separating information from misinformation is often challenging. Cadence, in the context of running, simply refers to the amount of steps run per minute, and is described using beats per minute, or 'bpm'. That sounds a bit dull for a path taking you to running joy, doesn't it? What cadence *feels* like is a tempo - a rhythm of footfalls - which sounds much more interesting, don't you think?

Any runner of any ability will benefit from reading this, whether it's a greater understanding of anatomy, finding the extra degree of extension, or the full pyramid of potential improvement. Based on 'feel' there are no hard and fast rules, no 'right or wrong', just easily understandable instruction and wonderful drills that have made a huge difference to me, and can start a running revolution.

I love the clear and beautifully crafted pyramid. Setting out the 'principles', getting people to think about how they are moving, performing a drill or two, and INSTANTLY feeling the differences … it is amazing sharing the experience with runners as they notice the changes.

The moving into the 'detail' … oh my goodness. Seriously, I think Salmons changed my life more than having children :)

Coaching this has been an absolute pleasure, and having a manual available for all is long overdue! I'm looking forward to seeing the changes out on the streets and trails. Whether it's a parkrun or a 100 mile ultra, this book will transform your running forever.

As a coach, I'm unbelievably excited about this book and bringing the PFM methodology to the world. As a competitive runner, I'm a little apprehensive about losing the PFM advantage!

It's all about the Salmons … oh, and *The Lemni*. Never forget *The Lemni*. That picture of me was on a 100 mile run by the way. 20 hours of being called the 'stick man'.

I hope others enjoy this journey as much as I have. If it doesn't revolutionise your running, you should read it again!! :)

Pip Haylett, Strategy Director at Kitewheel,
PFM Coach, writer Run247 and endurance athlete

Forget your Fitbit, Garmin or heart rate monitor; this book should be your new running buddy!

Cat Benger, ABCpure Coach, Kona Triathlete

Helen's focus on the art and science of running has enabled me to go from non-runner to competing in 100km mountain ultras in less than five years. She guided me along the very trail you're holding now, with my journey so far encompassing an Ironman triathlon, the Ballbuster Duathlon, the Engadin SwimRun, and over a dozen other ultra marathons - all without injury or incident, and with joy and a childish delight for the simple act of putting one foot in front of the other - again and again and again.

Helen's encouragement that I "explore this movement, listen to what my body says about it, and act upon the feedback accordingly" have enabled me to do things I never thought possible.

James Wilkinson

To be absolutely honest, I had no idea what to expect when you said you had written a book about the work you do as I didn't have a clue how this complex and practice-reliant knowledge could possibly be wrapped up in a book that would help someone run better. The incredible benefit I feel I got from coming to see you and work with you in person made me think: "That might not work, people need to come and see you. This is too brilliant, yet too complex to read about in a book and benefit from it." Oh dear, how wrong I was!!! Why? Because this book is You! It's like you are right there, talking!

Given that only a few months ago, AiM and PFM were completely new subjects to me, I might be a good person to judge whether the way you presented all this great knowledge in the book is easy to understand, or plausible for those not knowing much or even anything about it. And my conclusion is nothing but YES! It is! The way you divided the trail as such, and the individual chapters, the way you included the drills and mapped out the exercises, and mixed it with the research you have done and the knowledge you gained over the years, is not just easy to follow and to understand, but also really, really enjoyable to read. AND, it really does get you (or me at least) on your feet to go and try it all out!

Please allow me to say that to me, the knowledge you share in your book is so valuable that I feel every elite runner should know about this. But at the same time, you present it in such a charming, personally engaging and fun way, that every hobby runner, who is also interested in running more efficiently, with less injuries and less effort, will enjoy reading and practicing it.

The "tuning in to what your body is doing", the "creating access to all areas of your body", which can then result in greater running efficiency, the advice to "become the owner of your body, to look inwards, to take control, and be more self-observant" and to "tune into your senses", all this is speaking directly to my heart and my mind when I think about my very own running trail lying in front of me.

To me, your book is a clever, enjoyable, fun, and extremely plausible read not just about running, but about running better; it gets you off the couch to go and test it all out - like no one I have never read before - and yet, will want to read again and again and again, until those drills have become a part of my daily running routine, just like lacing up my shoes.

Whilst I felt with every page I read that writing this book must have been a great pleasure for you, I now also wish for you to get the feedback and success that it deserves. Of course, as with all books, not everyone may like it, but those who really love running, and love themselves enough to care about their body and health by aiming for more efficient running, those should love it.

Anke Esser, pro long distance athlete

I am sitting writing this email with a buzz of something in my body having gone through the latest draft of the book. In the words of that judge on Strictly ...   A ......mazing.

It's about the reader and hasn't lost any of your enthusiasm or humanity - it tips or leans toward the person you want to help - brilliant.

"letting bones dangle under an effortlessly perched head, he seemed to suddenly relax into his body and just started flowing......" Now there's a good read.

Ben Houghton, CEO & co-founder of Noggin

Helen captures the reader from the very start with her impressive use of words and her boundless passion. She teaches us that everyone can transform and LOVE their running. Eye-opening, well-written and thought-provoking.

Trace Baumann, Master Coach Total Immersion, Master Trainer Reflex Integration

---

I have known Helen for many years now, her infectious enthusiasm and passion for running and human function are second to none; and this is reflected throughout her beautiful book.

What Helen has done is to convey her incredible journey, her numerous successes in overcoming challenges (personal, technical and even societal), her zest for exploration and her deep understanding, all in the beautiful pages of her book.

I've enjoyed both spending time with Helen, presenting with her, learning with her, sharing and developing ideas, having many "a-ha" moments - reliving many of those in this wonderful book. Congratulations, Helen, on such a positive, informative and inspiring creation. So great that you're able, now, to share your passion and wisdom with many more people; helping them, too, to realise their potential.

Matt Wallden: CHEK Faculty, MSc Ost Med, BSc (Hons) Ost Med, DO, ND, JBMT Editorial Board

---

I thought I could skim-read it to accommodate my lack of downtime, but I couldn't; I had to read every word, because it's so damn good!

Mr Rob Pollock, MBBS, BSC, FRCS, Consultant Orthopaedic Surgeon, Royal National Orthopaedic Hospital, sub-12 hr Ironman

A LOST RUNNER
A BUDDING RUNNER
A REPETITIVELY-INJURED RUNNER
A TRIED-BUT-IT-HURT-TOO-MUCH RUNNER
A RUNNER LOOKING FOR THE JOY IN RUNNING
A RUNNER SEARCHING FOR MORE SPEED AND RESILIENCE
A TIRED-WITH-NO-PROGRESS-TO-SHOW-FOR-EFFORTS RUNNER
A CURIOUS RUNNER IN THE PURSUIT OF USING YOUR
BODY MORE EFFICIENTLY

AT SOME POINT ALONG MY RUNNING JOURNEY
I HAVE BEEN YOU, AND I KNOW THE WAY.

DESTINATION DELIGHTS:

Efficient Running is a 'look' to the observer and a 'sense' to the person. The 'look' exemplifies elegance and efficiency of movement; a body in harmony, gliding across the ground. The 'sense' is that of a more relaxed body, generating feelings of enjoyment and pleasure as each stride gives life to the next with global movement co-operation. Anyone - *everyone* - has the ability to recreate this, and the pages of this book mark a well-defined trail to lead you to these delights.

The trail follows a simple and progressive process to achieve joyful running efficiency. Not an airy-fairy joyful; this is a rarified state of being that I perceive as being generally missing in the running world. Running joy is what running efficiency generates.

MOVE AND THINK AND FEEL AND CONNECT.

By *integrating exercise with evocative vocabulary creating thoughtful movement patterns*, you'll discover the fullest potential of physical space your body can enjoy using, and simultaneously dial into the sensory feedback of your own internal awareness; their unification will guide you to your best running form choices - those that are Absolutely Right for you.

MY HOPE AND INTENTION
IS FOR YOU ALL TO SMILE AGAIN AS YOU RUN.
I INVITE YOU TO EXPLORE - AND POSSIBLY RECLAIM -
BOTH YOUR RUNNING BODY AND YOUR RUNNING MIND.

'YOU' IS ALL YOU NEED...
AND MAYBE SOME SHOES
IF YOUR FEET LIKE THEM ...

FOREWORD

I remember my first contact with Helen Hall. She called me up, introduced herself and immediately burst into the following self-promotional pitch: "Hi Gary. I'm ringing you because you do amazing things with feet. Now, I thought I did amazing things with feet, but it turns out that you do even more amazing things with feet and so I'd love to come and learn ..."

Right from the off, Helen wore her open-mindedness on her sleeve; her sheer internal belief that literally 'anything is possible' has not only lead to the production of this fabulous book in your hands but also to some incredibly unique achievements in the realm of running and ultra events. Her volume of experience in running around the world and her passion for both running and the runner is reason enough to engage in the material hidden within these pages.

Helen is a lady who knows what she wants and how she's going to get it. Already armed to the teeth with an idea of how people should run, Helen took any information I threw at her and elegantly moulded it into her running coaching ideas, not with the goal of developing a technique as such, but to give birth to an idea ... the concept of simply engaging the runner to self-discover what running is for them, through an exploration of the movements in their own body.

Something Helen and I have both shared is this idea that running techniques and methods exist because people struggle with their bodies; these 'methodologies' are 'lovely' ways to control those bodies and lock them into a position that aids the technique of running, which is all well and good, yet most appear to be still in pain. And when exactly was the last time you saw somebody running with a SMILE on their face??

Helen delicately inserts positive energy back into running. She has found a way to coach running without a method, and with no desire for you to control your body parts - in fact, quite the opposite. Helen's idea is to set them free, which will set you free, so you may run like the wind. I wholly invite you to allow Helen to guide you through her process, through the ten steps of the coaching pyramid, cover you in story, metaphor and wonder, as you begin to think less about 'doing' and more about poo on your shoe and oddly enough, as a result, run like you have never run before ... this is a book you literally read on the job!

Remember struggling to think of someone running with a smile on their face? It's my prediction that you will see so many more doing so ... and when you catch them beaming their way along the beaten paths towards you, you'll know that they too have done it Even With Their Shoes On :)

Gary Ward
Creator Anatomy in Motion

CONTENTS

Wholehearted Gratitude 8

The Beginning 15
    Gathering Information 16
    Introducing TTF 48

The Middle
    Part One 65
Level 1   Getting Your Head On Right 66
Level 2   Is There Poo On My Shoe? 113
Level 3   Oh, *That* Pelvis! 148
Level 4   Meeting In The Middle 177
Level 5   The Stride Is Be-hind Youuuuu 205
    Introducing WujWums 209

    Part Two 240
Level 6   The Silent, Non-Soggy Cuppa 246
Level 7   Salmons and Pentopodes 275
Level 8   Balancing Flounders 303
Level 9   Flying Down, Bouncing Up 322
Level 10 Power On, Power Off 342

The End 358

Appendices 363

What's Next? 374

WITH THANKS

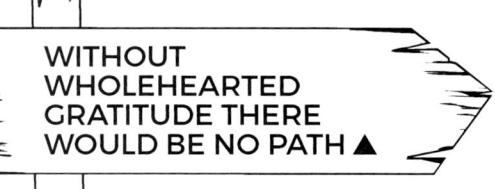

Thank You to Gary Ward, Chris Sritharan, my fellow AiMers, Brian Hall, Bryn Green, Pip Haylett, James Wilkinson and all the runners who opened their minds and presented their bodies to me for safekeeping and in doing so have been of invaluable help in honing my coaching skills and concepts.

I am forever in the debt of the wonderful man Gary Ward, his first book *'What The Foot?'* and the marvel that is his *Flow Motion Model*™, taught in his Anatomy in Motion classes. Of course, Gary would be the first to say the miracle is **our body** which 'flows in motion' but he is the pioneer, who mapped out our 3D movement, joint by joint, at each significant moment in gait, making sense of what we see daily in terms of human movement. It is his model that has enabled me to dovetail in-depth joint mechanics comprehension with the activity I love; applying that knowledge to empower the runner with better understanding of their own bodies is what I care deeply about.

My fellow Anatomy in Motion friends and I are all *unashamedly* still learning together; the subject of gait is complex, and we share regular 'eureka' moments on our forum when yet another piece of the fascinating FMM™ jigsaw puzzle falls into place effortlessly. As if it's another language, I now regularly dream in 'joint mechanics'.

And when a moment of dawning understanding happens to a runner in front of me, their curtain-raising insight into a new aspect of themselves that totally - *and for the first time* - makes sense, never fails to make my day; it's what makes my work so nourishing.

Daily at work and throughout this book, I draw heavily on Gary's drills to open runners' bodies for their running gains; to safely generate the space their body then has the potential to use. I have changed the names of the drills, simply because expressive terminology helps me, and the folk I work with, remember them!

With infinite gratitude, this book is also peppered with *Chris Sritharan-isms;* not just his own words and the ones he shares with us from others, but perhaps more importantly his influence on how I think and use my own words. Chris has worked alongside Gary for over half a decade now, and all AiMers know and love him for his *'Observe Curiously'* insights. I feel privileged to count Gary and Chris as my friends, their individual imprints stirring in me an internal dialogue demanding that I question my statements, seek answers through asking better questions, and generally examine the way I think and speak regardless of the subject matter. Editing this book has taken much longer than I expected as a result of them ... but I believe it was worth it.

This quote sums up what was going on whilst I learned and thought and ran and wrote ... and repeated, over and over again:

"SOMETIMES WE MAKE THE PROCESS MORE COMPLICATED THAN WE NEED TO. WE WILL NEVER MAKE A JOURNEY OF A THOUSAND MILES BY FRETTING ABOUT HOW LONG IT WILL TAKE OR HOW HARD IT WILL BE. WE MAKE THE JOURNEY BY TAKING EACH DAY STEP BY STEP AND THEN REPEATING IT AGAIN AND AGAIN UNTIL WE REACH OUR DESTINATION." - **JOSEPH B. WIRTHLIN**

I am, of course, the sum total of *all* my learnings from *all* my teachers, and like everyone, they go all the way back to childhood. I particularly remember Mrs Thornley, my grammar school maths teacher who looked on in horror as I informed her I would be taking pure and applied mathematics at A level. The 'gifted' gene passed down from my father was linguistics, and all the staff - especially the French teacher - expected me to go in that direction and achieve straight 'A's; but that wasn't going to help me in becoming a meteorological observer in the Navy. I needed physics, but to pass that at A level I knew I'd need a lot of extra maths tuition.

Two years later, I managed an O level pass at A level Maths (no further measurable progress apparently!) and a triumphant C in Physics. Mrs Thornley's patience - whilst I struggled in a field I felt a stranger in, and in the certain knowledge that I would bring down her average student score - still stirs in me great gratitude.

After school, my teachers were my RAF instructors and bosses (I changed my mind about the Navy!). They took in an 18 year old unworldly innocent, toughened her up, awarded her triumphs and punished her errors. Bernie Grant was my last boss, who saw me skilfully across the uniformed line into civvie street; I respect him immensely for showing me the merits of always looking forward, never back.

Since my time as an RAF air traffic control officer, my life has been spent learning from leaders in the world of bodies, structure, movement and health; Anne Vadgama introduced me to the effects of Vodder manual lymph drainage, Hildegard Wittlinger both terrified and inspired me to sharpen technique skills necessary to deliver results, and Professor Albert Leduc facilitated a development of those skills few have been as privileged as me to combine. Education continued with Paul Chek's exercise, lifestyle, nutrition and coaching concepts delivered with great knowledge, enthusiasm, compassion and commitment by Leigh Brandon, Matt Wallden, Dan Hellman and Angie Lustrick. Angie spoke so deeply from her heart, it opened the door to thought processes I would have previously dismissed. Even before he became my CHEK tutor, Matt was a positive influence on me through the world of barefoot running; Matt was the first person outside my immediate family to praise my work in such a way that I felt confident I was on a path that was going to take me somewhere exciting. I treasure this amazing man. Dan Empfield - the founder of the triathlon bike geometry - taught me the art of fitting the bike to the cyclist, that there's no such thing has having too many dogs and that great story-telling delivers the message. To all my outstanding teachers, thank you.

"EDUCATION IS NOT THE FILLING OF A PAIL, BUT THE LIGHTING OF A FIRE".- **WILLIAM BUTLER YEATS, IRISH POET**

In terms of creating this book I needed a lot of help! The years spent working with friends, family and clients generated experience and material, and when asked, these same lovely folk offered their time freely to provide you with animation for the video drills and end-range stances for the still photographs. I have helped them, and they helped me in return - beautiful reciprocity. Thank you to my two wonderful, endlessly loving and supportive boys Josh & Sammy Privett, James Wilkinson, Bryn Green, Wendy Jordan, Kirsty Hawkshaw, Alex Field, Karen Kennedy, Martin Jones, Beky Cann, Leyton Cheyne, Emily Hartwell and the inimitable Dave Newton for shooting said videos and stills. Wendy should be nicknamed

Hawkeye for spotting all the American spellings that sneaked in under 'auto-correct'; thank you to all my American readers for your patience as you read 'typos'!

James Wilkinson needs special mention here, being the wonderful model offering visual clarification of my words throughout these pages; holding all those challenging positions with a passive face (mostly!) took immense concentration, co-ordination, patience and strength.

Dom Scott listened to me and created the magical cover I dreamed of and a visual layout that brought to life my stick men scribblings. Dom's patience and creativity seemed to bring s-p-a-c-e to the reading experience that matched the intent in the words.

Ben Houghton's influence in making sure I kept relevant, in context and clear on the intentions at every level was a vertiginous learning curve, delivered with pure heart. And Thank Goodness for you Ben; turns out there was a lot more work to do after our sessions!

Cat St Clair, both an inspirational running role model and the person responsible for my seminal moment on the tube to Clapham Common, turned out to be a self-confessed grammar and punctuation snob, and amongst many corrections, has ironed out all the apostrophes that had no right to be there.

Special mention also goes to my 'grasshoppers', Bryn Green and Pip Haylett, who were the first two runners to become PFM coaches. Their unwavering belief in my message has been both humbling and inspiring. They run for the sheer joy of running and the fact they wanted to continue working with me once their recurrent injuries were history had wonderful synergy written all over it. Here is Pip's 'story' as a result of his first 50 mile ultra distance event, The 2014 Thames Trot:

"Thank you! I really enjoyed the 50 miles, despite the last minute changes to the course due to the flooding, and the fact that I was in California with work until the Friday evening before the race on Saturday, so was running with jet lag... and that my training and running buddy pulled out at the last minute with flu, so I was running by myself instead of with a partner as I had planned / expected ... despite all that, it was a great day out.

I think I got away lightly, with no injuries at all. I just washed my spyridons out at the checkpoints to get the grit / mud out, and it was all good! I admit I was pretty angry with whoever invented 'stairs' on Sunday, but I was back and running again after a few days. It's all about the amazing technique you have taught me, and I try to practice – and for that I am forever grateful.

Seriously, the running journey I have been on with you … having initially found Barefoot Audio, I can remember so very, very vividly the first run I went on with Apollo 3. I was running around Richmond Park, and can tell you exactly where I was on the 7 mile circuit when I first crossed my arms and found the counter-rotation … the hill I was going up when I first 'polo-minted' … and the smile on my face when I got to 'power-on' running ;-). Then the marathon, when I listened to Apollo 3 over and over to get me through the race. And then the courses last year (hills! I love hills now!) and now the recent 50 miles … well, it's probably changed my life more than having children!

I am enjoying running so much more than I ever did, have recovered from all the knee problems I used to get, and really look forward to getting out and amongst it, and being as efficient as I can. 'Out of breath' is not a concept anymore when running!

Next goals are 20 minute 5k, and 40minute 10k… and possibly another 50 miles, just because it was fun…"

Since then, Pip's run a 19:43 minute 5k and many more 50 milers, with his latest being a minute a mile faster than the same time the previous year. Not content with a few 100 milers, the furthest run in one go is currently 186 miles … now they've started, neither Bryn nor Pip seem to want to stop!

And my dogs, Elsa and Parker. What can I say? Thank you for giving me unconditional love, and daily perfect excuses to move and think and feel and connect.

27th September 2016 dawned with promise. It was the day after a dream in which I watched myself start writing this - my personal legacy - finally and effortlessly; so I did exactly that.

I am Perpetual Forward Motion, inspired by the words of my favourite Raramuri proverb, engraved on my 50th birthday bracelet gifted to me for my 5th Ironman event in Nice, France:

"When you run on the earth and with the earth, you can run forever."

And by Chris Sritharan, who said in response to my enthusiastic exclamation that 'bodies are never-endingly brilliant':

"And so are we, when we get out of the way".

And by Matt Wallden, of Primal Lifestyle who replied when I asked 'why do we bother?':

"We try, because it results in our optimal expression of potential".

And by Gary Ward, who after listening to me assure him that I COULD be a business woman, having just got hopelessly lost en route to a business development workshop, said:

"Nah. Who wants to be that? Instead remain in the pursuit of passion and inspiring your industry to change ... we don't do business. We do AMAZING things".

And by my husband Brian, who forms the 'other side of the coin' of whatever emotional state I'm in, creating equilibrium. He is always there - demanding (oh how folk who know him will chortle, right there!) that I be the best version of myself possible, to not rest until I have done just that.

Together, we are inspired by the 'Holstee Manifesto' that changed our lives when we saw it on a shop window in a tiny village in the south of France whilst on honeymoon.

We acted on our reactions to it and have never looked back. Google it and enjoy the entire script:

> "THIS IS YOUR LIFE. DO WHAT YOU LOVE, AND DO IT OFTEN … LIVE YOUR DREAM, AND SHARE YOUR PASSION".

When asked how many edits of the manuscript this needed, the figure 88 sprang to mind, partly because it felt big enough to be accurate, and also due to my fondness for the sign of infinity (my Perpetual Forward Motion logo). Each edit tweaked the language for flow and clarity. Every now and then, as new understanding came to light, material needed amending; more often than not, some kind of contextual qualification. No doubt, if I edited it again, I could find more improvements, but as you'll read, *"progress, not perfection"* is what it's all about. Whilst Perpetual Forward Motion is a wonderful thing, writing this book in perpetuity would seem fruitless. So 'this' - if I'm ever to get the message to you - is my "final best me"; according to all my current knowledge, 'this' is my favourite and most effective way of helping *anyone* master smooth, efficient, enjoyable running.

Once you've happily conquered the trail many times, getting to know yourself, learning how to read your body and listen to its needs, sifting through experiences to make the Absolute Right decisions for YOU, you might feel ready to transcend to even greater running heights; my collective ideas on how to help you triumph are already being tested and honed and will be ready for you. All in good time …

THE BEGINNING

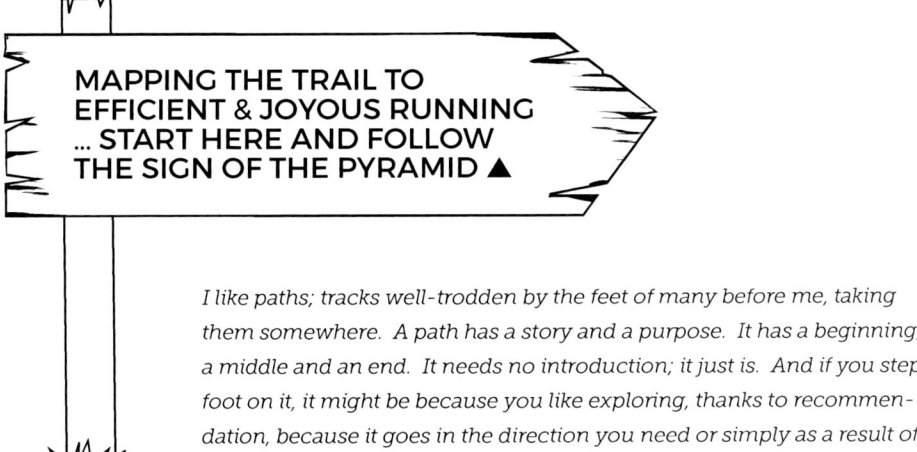

MAPPING THE TRAIL TO EFFICIENT & JOYOUS RUNNING ... START HERE AND FOLLOW THE SIGN OF THE PYRAMID ▲

I like paths; tracks well-trodden by the feet of many before me, taking them somewhere. A path has a story and a purpose. It has a beginning, a middle and an end. It needs no introduction; it just is. And if you step foot on it, it might be because you like exploring, thanks to recommendation, because it goes in the direction you need or simply as a result of bumping into it.

This book signposts a path; a trail formed by the feet of many folk before you. You might have picked it up out of curiosity, because someone mentioned it, or in the knowledge it marks out a route you want to adventure along. It has no introduction; it just starts.

The first steps take you on an easy traverse to the foothills of your destination - a warm-up if you will. We'll look at the lay of the land and get a better understanding of any energy conservation requirements for the work ahead. Zooming in on the footprints left behind will help to pace your journey; if you rush along, you might miss a turn or two, which would be a shame - everything along the path is worth investigating; for efficiency, for completeness and *especially* for the fun of it.

GATHERING INFORMATION

CONTENTS

Pathfinders	17
Trail origins	21
The voice along the trail	26
Finding the edge	39
Joyful running efficiency	43
Mapping your progress	46
Tissue Tolerance Factor TTF	48
Route: up the pyramid	50
Using stiles to help with sticky anatomy	53
Language of the trail	58
Injury, pacing and speed	60
Check noticeboard	63

PATHFINDERS

"HAVING SEEN THE MASSIVE RUNNING IMPROVEMENTS YOU HAVE BEEN ABLE TO GIVE TO HER, I WAS WONDERING IF YOU WOULD BE ABLE TO GIVE ME SOME HELP?" ASKED MICHAEL, HOPEFULLY.

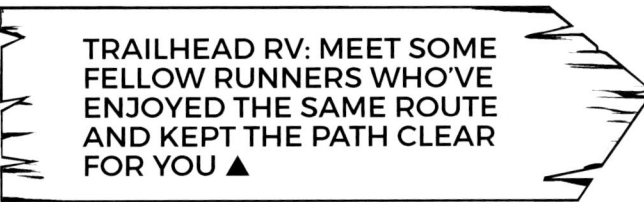

TRAILHEAD RV: MEET SOME FELLOW RUNNERS WHO'VE ENJOYED THE SAME ROUTE AND KEPT THE PATH CLEAR FOR YOU ▲

He'd watched from the sidelines as his partner-in-chronic-niggly-pain progressed into a faster-runner-in-no-pain. The way the process had made sense had sent a powerful message, and coupled with perhaps a touch of love-nest rivalry, his appetite for injury problem-solving had been reawakened. A long succession of similar stories, the initial symptoms of which might sound like a carbon copy of your own autobiography as you read on, formed the catalyst for me to start recording the process. Let's meet a few runners; in the spirit of Ralph Waldo Emerson, they went where there was no path and left a trail. Running Pathfinders ...

Michael - suffering with **cramp-like tightness in his lower back which developed whilst running and stopped him from running further** - followed the footsteps of Harriet, who came with the simple wish of being able to run consistently without something in her right leg giving her grief either during or after a run. For Harriet, **pinning down the problem seemed to be the biggest issue as it could appear anywhere between her hip and her knee**, and would take up to five days of anti-inflammatories to calm down. The next run would undo it all and she'd be back to square one.

She'd spent time and effort strengthening the muscles of her right leg and right buttocks, but to no avail. As it turned out, her right buttock and leg muscles were already *immensely* strong, as they'd been busy carrying the weight of her torso leaning over them ever since her pelvis had shifted over to the left. Her niggles were borne of compression and solved by the decompressive nature of 'space'.

"WOW IT WAS AMAZING! I SHOWED MICHAEL AND HE COULD SEE THE DIFFERENCE; HE SAID I GO FROM A STABBY WALK TO A FLOATING WALK! I DID 10K YESTERDAY AND IT FELT GREAT, BOTH LEGS FELT LIKE THEY WERE DOING THE SAME AMOUNT OF WORK!"

And later ...

"WELL I WAS DISAPPOINTINGLY VERY SOGGY, IT'S THE MOST RAINFALL CALIFORNIA HAS HAD IN 10 YEARS. IT'S BEEN MISERABLE (!) BUT MY RUNNING WAS NOT. I FLEW, MY GOD WHAT A DIFFERENCE!!!"

Michael, having watched Harriet unravel her joint mechanics, knew the score. He diligently put a few minutes aside several times a day to perform drills to open joints in each foot, being mindful to co-ordinate the flow of joint rotations up through the pelvis and into his spine. Following his first session outdoors, he stuck to the suggested guidance of walking to warm-up, walking the uphills and only running on the downhills, every other day. This was all *way* below his usual activity level, but he demonstrated patience because he understood the process: it wasn't about fitness, it was about **connecting the action with the thought with the feeling**. On his second session, the magic happened.

Towards the end, having practiced mindfully letting his 'nemesis' tension disappear and letting bones dangle under an effortlessly perched head, he seemed to suddenly relax inside his body and just started flowing. I have no other words to describe it and I'll never forget it. Neither will he. Michael was running in harmonious flow and by the time I caught up, back at the clinic, he was 'in wonder'. He'd just experienced running pleasure the like of which he'd never, ever encountered and he hadn't wanted it to stop. He was visibly moved, and I can still feel the powerful reaction as I remember the moment. I'm fortunate enough to see and feel running magic happen in front of me - regularly.

In a lovely chain of linked runners, Harriet had sought help having watched Russ succeed Liz. Russ came with a long list of running injuries after telling me he'd seen:

"A HUGE TRANSFORMATION IN LIZ'S RUNNING SINCE SHE STARTED WORKING WITH YOU AND I'M HOPING THAT YOU WILL BE ABLE TO HELP ME RUN FURTHER AND FASTER WITHOUT FALLING TO BITS".

He wasn't joking. His ten year running career had seen him with **pulled hamstrings, calf strains, piriformis pain, achilles pain, tight iliotibial bands, bi-lateral arthroscopies for knee pain, back pain and a sore neck**. Russ is amazed at what his body can do, now he understands it better and looks after it well. Liz, despite a history of **knee pain, shin splints, bakers cyst, plantar fasciitis and hamstring trouble**, loved being incredibly active and came looking to be able to run and not get injured. She has since achieved personal bests in running and having surpassed her expectations at her first duathlon event now enjoys what her body is increasingly capable of. Liz, in turn, had listened to the advice of her running buddy Gearoid, who arrived as a golfer-turned-runner with *"no injuries from golf!!!"*, but who'd picked up **plantar-fasciitis at the start of marathon training**. Along his movement journey with me he discovered efficient trekking, enabling him to hike up Mont Blanc with very little training, and complete an impromptu challenge in style. Gearoid came on guidance from his mate Alan, who opened the door (literally) on a life-affirming story that could fill a chapter all by itself; having just joined a gym, Alan had only popped in to ask about footwear and ended up on a journey that took him across the Ironman finishing line. Running Legends.

These willing and wholehearted folk - and many others you'll meet along the way - passed on their enthusiasm with so much passion, their energy instilled hope in others. Their eyes shone. Relating their 'eureka' moments (when great movement patterns unleashed unforeseen - by them - running prowess) provoked outbursts of superlatives. Their spontaneous joy and irresistible facial expressions spoke volumes.

RUNNING WITHOUT PAIN AND DISCOMFORT...
RUNNING FASTER... RUNNING FOR LONGER...
ENJOYING HILL RUNNING... RUNNING EFFORTLESSLY...
FEELING LIKE A RUNNER...
SMILING AS THEY RAN!

All of these delights were experienced on their journeys towards running efficiency. Of course they were thrilled at the time, but isn't that how running *should* be? Fun! Gratifying, even? And if you put good work in, it *should* generate progress, shouldn't it? "I ran a Personal Best", I'd hear. "Of course you did", I'd reply. "Why wouldn't you? You're running more efficiently than you were!" They would go on to eclipse their newly-discovered 'more speed for no more effort', with more speed for *less* effort and be enthralled with their own potential. Quite rightly so.

I watched many running transformations and life shifts - as we'll see, **movement and thought are inextricably linked and form a compelling team** - and wondered why folk seemed to think this was new information. Surely it was already out there, somewhere? But if my clients were anything to go by - and they seemed a pretty normal bunch of lovely folk - the evidence suggested not.

I've always believed that running 'belongs to us' as a mode of transport and that it should neither hurt, nor feel uncomfortable nor be innately injurious. Why *would* running hurt, feel uncomfortable or be injurious if we've evolved to be upright, on two feet, with more than one gear? It's just one up from walking, right? When we were very young, we weren't 'taught' to walk, we just started instinctively, referring only to our friendly internal expert, 'Sensory Feedback'. The sequence seems pretty standard: stagger (to great applause), topple, stagger, adjust-a-bit, topple-a-bit-later, repeat many times. We continued to practice without complaining about how long it was taking, until we graduated - no fanfare this time - into tiny upright humans getting around consistently on two little feet. Then, **seemingly without any further training, we were running away from the 'Tickle Monster'**. So if walking is coded into our DNA, surely we must be 'born to run' too? And if we can loosely agree on that rather sparse summary of human evolution, we could assume that running should be pretty straightforward, couldn't we?

TRAIL ORIGINS

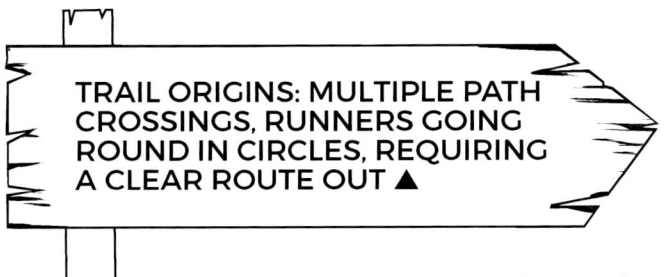

TRAIL ORIGINS: MULTIPLE PATH CROSSINGS, RUNNERS GOING ROUND IN CIRCLES, REQUIRING A CLEAR ROUTE OUT ▲

When I became an injury statistic, not only was it a surprise (how?) it came as a shock (why?). And when no-one could help me, I had to figure it out for myself. I knew bodies were beyond clever, so why couldn't I heal? I knew running was the most natural thing in the world, so why couldn't I do it anymore without pain? *How could that be?* Long before I'd even heard the phrase 'think outside the box', circumstances challenged me to think differently.

Provoked into self-investigation, I broadened my understanding of movement, and was able to reinstate my running status quo. More about that later, but for now the relevant point is that I was running again for the simple pleasure of it, for the joy orchestrated by flying through the air putting one foot in front of the other, effortlessly and seemingly endlessly ... I was running for the *state of being* I remembered from childhood, when the three miles 'out-and-back' down the country lane was a great adventure. I was back on the trails enjoying myself, whilst in clinic I was hearing **'ahh running, I used to love it, but it doesn't love me any more', 'turns out I'm not made for running', 'it's not for me, it hurts too much', 'every time I try harder, or go further, I get injured'.**

As adults - hopefully beyond toppling - why were so many of you getting injured, and so often? An isolated case might be considered unlucky. Multiples upon multiples didn't make sense. Having a clinic schedule full of folk injured through 'a natural activity', didn't make sense! *Why* were so many getting injured? Mad, and maddening.

> **FOOT STUCK DOWN THE PAIN & INJURY RABBIT-HOLE? EXIT VIA THE ▲**

And the variety of running pain stories! At one end of the 'no-joy-in-running-anymore' scales, there were folk arriving having been **told not to run again** because the problem had either been deemed irreversible or a direct finger of blame had been pointed at the activity of running. **Dodgy knees, dodgy hips and dodgy backs** came under this category quite often. Some came looking for a second opinion; some came simply to do 'their best by their bodies' and were amazed at what was possible. For very many, with help, guidance and patience, they *did* run again - not only joyfully and without pain, but with *more pain-free general mobility* than they'd enjoyed at the time they were instructed to halt running.

My bias towards my favourite activity might be skewing reality, but this phenomenon has played out so many times, it almost feels as if the world of 'health' has hierarchies of movement practice, with running being consistently demoted. Opinions are divided and make for curious reading: some experts tell us that steady aerobic exercise must be limited, and we should rush around vigorously for just a few moments a day to achieve optimum health; some advocate movement almost exclusively in the horizontal plane, isolating and strengthening body parts with minimal engagement of our feet; yet others are 'pro' strength training and 'anti' cardiovascular. Overall, despite the evolutionary running heritage many anthropologists theorise we've emerged from, it's as if running for longer than Usain Bolt takes to win our hearts is deemed somehow 'bad' for us in this modern world, and can't be trusted as a form of healthy exercise. Sure, I agree we should avoid running in a manner that is harmful, but is consigning the 'next gear up from walking' to a shelf of low-importance really the answer? Does that make sense to you? I find myself asking 'Why?' frequently and currently have a warrior's quote printed into my mobile phone cover: "I choose to listen to my inner voice, not to the random opinions of others." Perhaps it's my Northern roots, but it spoke straight to my heart.

At the other end of the 'where's-the-running-joy-gone' scales, and just as devastating to the person concerned, were the cases where **the repetitious nature of the injury drove them mad with frustration and now they were close to giving up** on their preferred movement activity. 'Groundhog Day' seemed to arrive at exactly the same mileage or intensity, no matter how much attention they had given to all the 'right' things - RICE (rest, ice, compression, elevation), massage, roll, stretch, more supportive footwear, go back slowly ... the list goes on. You may well have been here many times yourself. Here, hamstrings (back of thigh) and 'below-the-knee' injuries prevailed: pain anywhere in the sole of the foot (commonly labelled plantar-fasciitis and when present across the breadth of the foot, metatarsalgia), the 'dreaded' top of foot pain (ToFP), unstable ankles, Achilles tendonitis and the ubiquitous running calf strains.

Again, with joined-up thinking, solving the mystery of the pain source was often simple, with improved joint mechanics creating space for healing. The vicious spiral would be halted and given no choice but to reverse direction. So often, it's not the pain site itself that's the problem, *especially* when the pain is only on one side. If only one big toe, foot, ankle, calf, shin, knee, hamstring or hip hurts, one of the first questions to ask is why doesn't the other hurt? **Unless you're recovering from an obvious impact to a particular area, why wouldn't both sides hurt? After all, you're not hopping. You're running, aren't you?** In my experience, this is a new consideration for many, and as soon as I highlight it to a runner stuck in a repetitive injury nightmare, I can see it hits home. As a point of note, I can honestly say I rarely see symmetrical, repetitive injury patterns despite the activity clearly requiring just as many 'rights as lefts'.

Along the spectrum between these two poles of joyless running, I'd see folk who'd stopped running almost as soon as they'd started, those who'd resigned themselves to only being able to run 'this' far or 'that' fast, and others who'd simply started to question what they'd previously been following in good faith. These runners arrived seemingly sharing common ground split three ways: of having been attached to an idea of running form they'd heard of or seen; or having depended on (literally and figuratively) a certain type of physical support they'd heard of or seen; or were wedded to a way of developing their fitness they'd heard of or seen.

> 'HOW' THEY WERE MOVING, 'WHAT' THEY WERE WEARING AND 'WHY' THEIR SCHEDULE LOOKED AS IT DID WAS DOWN TO RECEIVED WISDOM THAT CARRIED SUCH WEIGHT, IT WAS OFTEN FOLLOWED WITH GREAT DILIGENCE, DESPITE BODILY PROTESTS.

Perhaps one of these scenarios is resonating with you? Maybe you've been influenced by one of the following:

"Lean into the hill. Pick up your knees. Pick up your feet. Circle your legs. No pain, no gain. It's running, it's going to hurt. Hit your bum with your heels. Pump your elbows. Support your arches. Wear more cushioned trainers for hard surfaces. Calf guards are the answer. Try harder. Race on Sunday, hills on Monday. Three hard sessions a week, and one recovery jog. Jog to warm up. Stretch to warm up." **Any of these sound familiar?**

That I was seeing the results of these themes in clinic on a near-daily basis bothered me. There seemed to be some words missing from the instructions emanating from both the clinical environment and the running industry. Rather than "don't run", perhaps "don't run until you've figured out WHY you run in a way that seems to instigate pain". Instead of "wear this", maybe "wear this as a temporary measure whilst you figure out WHY you need support in the first place". Complete the instruction "hills on Mondays" with "if you feel fully recovered, with a spring in your step and all heaviness from the previous hard session gone, and remember to give your body a rest if you raced on Sunday!" Qualify that whilst 'calf guards work for some', the fit is all-important, and they don't suit all calf shapes.

Working in the field of lymphoedema for many years, I feel as if the topic of sports compression deserves a chapter all to itself to unravel the many misconceptions surrounding it, but given this is only the beginning of the story, I'll keep it simple. These garments are designed to create a stronger venous and metabolic waste fluid return through the squeeze formed by a muscle contracting against the restriction of an artificially tight skin. So unless you want to make your running harder, they're best served up for an active recovery, post running.

As for "run like this", I admit, I'm struggling to complete a phrase I actively run away from. Let's remaster it. *"Explore this movement, listen to what your body says about it, and act upon the feedback accordingly".* There. That's better.

THE VOICE ALONG THE TRAIL

Have you ever stopped to consider how vast the world's running toolbox seems to be? Full of must-have shiny new gadgets, quick-fix strategies, how-to instructions from a variety of contradictory sources, and a plethora of external accessories to help you feel better, go faster, run further. All there to 'support' your activity. Yet research has emerged saying the injury rates remain the same, in spite of all the paraphernalia. I feel runners are being distracted from their intuitive and inherent movement abilities, and it makes me so cross. Over the years, I've clambered up on my soapbox more than a few times, ranting that the running world needed another voice to get behind the runner whilst they searched for their 'just right'; one that was fluent in the transfer of learning; that returned the authority for comfortable movement back to the runner; that related directly to the runner, fully explaining how, what and why he or she might be feeling and thinking 'this or that'; that could throw light upon what might be 'better or worse' rather than 'right or wrong'. Where was that voice of common sense?

> THERE WERE JUST TOO MANY TALES OF RUNNING SETBACKS, CREATING A TIPPING POINT OF UNNECESSARY WOE AND A CALL FOR ACTION.

And who am I to stand up and be heard, you might ask? Well, I'm the accumulative product of all the characters on page 1, so I've probably been where you are now; if not exactly, then close. Amongst other things, I'm a runner and running coach with a conversation-ice-melting-claim-to-fame of being the first 'barefoot' Iron(wo)man in the world, and with an injury history so long I recently realised I'd forgotten my very first surgery, resulting from an unlucky running fall (I don't make a habit of toppling, but tilted pavement slabs can be really treacherous if you land higglety-piggelty).

Pain instigated my own journey towards efficient running. It turns out that necessity is the mother of both invention, and 'Taking Matters into your Own Hands'. Shin Splints & Sciatica. The 3 S's. The bane of my life because, either together or alone, they made a misery of the one constant that had kept me sane since I was at grammar school – running. I ran as soon as I was 'old enough'. I held the record for the mile walk at junior school, because

> ## "NO, NO! THE ADVENTURES FIRST, EXPLANATIONS TAKE SUCH A DREADFUL TIME."
> ### LEWIS CARROLL, ALICE IN WONDERLAND ▲

we weren't allowed to run it – we were 'too young'. I ran the inaugural Stratford-upon-Avon Half Marathon aged 17; I arrived at the event having trained for the full distance, but with 2 months to go before my 18th birthday, they wouldn't allow me to run it. With knock-knees and gym knickers, you see me here telling the announcer off because he'd got my name wrong. Always was a stroppy Yorkshire girl!

I can't remember when the pain started. Have you ever said that? Crikey, if I had a penny for every time I've heard that in clinic or when coaching …! For so many, the pain has been there so long that despite delving into memory banks they still can't fathom what exactly 'set it all off' and when. Sometimes, things just happen because they were ready to. Running miles in British service-issue DMS boots (no, not Doc Martens, 'directly moulded sole', aka dreadful rubber soled ankle boots, as seen in the Imperial War Museum!) with packs on backs and pine poles on shoulders during Royal Air Force officer training, probably contributed heavily to the 'why' in my pain history, but that was long before the 'when'.

I followed instructions. I did the exercises; wore uncomfortable insoles I was told I would 'break in' (what with? Eh? *My feet??*); picked up pencils with my toes; sat cross-legged on the floor; slept on strange shaped pillows; sat in special seats in the car, at the desk and at the treatment couch; I dutifully 'rested', not doing the very thing that I loved - I mean, what kind of a solution *is* that? I tried them all. You probably have too. Some helped a little; some didn't at all; the pain was always there – the only variance was the degree.

Then, in 2002, a breakthrough.

It started with the most unlikely predecessor to a barefoot shoe you could imagine – the original and enormous-soled MBT trainer – with the ground far, far away from the actual sole of my foot. Some of you may remember them. But the 'B' stands for Barefoot, so perhaps it was a clairvoyant peep into the future? Whatever it was, after 21 years of constant sciatic feedback of the grumbling-through-to-yelling varieties ... the pain disappeared. Extraordinary. Theories at the time revolved around postural improvements both in muscle tone and body alignment. All my lymphoedema patients were cajoled into wearing them, to optimise venous return and drag the lymph along, willing or not. The successes were so many and varied, that having trained alongside two osteopaths and a chiropractor on the first MBT training course in the UK, I opened Ten-Point, the first MBT shop in the UK.

Running in MBTs myself, and helping to improve people's walking and running gaits in them, filled my life for quite a few years. There wasn't much choice floating around the footwear industry in the mid 2000s; running shops focused on ever-growing heel cushions, springs, stability posts and so-called crash pads (and if you're wondering, that's the name the *industry* gives the flared section of cushioning around the outside of the heel area. Interesting, eh?). Many runners ran with what some consider to be a walking gait pattern - heel to toe - with all that cushioning protecting them, they could, couldn't they? Whilst my thought processes are more refined now compared to then, it still strikes me as remarkable that - for me, as well as for many others I've since worked with - adjusting *first contact* with the ground to somewhere forward of the heel bone itself, whilst letting the heel descend and 'kiss' the ground almost immediately after, sorted out those shin splints almost obscenely quickly.

And so I continued on my life's journey, routing via a not-quite-straight-and-therefore-endlessly-engaging path. And, having said goodbye to my 3 S's, I made steady forward progress. During my divorce, I was told my running symbolised 'running away' from my problems. Even if it was to some degree, within 30 seconds of starting a run, the solution to whatever was bugging me at the time would appear - whether I was looking for answers or not. Running has been my waistline friend, my health and my sanity. For me, running wasn't an option. It was a part of me, and helping others find solutions to get back to their own running was just as important, because I understood their frustrations. Always on the look-out for another way to do the same thing – improve running enjoyment and offer people choice – I found Newton shoes and a delightful tale of two philanthropists. They wanted to use their fortune to introduce the cushioned running world to a new concept in running footwear: a non-cushioned, lower-heeled, forefoot-lugged, garish-coloured marvel.

Well, we flew on our first run. I PB'd my 5 mile loop by 8 minutes!! Whilst I knew the stats - that every 100 grams on your feet is 3% effort, and that MBTs were (very) heavy - they had been the only shoe I could find where runners were able, through the technology in the sole, to improve their internal awareness and gain more information about what their bodies were up to above their feet. As one door closes, another opens ... now we could move in a better way, AND not be weighed down by a couple of bags of sugar on each foot!

Progress.

The launch of Newtons in 2007/8 heralded the very beginnings of mainstream awareness of natural running, minimal footwear and 'barefooting'. I'd already met Matt Wallden, the wonderful, forward-thinking, inspirational MD of Primal Lifestyle at the Back Show at Olympia. Wearing my much-loved Feelmax toe socks from Finland, I'd been able to try on his Vibram Fivefingers (VFFs) with ease. There was something in the air. Pose Method and Chi Running were being discussed, on-line forums were becoming popular and experiences were being shared. I'd been barefoot and pregnant in East Africa, only to come home and be totally unable to fit into any 'normal' shoe I'd previously owned. My children's feet were perfect until they went to school in the UK and started wearing 'proper shoes'. (Sorry Joshy & Sammy - I can only apologise that I didn't know then what I know now!). There was definitely something about shoes that changed feet, but not enough people were talking about it.

We took the plunge. It's so long ago, it now feels like it happened overnight, but I'm sure it didn't. Wearing our first pair of Vibram Fivefinger KSOs, we headed off for our first run. I still remember it. It was dark, it was somewhere off-road, we got lost in the moment and then *actually* got lost, we laughed, we felt the cool mud squeeze up and squelch between our toes, our arches were stabbed by cruel stones hidden along the path, we ran further than we'd planned, and even that was further than we ought ... and all three of us probably had one of the best - most joyful - runs of our lives. We were hooked.

This was unchartered territory and without a manual, so naturally we made lots of mistakes, or perhaps a better term might be 'learning hiccups'. Clearly, it was all meant to be part of the journey, because here I am writing the book about it all, saving you from the same gaffes. My own running and run coaching was now almost exclusively done in Vibram Fivefingers, but choice was important to clients and customers, so the search for great footwear that allowed feet to be – well – feet, continued in earnest. Running form was explored and honed entirely unshod along the five mile local 'Pednor Loop' country lane – it's amazing what you learn about the mechanics of the human frame in motion when you are totally connected with the ground. Returning from one such session, I was stopped by a lovely older lady with blue hair driving a matching blue Volvo estate. She wound the passenger window down and asked "Are you ... alright?" Confirming that indeed I was, she hesitantly pointed to the apparent loss of my senses ... "you seem to have – er – forgotten your shoes, dear" ... :)

I was asked so many times "how far can you run in them?" (referring to the Fivefingers) I decided to go and find out. After an endlessly frustrating summer trying to sort out a hip flexor injury I'd created by riding too big a gear on too high a saddle (I was a cycling newbie back then), I began my ultra distance running journey in the Fivefinger Flow. I completed two of the three days of the Druid's Challenge (29 & 27 miles respectively) in November 2009. With ten miles of the second day left to cover, the hip flexor finally 'went', so naturally I dragged my right leg between my poles (now crutches) to reach the end, only to be casevac'd home, and scolded for my stubbornness. Blasted broken hip flexor became my nemesis.

With an uncompleted multi-stage ultra behind me, I overheard someone say "she couldn't do it". "Couldn't do what?" I demanded. "Ironman", was the answer. So I signed up for it. During training, I fell off my heavy winter bike by losing the back wheel descending a muddy country lane, and slightly broke my ankle – I say slightly because it wasn't until the black bruising subsided from my hip and thigh that I even noticed my ankle was crippling me. The X-ray confirmed the break but by that time I'd been hobbling on it for a couple of weeks, so a cast seemed overkill. Good decision – nine weeks later I ran the Berkhamsted Half Marathon. Not long after that, I fell off my brand new carbon race bike. This time I was standing still, telling a story. I got over-excited, over-balanced and keeled to the side of my still-clipped-in foot. Have you ever seen that happen in front of you? 'You've Been Framed' material - absolute, pure comedy. Desperate not to damage my brand new race bike and realising I was going down whether I liked it or not, I lifted my incredibly light bike out of the way – saving it. Phew. I saved my beautiful bike and broke two ribs, with three months left before Ironman. There's nothing like a ribcage injury to focus the mind on the need to optimise running technique. In Austria, after 2.4 miles of swimming, 112 miles of cycling, 26.2 miles of running, with a 26-page race report documenting the ridiculous amount of ablution stops (it was very messy), I became that conversation-ice-breaker; the world's first barefoot Iron(wo)man.

Now I'd done it, I was satisfied. Wearing my medal in the shop (sad Yorkshire girl) I was asked "Which one?" "Austria" was my proud reply. My next adventure began with the words that followed, "Ah yes, the 'soft' Ironman".

Red rag to a bull ...

Training began almost immediately, followed by a bike crash six weeks later, where another lack of handling skills, plus a bit of bad luck, saw me wrapped around a concrete post. A gradual loss of power and feeling to my left arm, preceded the final event that indicated I ought to seek help: not being able to reach up to give my 6' 2" son, Joshy, a hug when he came home from university.

In December 2010 the wonderful Mr Sabin kindly gave me back full use of my left arm by performing a double discectomy with spinal fusion across three vertebrae in my neck. Within 24 hours, all symptoms had completely disappeared. Five days later, in the snow up at Coombe's Hill, I ran 50 yards because with skilled, non-impactful, barefoot running, I could. Frustratingly, eight weeks later, and just as I was about to get back on my bike, the umbilical hernia that had popped out at the same time as the two discs had to be repaired.

Permission was granted to 'start very gentle exercise' at my six week check-up. I nodded obligingly, opting to omit the news that I'd just returned from a warm weather training camp, where (gently) cycling 112 miles had been our final day's action.

On 21st May 2011, five months after major neck surgery and three months after abdominal surgery, I completed Ironman Lanzarote ... arguably the hardest Ironman of them all. I was 40 minutes faster than my first 'soft' Ironman, with just as many loo stops. As far as I was concerned as I grabbed the finish-line banner, wrestling it off the glamorous banner-holders, I'd won.

That Ironman was special. I had been told I couldn't – and shouldn't. But a challenge isn't a challenge if you know you can do it. In my heart of hearts, I knew that if I used my body as well as I possibly could, as well as I believe it was designed to be used, then I ought to be able to do it. After all, a bone knits together in about three weeks, and the knit is strong by six weeks. So I figured I had time to heal and get strong if I used my body with joint and soft-tissue thoughtfulness. This is what I passionately believe efficient running to enable – fluid, flowing, comfortable, sustainable running with minimal injury risk, through joint-friendly movement. I simply find it more enjoyable and more comfortable to do with less on my feet than most.

So what does an opinionated Northerner wear on her feet when she gets married? Sequined Vibram Fivefingers. And what do Mr and Mrs Hall do on their honeymoon? Run round the vineyards of Languedoc in 'his and hers' Fivefingers, preparing to face the demons of her unfinished Druid's Challenge ... of course!

And, at the 11th hour of the 11th day of the 11th month of the 11th year of this century, we set off – Mr Hall for his first 31 mile ultra distance run, and me (now Mrs Hall!) to complete the three day 84 mile Druid's Challenge – because we could.

Remembering the start still catches me at the back of my throat. I didn't know I could do it, but I thought I could. So I tried. Not famous for paying attention, I got lost every day ('just follow the acorn signs' they said – how difficult can it be?) ... but finally, I found the finish line. More emotional than the first Ironman; more emotional even than the second Ironman. Completing Druid's Challenge was utterly overwhelming. And now I could tell people that so far, the furthest I'd tested the concept of barefoot - and efficient running - was 87 miles.

Couple show Iron strength
Wife pips husband to the post of gruelling challenge

Mr Hall, having supported me through two Ironmans, now wanted to give it a go himself. Upping the anti, he opted for his first triathlon to be the hardest Ironman in the world, so back to Lanzarote we went. This time I ran in the new Fivefinger Seeyas: ultra-thin, super comfortable, and - I discovered - without heat insulation. I ran faster than I'd have liked to until I was able to slow up a bit when the sun finally went down. The ground was H-O-T!! That probably got me my 'win' by ten minutes, and in my mind, reinforced my life mantra:

'IF YOU THINK YOU CAN DO IT, YOU PROBABLY CAN.'

A fortnight later I was itching to run again, but knew I ought to allow a little more 'recovery' time, so with my returning energy, decided to do a bit of gardening. Actually, I don't do gardening; I have a track record of knocking off green things rather than anything nurturing, like growing them. I decided to play safe and do some landscaping instead, laying fifty slabs of Welsh slate over my dying green bits. I was a bit stiff after Ironman; I couldn't move after gardening. I'd managed to prolapse a disc and couldn't feel my right foot … and I was third 'man' on the Barefoot Relay Team for the Classic Quarter in just over a week's time …

Turns out, by using the muscle memory of skilled running, trotting twelve miles along the beautiful, if rather lumpy, Cornish coastline with a prolapsed disc is do-able without pain. Not at speed, but do-able. The Adventures of Team Shambolic – featuring Matt Wallden, Tim Bishop, me and the world's barefoot best-friend 'Barefoot Ted' – is its own story. Suffice to say we had a blast, raising eyebrows along the 44 mile trail with our 'non-standard' attire; never mind our footwear choice – Barefoot Ted ran in a jumper and cut-off jeans with a leather gourd as a hydration pack!

My Efficient Running Barefoot Journey continued apace, immersing me in exciting projects and more adventures. The most experienced training provider in the UK, YMCAfit, approached me to write a manual to teach their instructors how to coach Natural Running, bringing the skills – and the joy – to more. The innovative British footwear company, inov-8, brought me in to coach the finalists of their "8 weeks to be a Natural Runner" competition; accompanying those eight runners - from a wide variety of running backgrounds - on their minimal/barefoot journeys was an honour and a real pleasure.

Having established that you *could* cover 87 miles over three days, looking pretty much the same at the end as at the beginning (although I did *feel* a lot more tired than I looked), it was implied that the night-stops allowed for rest and recovery and "it isn't possible to hold form" for 50 miles straight. Well, without having tried, I couldn't possibly argue. Off I went again. Anticipating any cynical references to easy route choices (I didn't want to have to do *this* one again) I opted for the 'underground' extreme ultra of Caesar's Camp; one for the purists, with no 'cheat sticks' (aka trekking poles) allowed. Five laps of a ten mile course across the military training ground of Dartmoor; no roads, no civilisation, 1520 feet of elevation gain per lap, rough tough stony terrain, funeral dirges played and abuse hurled at you through base camp to make sure spirits are thoroughly dampened as you pass through, and with a late start so you ran as much of it in darkness as possible.

It was my usual disorganised preparation. I had not one, but two run coaching sessions booked the day before, and by the end of the day I'd run ten miles and walked three miles to and from train stations. So a half marathon in my legs the day before they were going to be asked to go further than they'd ever done in one go ... by a long way. Not ideal, but nevertheless, we set off in high spirits, me and my RB (running buddy), Jason Smith. Until lap three that is, when a broken toe suffered on lap one was causing him so much grief as he stumbled in the dark, that I had to send him home.

I remember passing a lovely chap at about 45 miles who said "Wow, you're still on your toes!" Not literally of course. I was just noticeable for not landing on my heels, which was pretty much what everyone around me was doing by then. Landing on my heels would both have felt horrible to me and braked me; with such an enormous challenge to attempt, the *last* thing I needed was to make things harder! I gave myself two challenges that day: could I run 50 tough-terrain miles in 'simulated barefoot' shoes, without injury or losing form *and* do it without recourse to gastric-distress-inducing sugar binges? Do you even need to ask? *Of course* I did it!!! I truly believe we can do a lot more than we think and that it's 'us' who put the limitations on our bodies, not our bodies. Our bodies are incredible.

I'd been studying breathing mechanics which meant a challenge was inevitable to answer big questions that weren't addressed in the textbooks, and to test breathing concepts in the running arena. My gorgeous and deeply loyal friend and work colleague for nearly ten years, Wendy Jordan (*Hawkeye*), wanted to run the Amsterdam marathon, so that was earmarked as the challenge venue. Having spent many fruitful and enjoyable hours practicing, I had a list of running factors to investigate. I felt it should be possible to run as fast as nose-breathing would allow for an entire marathon; to still get a halfway decent time (for those that consider 'time' to be the be-all-and-end-all); to feel less fatigue because everything was being fully-oxygenated; to not need to take on fluids as much because the swallowed saliva generated would self-hydrate; to complete it both fasted *and*

without adding fuel because if your effort level enables nose-breathing, you must still be in the aerobic, fat-burning energy system, negating the need to top up with carbs; and to recover quickly, given I'd be fully oxygenated throughout. And when I say nose-breathing, the rules were clear - my mouth was to stay *shut throughout*. Quite a lot of boxes to tick, but I was curious ...

Poor Wendy had to put up with a silent first 10km whilst I hand-signalled our route through the 42000 participants. Then our running paths separated when she stopped at the next aid station and I didn't bother until 35km ...

I was quietly (er, silently!) surprised at how well I was running. With poor preparation (as usual, too busy coaching everyone else to have time for my own training), I'd started 'well within myself' ... then, with the ability to breathe in and out through my nose as my 'pacer', I let myself increase speed, knowing I was still running aerobically (even though my heart rate was averaging high 150s). It was looking good for an easy sub 4hr marathon. With less than 10km to go, folk back home stalking me on the tracker app were expecting 3:43 ... then I got bored.

When I crossed the finish line and called home I was greeted with "Were you injured?" "No." "Were you sick?" "No." "Were you in pain?" "No." "Did you have to walk?" "No, but I might as well have been." "Then why did you go so slow?" "I was bored". Oh dear! It turns out I'm not a 'fair-weather runner' - I'll run in anything - but I AM a 'fair-scenery runner'. I run for the pleasure of running, enjoying the sky, the panorama, nature, fresh air, fresh smells. Capital city industrial areas, running up and around four-lane flyovers and admiring airport-sized warehouses just doesn't cut it for me. In the industrial backwaters of Amsterdam, it was all

I could do to keep 'running'. Nothing hurt, nothing was tired, there were no aches, niggles, there was no fatigue. I was just so bored I couldn't be bothered. There was simply no pleasure in it. 'What on earth was I doing there?' I asked myself in my head (and I bet I wasn't the only one!).

Then, with about 500m to go, the industrial buildings suddenly gave way to event hoardings and the Olympic Stadium was finally visible. I decided that with only 500m to go, I could – after all – be a bit bothered. Crowds roared and clapped, massaging my ego and encouraging my now 'bothering' legs. I smiled through closed lips and clapped them back. Not soon enough, I was (now proper) running through the stadium entrance. Even now the memory takes my breath away ... with 100m to go – along the final straight – I was so emotional, my heart got stuck in my throat and I had to drop my jaw and take my first gasp of mouth-air in lieu of suffocating. So, 26.1 miles nose-breathing, 100 yards not. Mission accomplished I feel - after all, survival is everything. 4 hrs 12 min (I think. Or was it 11 min? Times really aren't my bag!). And after that, the ONLY thing to do was eat a massive portion of Dutch apple pie and copious amounts of cream with my roomies, then party until the wee small hours. Turns out, nose-breathing leaves one well oxygenated, unfatigued and with growing DOMS (delayed onset muscle soreness) *only* in ones diaphragm!! Who knew?

More recently, Wendy wanted another challenge - a team one this time. "How about 100km non-stop?" *What is it* with folk and this obsession with numbers?! 87 miles over three days isn't enough and 51.9 miles (must have dog-legged there somewhere) in one go apparently doesn't look as impressive as 100km. So off we go. The ever-smiling Beky Cann got sandwiched between two PFM Coaches, me and Bryn - who got in touch with his feminine side and stood in for a sadly-poorly-on-the-day Wendy; 'Girls on Tour', regaled in bright pink T-shirts with sparkly blue lettering, trotted across The Ridgeway in search of adventure. I kept waiting for fatigue and aches and that horrible feeling when a muscle is red and angry inside its 'bag', inflamed and wanting to stop, not painful as such but feeling internally 'raw'

- you know the feeling? It just didn't happen. Hand on heart, I was relaxed and comfortable until 85km. Even then, whilst I was stiffening a bit in the cold, it was the dark that led to a lack of visual interest and inevitably ... boredom!

And don't think I don't know what you're thinking. I'm ready to run away as fast as I can if I hear the phrase a hundred miles anywhere near me ... but I do have a three-year plan to conquer the 400km of Cape Wrath. I'm curious; eight of the toughest running days I'm ever likely to encounter ...

FINDING THE EDGE
....

The irony of dubbing myself the 'Queen of Efficiency', whilst spending much of my time introducing ways of transforming running habits one runner at a time, had become untenable. To be truly efficacious I was told (I had to google it ... *gorgeous* word!), I required results in numbers with a lot more zeros. Lovely though it was to have runners visit me by recommendation, the requirement to 'see me' was loaded with limitations: whilst folk *have* travelled far (even from abroad), the majority of those I saw lived close enough for it to be a feasible project; and all who know me are familiar with my aversion to early mornings, leaving only a certain amount of awake hours left in any day.

An extended reach to runners began in 2011 through a collaboration with the beautiful-from-the-inside-out singer/songwriter Kirsty Hawkshaw. We created virtual-coached running albums to specially composed music via our Barefoot Audio label and available on iTunes. It continues to be a slow-burner, but I'm an optimist and still hope it will bear fruit by virtue of its usefulness. Hindsight tells me that we limited our early influence in the running arena by labelling ourselves with the heart we wore on our sleeves. Such naivety! No matter. All part of the meandering adventure.

In the intervening years I continued my education, accumulated greater wisdom and understanding, and learned to approach the 'noise' around footwear choices calmly, whilst remaining passionate about what - or rather what does not - adorn my own precious feet.

And, although I owned knowledge through nearly four decades of running experience, back in 2011 I still struggled to explain myself in any kind of scientific way when challenged by those with a strong affinity to 'their way' of running. The gift of being able to articulate the 'why' came through serendipity: I was recommended by Oliver Selway, author of "Instinctive Fitness", to read "What The Foot?"; then I met and learned from its author Gary Ward and Chris Sritharan of Anatomy in Motion, and spent years mastering Gary's Flow Motion Model™ of gait. With beautiful synchronicity, the 'how' - **integrating exercise with evocative vocabulary creating thoughtful movement patterns** - can now be validated with the emerging understanding of neuroplasticity. Gracefully described in his second book

"The Brain's Way of Healing", the fabulous Norman Doidge (with reference to neurofeedback principles) expresses that to:

"DEVELOP INCREASED AWARENESS … CAN LEAD TO NEURAL CHANGES AND NEURODIFFERENTIATION. (PUT DIFFERENTLY, WHEN FELDENKRAIS TRAINED HIS PUPILS TO REFINE THEIR SENSORY AWARENESS OF HOW IT FELT TO PERFORM A MOVEMENT, HE WAS TRAINING THEM TO MAKE MORE USE OF THE FEEDBACK PROVIDED BY THEIR SENSES.)".

… MAKE MORE USE OF THE FEEDBACK PROVIDED BY THEIR SENSES …

Isn't that mouthwatering? Doesn't that sound empowering? As if there's another running choice around the corner? Too much choice is paralysing, but on the other hand, it doesn't feel like choice when it's laid out as a battleground; running publications and social media abound with the war of words over 'cushioned versus minimalist', 'supported versus barefooted', 'heel-striking versus midfoot/forefoot landing'. There's an amazing quote right at the beginning of the film 'Arrival':

"LANGUAGE IS THE FOUNDATION OF CIVILISATION. IT'S THE GLUE THAT HOLDS THE PEOPLE TOGETHER. IT'S THE FIRST WEAPON DRAWN IN A CONFLICT".

The scene was so powerful it drew me back in after the film had finished. We don't need any more argument. All forms of expertise are a resource, after all. My offering is that together we might consider another side to the running coin. In addition to 'heads *or* tails', 'this *or* that', let's find the edge … '*and you*'. On either side of divided opinion, is 'you'. Put another way, the infinite cleverness of 'you' sits in the space between 'this' piece of conventional wisdom and 'that' piece. The filling in the sandwich should always be the most interesting bit …

The pages of this book mark a well-defined trail, whose purpose is to lead you to the discovery of unused physical space in your body and to pick up on the spoor of your own *internal* expert, guiding you to *your* best choices. This sensory feedback arises from movement awareness and gifts the unequivocal *Absolutely Right for You.* 'You' is the bit that no-one can argue with, can they? And if they did, would you listen?

> "RAISE YOUR WORDS, NOT VOICE. IT IS RAIN THAT GROWS FLOWERS, NOT THUNDER"
> **JALALUDDIN RUMI, PERSIAN POET**

To add zest to my writing speed, it was pointed out to me that if any of the hundreds and hundreds of runners I've helped over the past fifteen years or so - either through one2one coaching, workshops or audio downloads - hadn't been on the receiving end of some form of provocation to follow the path that led them there, they would have been forced to continue their search for 'the answer', which they might never have found. Whilst I naturally scoffed at such a bold statement - that's the culturally-entrenched British self-deprecation gene in me - it did make me stop and think. Actually, how often do we miss what's right under our nose? How often do you stare at what you're looking for but simply don't see it? In the case of running, it's you! You're the hidden gem. We haven't got to the 'how' yet, **but whatever you want from your running - pleasure, to get off the 'plateau' you're on, to be free of injury, to achieve a Personal Best, to experience the joy *of* running, to run *in* joy, to just *start* running - an *attentive* you is all you need.**

And, right there, lies the crux of it all. A three-syllabled word that you might even have missed if you're a scan-reader.

Let's google the most popular activity in the world: Fitbit's statistics will reveal it's running. Wonderful! My favourite. One you're probably interested in too, given you've picked up this book. So why do so many look like they're hating every moment? It's true, isn't it? Faces either screwed up in effort, or looking gormless in a slack-jawed, open-mouthed kind of way. 'Plugged-in, glum and dumb' is another look I see daily. Plodding at one pace and one rhythm, to the beat of whatever is blocking out the world they're moving in. Runners dis-engaged, both internally *and* with their surroundings, looking about as far from being attentive to anything as is possible. Frankly, the epitome of *not* attentive. You see them everywhere, don't you? Just this morning whilst walking the dogs in glorious sunshine, I stepped aside with a smile to allow a runner past on a narrow trail in the woods. No acknowledgement and certainly no reciprocal smile. Eyes and ears closed off, and to this depressing picture add 'and body bunched up'. It's as if people are trying to run in less space than their bodies actually occupy. If you haven't noticed this already, now I've mentioned it you'll probably see it everywhere. It feels so prevalent it's like an epidemic of 'running small'! Why *wouldn't* running be hard if you're trying to do it from inside an invisible sack? No wonder they don't look like they're enjoying themselves. It shouldn't be this way. It doesn't need to be this way.

> WHETHER YOU GREW UP WITH "PLANET EARTH" OR ITS PREDECESSOR "LIFE ON EARTH", WE ALL KNOW THAT THE ENTIRE ANIMAL KINGDOM SHARES THE ABILITY TO CHANGE SPEED - TO HAVE DIFFERENT GEARS - HOWEVER MANY FEET, FINS OR WINGS PRESENT. AS SIR DAVID ATTENBOROUGH SHOWED US, IF A MATE IS CALLING, EVEN THE SLOTH CRANKS UP THE PACE. ONE SPEED ISN'T HUMAN … IT'S NOT EVEN ANIMAL.

If your car couldn't get out of second gear, you wouldn't drive around in that gear forever, listening to the engine's protests, would you? You'd take it to the garage to find out why and fix it. Forward motion in an upright human has many smoothly changing gears and you should be able to get a kick out of them all. Paying attention to how you're using your body, giving it space, noticing what it's telling you and responding quickly and appropriately to the feedback is how you keep the engine ticking over nicely, enjoying the ride.

JOYFUL RUNNING EFFICIENCY

Happy, smiling, joyous faces are what I have the privilege to see when I'm coaching, and they're infectious.

> **"ONE CAN NEVER CONSENT TO CREEP WHEN ONE FEELS AN IMPULSE TO SOAR"**
> **HELEN KELLER, AMERICAN AUTHOR**

So now, having decided my voice is loud enough and works best when things are simple and make common-sense, I find myself *compelled* to write this book, and walk as many runners as I can reach in one lifetime through a simple and progressive process to **joyful - yes, JOYFUL - running efficiency. Not an airy-fairy joyful; this is a rarified state of being that I perceive as being generally missing in the running world at the moment. Running joy is what running efficiency generates.** As Heather put it:

> "I ENJOYED AN HOUR AND 20 MINUTES OF BLISSFUL AND UNEVENTFUL RUNNING ON SUNDAY AFTERNOON: HEAVEN!! NOT A BLIP, NOR A NIGGLE, A TWINGE OR A DOUBT EVEN AFTER STOPPING FOR A CHAT AND THROUGH A VARIETY OF PACES, HILLS AND A RACE THROUGH THE WOODS AT THE END WHEN IT WAS GOING DARK AND I COULD NO LONGER DEFINE THE GROUND!! LOVED IT!!"

And just to be absolutely clear, what I propose in the following pages isn't 'my way'. There is no 'Helen Hall Method of Running'. How egocentric would that be? What I aim to disseminate via all modern means of communication possible is '<u>Our Way</u>' of running. Given the unambiguous and calculable nature in which each joint rotates in all its dimensions, every bit of every step is describable, internally palpable and replicable. We have efficiencies of movement encrypted into the shape of our bones, the articulations of our joints, the interwoven nature of the soft tissues and within the responses to activity of our changing, living brain.

Scan to watch

Rudisha Breaks World Record

That said, what does Efficient Running look like? Do we have any kind of benchmark? In the same way we can all appreciate a great tennis back-hand even if we don't play, we're all able to recognise effortless, elegant running. For a quintessential example of the latter and the opposite of it side by side, you need look no further than the London 2012 800m final; David Rudisha of Kenya took both the gold and the world record looking as if he wasn't going to break sweat, and the youngster Nijel Amos of Botswana came in second with limbs flailing everywhere. The QR code takes you to the Men's 800m Final London 2012. I'm watching it as I type and even though it's the nth time, it's still giving me goosebumps. You don't need to be an expert to know that Rudisha looks relaxed and Amos doesn't! (In my opinion, Rudisha looks the *most* relaxed, and he won. Just saying).

If I did start by running away from something, it formed the bedrock of all the choices I've made since then, and therefore I can be nothing but grateful for everything I've experienced. Now I know I'm running *towards* something. I feel thankful that the universe saw fit to offer procrastination, the art of which I perfected and which led me to wait until now - unfettered by the burden of proof - before putting as loud a common-sensical voice as I can to the bones of what I've been teaching for years ... that **running questions are answered with the only truth: the runners' body.**

> "LIFE WAS ALWAYS A MATTER OF WAITING FOR THE RIGHT MOMENT TO ACT."
> **PAULO COELHO, BRAZILIAN LYRICIST**

My intention for this book is to help you 'notice yourself'. Your running questions will be answered with the only truth: your body. I invite you to embrace the notion that 'you' really is all you need for your running, and to enjoy the journey along this path of discovery. My goal is to make the process accessible to you and to be simple, because it IS simple. This all started with Running Pathfinders, who spread the word. The trail is laid, ready to be tramped into a deep groove of running information trodden around the globe. Running Shifts ...

MAPPING YOUR PROGRESS

TRAIL WAYPOINTS ABOUND TO KEEP YOU ON TRACK; MAP YOUR PROGRESS AND ENJOY PUNCHING IN ON THE CHECKPOINTS ▲

This is not - nor is it meant to be - a scholarly works. The subject is practical and, I believe, should be fun. So my goal is to engage, whilst encouraging you to reframe how you approach this most natural of human movements. To that end, it's written as if I'm talking to you. When I record the audio version, I'll be doing exactly that. I'm writing in the way I talk to runners every day. They have responded well, so I hope the written version translates just as well; that my enthusiastic message carries over to you, wherever you happen to be.

My life story is my running story, which isn't over yet and which I've offered in brief (there's a lot more!) simply to show you the nature of the source of the following information. I'm not a theoretical running coach. That would be akin to a theoretical surgeon never touching a patient. Neither am I a biomechanics expert, here to argue the ins and outs of muscle attachments. To a certain degree, I learned anatomy through experience, and bolted knowledge to it. I didn't acquire knowledge and bolt experience to it. I invite you to do the same, just as would happen if we were face to face:

"EXPERIENCE NEW MOVEMENT PATTERNS AND RUNNING SENSATIONS AND BOLT KNOWLEDGE TO THAT EXPERIENCE" - **BEN HOUGHTON**

In order to make sense of it all - to help you convince yourself of your experiences, and to do it safely - I do need to give you some basic anatomy though. Just enough. I hope you decide I've got the balance of 'tech' information right as you journey through the pages. If I feel a greater degree of detail is helpful, I'll partition it so you can check in with it at your leisure, or not at all. It'll be your call. I'm here to tell stories to illustrate what you're going to be experiencing, not to lecture.

And to smooth the path of running discovery, it would surely help if you're aware of all the practical considerations before you start. In truth, I would feel remiss if I didn't invite you to ponder on the most commonly forgotten issues when performing either a new activity, or a familiar activity in a different way. The very words 'new' and 'different' in the context of physical activity should sound an alert: new loads on parts of your body not used to them, mean you might notice muscle soreness or stiffness. You've probably felt that before. New movements in the gym or extra efforts up the hills commonly result in hard-working muscles talking to you about it for a few days. This phenomenon is called DOMS, or delayed onset muscle soreness. Everything is fine at the time, but the following day the stiffness is noticeable, often growing worse on the second day after the efforts and finally subsiding on day three.

Noticing physical changes isn't a negative at all. After all, *"without change, there is nothing to be said"* - Philip Ball, Critical Mass. The considerations are twofold: rate and intensity of change, and they form an inverse relationship. Redistributing the bone and soft tissue workload can occur almost instantly, but time is required to embed the strengthening of both newly-busy muscles and tendons as well as the brain-driven new motor programmes that action the movement. If changes within your body feel less intense, you can move on more quickly. If your body reacts more strongly, then progress has to slow to accommodate the changes. This - rather than your enthusiasm - should be the driver for the rate you progress through the book.

When I'm present, I can guide the runners who want me to 'tell them what to do and when to do it', whilst encouraging them to lean into their own sense of capability, to tune into their tissue tolerance factor ...

- SOMETIMES, WORDS JUST FALL OUT OF MOUTHS INTO THE UNIVERSE, AND THEY'RE SO WEIGHTY, SO MEANINGFUL, SO USEFUL, THAT THEY NEED PICKLING FOR IMMORTALITY. TISSUE TOLERANCE FACTOR, TTF, IS YOUR NEW METRIC.

TISSUE TOLERANCE FACTOR: SELF-ASSESSMENT TOOL

TTF 1
You cannot even walk without feeling restricted or in pain through tension in soft tissue (not just tight muscles, muscles so tight you feel restricted); you wake up with it even after a night's rest.

TTF 2
You can walk without tension restriction/pain, but notice its restriction as soon as you run; it's less noticeable first thing in the morning.

TTF 3
You notice the restriction/pain after a couple of kilometres; it may or may not be noticeable on waking.

TTF 4
You notice the restriction/pain after roughly 5km or 30 minutes of running; it's rarely noticeable when getting out of bed.

TTF 5
You notice the restriction only towards an hour of running; pain is now rare and it's only a memory on rising.

TTF 6
You notice the restriction only after a run. No pain, just discomfort.

TTF 7
You notice the restriction on the day following a run.

TTF 8
You notice the restriction only when active on rough terrain.

TTF 9
You only notice restrictions when you've greatly exceeded current tolerance times/intensities.

TTF 10
You rarely notice any restriction.

> **"NATURE DOES NOT HURRY, YET EVERYTHING IS ACCOMPLISHED" - LAO TZU, CHINESE PHILOSOPHER ▲**

You still have to gauge your own body state, but now you've got numbers to line up with your self-assessment and help you feel comfortable about what you've done and where you're going. Using the descriptions, you can evaluate with reasonable accuracy 'where you are', empowering you with the self-confidence to progress onwards only when the next stepping stone is within reach. Pacing is so often the solution, in life and in running, which of course, *is* life ...

ROUTE: UP THE PYRAMID

"SOMEWHERE BETWEEN THE BOTTOM OF THE CLIMB AND THE SUMMIT IS THE ANSWER TO THE MYSTERY WHY WE CLIMB"
GREG CHILD, AUSTRALIAN AUTHOR ▲

From wikipedia.org:

"A PYRAMID'S DESIGN, WITH THE MAJORITY OF THE WEIGHT CLOSER TO THE GROUND, AND WITH THE PYRAMIDION (THE UPPERMOST PIECE OR CAPSTONE) ON TOP MEANS THAT LESS MATERIAL HIGHER UP ON THE PYRAMID WILL BE PUSHING DOWN FROM ABOVE. THIS DISTRIBUTION OF WEIGHT ALLOWED EARLY CIVILIZATIONS TO CREATE STABLE MONUMENTAL STRUCTURES. IT HAS BEEN DEMONSTRATED THAT THE COMMON SHAPE OF THE PYRAMIDS OF ANTIQUITY, FROM EGYPT TO CENTRAL AMERICA, REPRESENTS THE DRY-STONE CONSTRUCTION THAT REQUIRES MINIMUM HUMAN WORK."

So THAT'S why I love pyramids! ▲

To further enhance the degree of astute self-control you'll exhibit during the physical demands of your running development, the route journeys up the side of a ten-floored pyramid. Each chapter (read: lesson) is a level of the pyramid, and the goal is to climb your pyramid at the speed dictated by your TTF and the guideline parameters discussed at the beginning and end of each stage. These 'barometers of ability' at each level, give you

something to engage with, over which you have control. No-one else. The buck stops with you. This is a GOOD THING. No-one else cares as much about you as ... you. You will make good choices because you'll be working the answers out from the inside. Remember:
This is a *living pyramid*; it's yours to explore as you climb - to breathe life into - at the

RUNNING QUESTIONS ARE ANSWERED WITH THE ONLY TRUTH: THE RUNNERS' BODY

rate that feels comfortable to your body, even if that's slower than your eagerness! If you feel the pre-requisites are holding you back from moving up to the next level, you might have missed the good physiological reasoning expressed on the pages. Dive back in and re-read them - I aim to look after you, to pace you safely and productively, not to hinder you.

Intention underpins the design. The pyramid's levels build the *Detail* of running skill on top of the foundational *Principles* of non-injurious movement patterns. In accordance with understanding going back over 4500 years, we're building a *"stable monumental structure"*. Doesn't that sound fabulous? To achieve that, layering skill over awkward, uncomfortable movement won't work. Put another way, sweating the small stuff isn't going to improve your running prowess if you ignore the elephant in the room (that'll be your *forward lean/ tightrope tracking width/high impact landing/plod *delete as appropriate).

Principles form the wide base of the pyramid, and to a great degree, the width of the pyramid at each level relates to the time you'd expect to spend there. Please allow that time to embed the new motor programmes; wait for soft tissue to strengthen before taxing it further, and be patient.

"THE HURRIER I GO, THE BEHINDER I GET"
LEWIS CARROLL, ENGLISH WRITER ▲

On your way up the pyramid, life might get in the way and you could hit a stumbling block. For some, the best action is to head back down a level or two and regroup. For others, whilst the running might have to stop, the movement drills within the levels can continue, maintaining joint mobility and soft tissue health. As the thought 'the best way up to the top is the one that's right for you' popped into my head, the image was that of the cool composure of the tortoise versus the cockiness of the hot-headed hare, and how appropriate the fable is to running adventures in real life. I've presented a couple of scenarios describing very different routes up the pyramid at the beginning of Part Two (page 240) as by the time you've reached that stage of the journey, the timelines and strategies will make more sense. As Dr John Demartini says in his book *The Breakthrough Experience*: *"Nothing of value comes without a price"*. **The value is the triumph of summiting and the view from the top; the price is 'only' that of self-control, of pacing yourself, of moderation, of tuning into the radar of sensory awareness and responding to what you notice ...** but of course, human nature being what it is, it's a big ask ... hence possibly (sorry) labouring the point.

USING STILES TO HELP WITH STICKY ANATOMY

TAKING YOUR MOST COMPLETE 'YOU' FORWARD: THE IMPORTANCE OF STILE ETIQUETTE ▲

Knowledge breeds understanding, so let's dig deeper. Not too deep - just a few anatomical concepts reframed for day to day use, and of relevance to you as an efficient runner.

This information will help you embrace the purpose of the drills dotted throughout your journey up the pyramid, which initially seem to disrupt the flow of your running. And I know so many of you *loath* running interruptions; as if a brief pause or a stop or - heaven forbid - a walk section, isn't part of running or means somehow you've failed in your run! Throughout your running adventure along this route, there'll be *many* intermissions, where you'll pause to perform a drill. Think of them as stiles along trails; you have to stop running to cross them, but once over, your run can continue. I offer them to you in the certainty that without them, the route to your destination would probably take much longer, and be significantly more arduous.

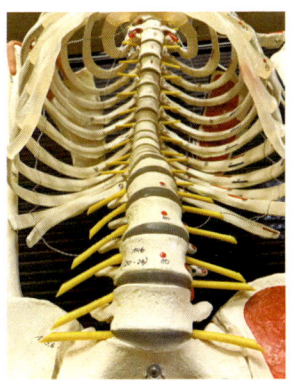

Let me explain. For a moment, let's consider the +200 joints in the body as doors (the experts can't agree on the total number and a rough count is perfectly acceptable for our purposes): if all the doors are open, we'd be somewhat floppy (Bill and Ben the Flower-Pot Men might spring to mind if you're a 60's-70's baby!); if all the doors are closed, we could be mistaken for a scarecrow - we might sway in a stiff breeze but that would be about it; for efficient, fluid movement to occur some doors will need to open and some will need to close with perfectly synchronised timing. Conceptualising joints as doors seems to help people better understand movement, perhaps because they're more relaxed connecting to something less 'biology' and more 'day-to-day' humdrum; if it works for you, feel free to substitute as you read on. I'll continue on your behalf for a while, and then leave you to carry on if you want to.

As you might already know (especially if you've read the already-mentioned brilliant book *'What The Foot?'* by the visionary Gary Ward), there are 33 joints in each foot and 26 joints in the spine. These are figures that tend to invoke disbelief in those I'm coaching, so I'm just going to repeat: there are a total of 66 joints/doors in your feet and 26 joints/doors in your spine. Now that's a good chunk of the total joints/doors in your body, regardless of which 'expert's number' you hang your anatomical hat on.

And in your case, of these couple of hundred joints/doors in question, are they all freely mobile in all the dimensions they're supposed to be able to move in? Are you aware of any limitations in movement anywhere? What about clothing restrictions? Have you ever even considered how tight you're tying your laces, or whether that strap around your chest - be it a heart rate monitor or a sports bra - restricts the joints where the ribs meet the spine? Does that 'racer-back' bra-top allow for freedom of movement of each shoulder blade around the back of the ribcage? Have you considered that if one area is limited, then another area might try to 'take up the slack' to enable you to continue doing whatever it is you want to

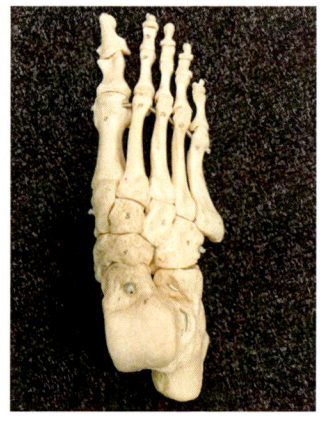

do? For some, this might seem far-fetched, but if it wasn't the case, how do you suppose you *continue getting around?*

The spinal column has 33 individual bones that interlock with each other. The top 24 are moveable and interact with the skull, the shoulder girdle and the pelvis. The Prophet Ezekiel connected 'Dry Bones' way back in the Old Testament and African-American author and composer, James Weldon Johnson put them in the right order in the song 'Dem Bones' (who needs Anatomy & Physiology textbooks?). The irrefutable point being there are MANY doors that can open and close - and in many directions - enabling pain-free, fluid motion!

> "IT ISN'T THE MOUNTAIN AHEAD THAT WEARS YOU OUT; IT'S THE GRAIN OF SAND IN YOUR SHOE" - **ROBERT W SERVICE, BRITISH-CANADIAN POET** ▲

If bones don't move in all directions they're designed to (read: restricted joint rotations), then the soft tissue response (read: muscle activity) is going to be proportionately limited. It's no good *thinking* you're running with the full potential of the fabulous butt cheeks you've pumped hard for in the gym, if half the bones they connect to don't move. We can all see that runners' femurs (thigh bones) move as one foot lands in front of the other, but their pelvises should move freely in all directions too because the buttock muscles attach to both, across the hip joint. This links in with Gary's Big Rule #2: *Joints Act, Muscles React* (do yourself a favour, visit the 'other side of another coin' and buy the book; *www.whatthefoot.co.uk*).

If your pelvis doesn't or can't move when you run - and only your legs move - the glutes' reaction in the generation of forward speed will be limited. The gluteals are the biggest muscle group, and if restricted joint movement means you're not using them to their best advantage then either you'll go slower, or you'll be forcing the use of smaller muscles with less 'bang for your buck' to achieve the same speed. Smaller muscles wouldn't be as effective, would notice the workload quicker, fatigue earlier and could well get grumpy over time through being over-used. Equal (or even less) speed for more effort would surely qualify as the *exact opposite* of efficiency.

> BUTTOCK MUSCLES ARE LAZILY REFERRED TO AS 'GLUTES' BY SO MANY THESE DAYS THAT WE MIGHT AS WELL JOIN THEM. GOING FORWARD, WE WILL!

And if the pelvis doesn't rotate freely and easily in three dimensions, that has a knock-on effect on the thigh bone that sits in it at the hip joint, which would then affect the knee joint, and then the ankle joint, in turn influencing the small matter of the function of 33 joints in *each foot*.

And vice versa.

Heading north, if the pelvic movements are in any way restricted, the knock-on effect travels through the lumbar (lower back) to the thoracic spine (think 'ribcage', think breathing, think aerobic capacity) and upwards to the cervical spine (neck) with consequences for the dominantly-held head and jaw position. Your head contributes to about an eighth of your bodyweight, and when it sits 'off centre', extra loads are generated for your body to manage. The effects also spread outwards, affecting the shoulder girdle (to include the rotations of the shoulder blades around the ribcage), the arms, the wrists, the hands and fingers.

> "JOINT MOTION INSPIRES ALL MOTION IN THE BODY. NOT JUST MUSCULOSKELETAL AND BIOMECHANICAL MOTION, BUT MOTION IN NERVES, MOTION IN THE FLOW OF FLUIDS, MOTION IN THE ORGANS AND MOTION IN THE MIND."
> **GARY WARD**

And vice versa.

We know the joint motion available at each intersection of bone - scientific folk have determined that through the shape of the bones articulating with each other. And we know the body's preferred combinations of those joint rotations at every significant moment in gait. It's all mapped out in Gary Ward's Flow Motion Model™. We also know that when a joint/door is restricted, another joint/door will help out. We know that 2 + 2 = 4. But so does 3 + 1; one arm might not be able to swing much, so the other arm might swing more to help out. Some call it a 'compromise'. I like to think of it as a balance adaptation; compromise sounds so limiting and the reality is our body's choices for adaptations in terms of joint motion combinations run into six figures. Hardly limiting! Heraclitus, the pre-Socratic Greek philosopher put it beautifully:

"OPPOSITION BRINGS CONCORD. OUT OF DISCORD COMES THE FAIREST HARMONY."

So whilst our body *can and does* make its own adjustments according to what is and isn't available in terms of joint motion, leaving one area working hard whilst another stays slumbering might create balance of sorts, but it doesn't seem either fair or effective in the long run. If we're going to travel along at a variety of paces on two feet as efficiently, as comfortably and as effortlessly as possible, we need access to all areas, as symmetrically as possible.

Back to the trail stiles I introduced earlier. In all their glorious real-life variety, they provide practical solutions to allow access through or over obstacles, enabling travel to continue along a desired route. Analogously, our 'drill stops' will do the same. We'll stop regularly at 'stiles' along the trail, where we'll use specific drills as:

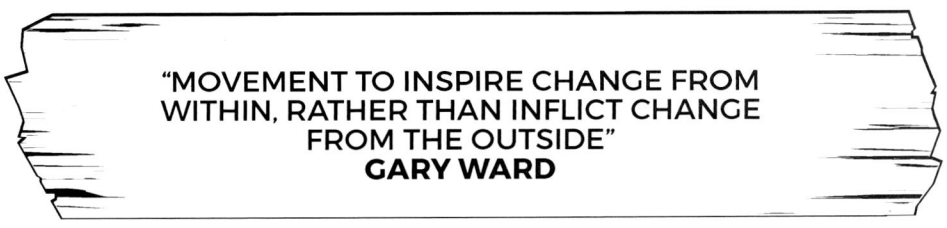

"MOVEMENT TO INSPIRE CHANGE FROM WITHIN, RATHER THAN INFLICT CHANGE FROM THE OUTSIDE"
GARY WARD

... with the goal being to overcome obstacles or resistance within our own bodies.

Optimising joint motion via specific drills performed with focus and intention is where the great gains originate. I cannot emphasise enough that 'trying' doesn't work. Even the word sends my shoulders up to my ears. Hearing the word rattles in my head like a whine. You cannot run 'like this' or 'like that'; you can only run in the way your body's invisible lines of tension and restrictions enable you to. *Its* way of running is its current *safest* option. And if the shapes you make when you run feel uncomfortable or painful, lumpy or 'not quite right', the solution is not to 'try doing something else' but to find and ease the restriction related to it, and enable *your body* to find a better way. At all costs, avoid pulling things that hurt. That rarely ends well.

LANGUAGE OF THE TRAIL

> "WORDS, ONCE THEY ARE PRINTED,
> HAVE A LIFE OF THEIR OWN"
> **CAROL BURNETT, AMERICAN ACTRESS ▲**

This book is **all** about language and context. The biggest challenge in writing it has been to be careful that my chosen words impart the message that's least coercive but still persuasive, in order to encourage change where change is required - to allow change to happen - but not to *make* change. There's a world of difference if you sit with it quietly enough.

For a start, let's take the heat out of the commonly-used term 'heel-strike versus mid-foot', and going forward, talk instead about the location of the 'first contact', or 'first ground contact', as a reframed, non-contentious line of investigation. We're going to give 'first contact' a safe home. And by changing the word, we might improve the timing of everything, and *that's* giving me tingles ...

Then, dog-ear this page, read it prior to each session and relabel as many of your personal 'athleticism's' as you possibly can. Here are a few to start you off:

FOR 'TRY', USE **LET**.
⬇
SEEK OUT LINES OF TENSION, **DISCOVER** WAYS YOUR BODY ENJOYS **RELEASING** THEM AND THEN - WITH THAT INCREASED FREEDOM - **EXPLORE** HOW TO USE THAT NEW SPACE.
⬇
REPLACE 'PLACEMENT [OF ANY BODY PART]' WITH **SENSING STUFF**.
⬇
RATHER THAN 'DO', **EXPLORE**.
⬇
BE KIND. IF YOU CAN'T BE KIND TO YOUR OWN BODY, THEN WHO WILL BE?
⬇
FOR PUSH, **E-A-S-E INTO**.
⬇
AVOID 'STRAIN': IT'S A RED FLAG - **BACK OFF!** IT DOESN'T MEAN 'DON'T EXPLORE', IT'S YOUR BODY SIMPLY SAYING MOVE MORE SLOWLY AND/OR DON'T MOVE AS FAR IN THAT DIRECTION FOR NOW.
⬇
TO 'ACTION', ADD **THOUGHT**. IF YOU'RE NOT THINKING ABOUT WHAT YOU'RE DOING HOW IS YOUR BRAIN GOING TO BE FULLY ENGAGED WITH WHAT'S GOING ON? HOW WILL YOU EVER EXPERIENCE THE AWESOMENESS OF MAKING ... "MORE USE OF THE FEEDBACK PROVIDED BY [YOUR] SENSES" ...?
⬇
DELETE 'NO PAIN, NO GAIN'. THERE IS NO SUBSTITUTE. IT WAS JUST NONSENSE RIGHT FROM THE START.

▲ ▲ ▲

INJURY, PACING AND SPEED

If you're injured, get better before you start! This book doesn't attempt to be - nor wants to be - the solution to your pain. Nobody can 'fix' anybody. If your body isn't 'self-fixing' within a reasonable healing time, seek help - not to 'get fixed' but to find out what's impeding your innate self-healing. Finding a practitioner who applies the Flow Motion Model™ principles would be a great start...

Even uninjured, folk often progress quicker with a little help. Very soon we'll have an arsenal of PFM Coaches to help you along, trained to observe movement as postural behaviour; the result of the interaction of reflexes and their relative strength forming the background for voluntary motion and skill development. Watch this space...*

To help reinforce the wise choices you'll make for yourself in the absence of me being actually right next to you, check off the following reminders regularly:

 CHECK 1: Volume of repetitions is generally not the problem; volume of *unkind, thoughtless* repetitions is.

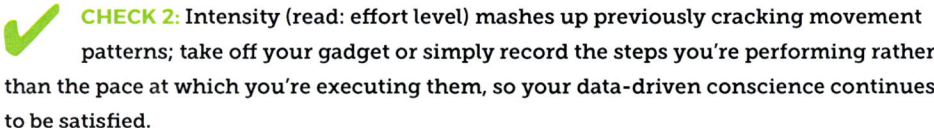 **CHECK 2:** Intensity (read: effort level) mashes up previously cracking movement patterns; take off your gadget or simply record the steps you're performing rather than the pace at which you're executing them, so your data-driven conscience continues to be satisfied.

CHECK 3: Soft tissue comes in a variety of colours according to the amount of blood circulating through it, so it's understandable that a premise exists stating that pinker soft tissue adopts training changes quicker than white soft tissue, through these blood flow differences. Personally, I have a sense that pumping muscle tissue *needs*

---

*Reflexive Health is part of the future of injury prevention, and PFM Coaches will be right at the forefront of the application of new understanding. The understanding of Reflexive Health has been growing since Sir Charles Scott Sherrington "almost singlehandedly crystallized the special field of neurophysiology" (- John F Fulton, Journal of Neurophysiology, 1952) with his 1906 published lectures titled "The Integrative Action of the Nervous System". I've got a strong feeling that it won't be long before objective analysis of reflex health becomes synonymous with movement investigation and re-education.

more blood flow and so has it, the white stuff has as much as it needs - which is less - and between the two there is perfect balance. After all, and putting injury aside for a moment, a stronger muscle with a weaker tendon isn't a stronger muscle you can use without risk of breaking it, so what would be the point of it? Regardless of the background physiology, if we bypass suggested figures of eight days for the tissue response of pinker stuff to bed in, but pay attention when the experts mention eight weeks for the whiter stuff to catch up, that paradigm sits happily in my grey stuff and in practice seems to work well. In essence, some *time* - and probably more time than you might have initially thought - is required for soft tissue to become accustomed to new work-loads.

> "SPEED WILL FOLLOW WHEN THE MECHANISM OF THE MOVEMENTS IS MORE ASSURED"
> **RAFAEL SABATINI, ITALIAN-ENGLISH WRITER ▲**

On the subject of speed.

I know, I know. I hear you. "But you said: more speed for no more effort." Yes, I did. But for most (not all) this is a result of a process rather than the result of a simple thought changing an inefficient action (I'm not going to give that one away yet. All in good time. You have work to do first). There's magic in efficiency of movement, but there are no miracles.

If you've been injured and in pain, the journey towards better running efficiency must include a *process of healing*. Too often, I've received emails from runners saying, "I did OK [at the 5km/10km/half marathon/full marathon/ultra] but I was much slower than normal". For 'OK', *across the board*, this meant they were not experiencing the previous pain that had brought them to me the week or the month before; we're talking pain bad enough to jeopardise their ability to have even started the event. As if to reinforce my deep sigh (as Chris Sritharan says "We're all (nice) idiots"), I'm looking at one such email right now. You might be using your body in a kinder way, but if areas are damaged, they still need time to heal.

There are no negatives; it's all a win-win. Being kind with the rate and intensity of change allows your body both healing time *and* a chance to 'get' the new movement pattern. This gives the green light to the process of neuroplasticity, where the motor neurons firing together, start to wire together. They then work more efficiently to generate the optimum timing of joint rotations to lead the dance of the soft tissue response. Time. The greatest embedder of strength and depth in new movement patterns.

> "EVERY DAY IS A GOOD DAY WHEN YOU RUN"
> **KEVIN NELSON, AUTHOR**

The last thing I want is for you to read this and stay squashed up on your sofa, but I can't *literally* be with you. So as you explore your running form, take it easy ... please ... and, have fun as you run! Perpetual Forward Motion (PFM) is here to create a shift in running perceptions, and together we can rid the streets of one of my pet hates - glum runners looking as if they're hating every minute, putting off other potential new runners in the process. Let's fill the roads and trails with cheerful faces and graceful movers!

My passion is to show as many as I can reach that if you want to run - for joy, for pleasure, for health, to be inspired, to be inspirational, to self-challenge - you *can*; safely and enjoyably by harnessing that which you already have: your body and your senses. You'll discover you can use your body via your senses to create change in your brain; you'll then be able to use those changes in your brain to fire co-ordinated motor programmes that gift movements which both feel and look elegant and effortless, are faster for no more effort, and are sustainable for as long as you need them to be. Be inspired by your changing body and embrace its ability to tell you what it needs to; 'listen' with the intent to act upon what you 'hear'; don't ignore what you don't want to see, hear or feel. And at every level of the pyramid, you're looking for:

> "PROGRESS, NOT PERFECTION"
> **DENZEL WASHINGTON, THE EQUALISER**

... who even knows what 'perfect' is?

CHECK NOTICEBOARD

Helen,

It is many years since I ran any sort of distance & having taken up running again in the spring, I found it all hard work. I had become the middle-aged jogger that in my youth I swore I would never be. Following your course I felt empowered with knowledge & confident that I could once again run. So with no real plan or training schedule I entered the Lisbon Marathon.

On Sunday 9 December I completed this marathon in 3.55.14. I can honestly say I utilised everything I learned on the efficient running course during this run. From the start I practised relaxing my feet, standing tall, correct breathing position, working my polo & all the other techniques taught until I thought I was running with maximum efficiency. And when I discovered I was slowing down or aching somewhere, I just revisited my technique, listened to Helen in my ear & everything went back to the way it should be. At halfway I was feeling so good I had secret visions of reeling in the 3.30 pacer & I believed 3.45 was a given. However I was to discover lessons learned were especially important in the last 8k when I suffered from seriously tight hamstrings and glutes & was forced to slow down considerably. Perhaps next time....

I am still a plodder but this plodder continues on his learning curve even more confident in the knowledge imparted on the course.

Regards
Ted

THE MIDDLE

10: CRUISE INTERVALS

DETAIL 9: HILLS 3

DETAIL 8: HILLS 2

DETAIL 7: HILLS 1

DETAIL 6: CADENCE & PACING

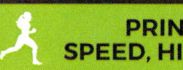 PRINCIPLE 5: SPEED, HIPS & HALLUX

 PRINCIPLE 4: ROTATIONS AND BREATHING

 PRINCIPLE 3: HILLS WITH GLUTES

 PRINCIPLE 2: WEIGHT SHIFTS

↑↑↑ PRINCIPLE 1: UPRIGHT ↑↑↑

THE PYRAMID CLIMB
TO EFFICIENT & JOYOUS RUNNING

ALTITUDE: TEN LEVELS
SUMMIT IN: HOWEVER LONG YOUR BODY NEEDS
AVERAGE GRADIENT: WHATEVER YOUR BODY ENJOYS

PART ONE
CREATING STRONG FOUNDATIONS THROUGH STABLE PRINCIPLES

Are you familiar with the often-quoted phrase of Benjamin Franklin, the Founding Father of the United States: *"By failing to prepare, you are preparing to fail"*? Even if that's the first time you've come across it, you're probably aware that regardless of the context the further you have to go, the longer the preparation really *ought* to take. In the main, I think we tend to develop this wisdom by ignoring it first and learning from the uncomfortable consequences of being unready. As American author Nicole Krauss succinctly puts it:

"WHEN YOUR PANTS ARE DOWN AROUND YOUR ANKLES, THAT'S WHEN EVERYONE ARRIVES".

So, whilst I risk being accused of repeating myself, I don't want any of you toppling over with your knickers at half mast; **the climb up the pyramid isn't a race to the top.** Some of you are so competitive that you will regardless (I get it, that's your *modus operandi*; so if you know that's you, *please remember* the TTF chart!), some will want to but will exercise caution having been bitten by that speed monster once too often, and some of you will happily mosey around and get there in your own good time because that's the way *you* roll. There's no right or wrong way to get to the top, but there *is* an efficient way; the one where progress is continual, or with minimal backward steps. Moving up the ten levels is a process that has a pace forged into it by previous footprints. Clear checkpoint markers define what's needed for the section ahead, so use your eyes and your senses and if in doubt, use the wise words of the recording artist, Auliq Ice, to guide you:

"IF YOU'RE NOT FAR ENOUGH ALONG TO BE ABLE TO DECIDE, YOU'RE NOT READY."

By pouring intent into every chapter and taking you step-by-step through each level, I'll make sense of it all - the whys, the hows, the what nows - and hopefully avoid any danger of bumping into you running with my book in your hand; whilst it would seem like great marketing, it would be as bad for symmetrical use of your body as the ubiquitous single hand-held running bottles …

LEVEL ONE
GETTING YOUR HEAD ON RIGHT

LEVEL ONE CONTENTS

Where you stand 70
Why does vertical matter? 72
Checkpoint One 77
Touchdown and the Achilles tendon 80
Stretching 86
Getting your head on right 92
Helpful hills 98
Feet 105
Questions 107
Checkpoint One Noticeboards:
    Checkpoint One Summary 109
    Leaving Level One 110

PRINCIPLE 1:
INTRODUCTION TO EFFICIENT RUNNING AND GENERATING AWARENESS IN THE SAGITTAL PLANE

So, you know how runners are always talking about calf issues, shin splints, knee niggles and back pain? I hear it so often, it seems the natural place to start helping. Here, at the base of the pyramid, we see the first signs of what to expect over the next section of the trail:

 This segment is where you'll notice where upright actually is, and appreciate the importance of being there ...

As any runner who's worked with me knows, stickmen hold the key to success, so Dom designed me some fancy ones. Which one are you? Do you know? Or do you just *think* you know? Or maybe you know which one you'd *rather* be? Does it even matter? Remember the stats about your head: that it's about an eighth of your bodyweight and if it's sitting forward of the base of the spine a tonne of muscles are going to be working hard to stop you face-planting? That's the 'lady' on the far left (who could just as easily be a chap!). You'll see 'her' everywhere. Some of you are there because that's where you thought you were *supposed* to be. We're going to explore what your body says about that shortly, but just for now we're simply painting pictures to make concepts easy to relate to.

"How many degrees of 'forward' counts as non-upright?" is a *really* good question I get asked a lot. I see many degrees of 'forwardness', from 'just off vertical' to hinged more than 45° at the hip - for all the world looking as if they're ramming their way through their run.

Regardless of the degree of modification, if the runner feels the benefit when they find *actual* upright, then it can be considered an improvement that matters to your body's joint mechanics. When Russ made the tiniest of adjustments, his calf pain disappeared. When a 22.5 stone Kevin was shown video footage of his somehow gravity-defying-near-50° lean he instantly grasped why it was such a struggle to breathe, never mind make forward progress without everything hurting. 15 months later, 6.5 stone lighter and upright, he became an Ironman (remember, that's a marathon *after* swimming and cycling for most of the day!).

NOTHING GOOD IS GOING TO HAPPEN UNTIL YOU'VE FOUND PROPER UPRIGHT.

Many running injuries lie in the sagittal plane of motion - examples are sole of foot pain, top of foot pain, metatarsal stress fractures, shin splints, Achilles tendonitis, calf issues, runner's knee (patello-femoral pain syndrome, or PFPS), hamstring strains - in fact, all the repetitive injuries listed on page 23. Lower back, neck and shoulder pain and headaches can also come under the 'sagittal plane' header, given the precious commodity all the connected muscles are hanging onto. You might already be musing that this could be what you feel in yourself - and see in others around you ... runners galore, trying their best whilst stuck in poor 'sagittal alignment'.

Anatomy Dog-Leg: For our purposes, just think of movement in the **sagittal plane** as **movement visible from the side of the body**. For instance, ankle/knee/hip bending and straightening (flexing and extending, respectively); rocking your body backwards and forwards

---

There's another fella running towards the pyramid ... maybe this is you? Fondly known as 'roadrunner' (meep, meep!) and beyond upright, this runner's ribcage stays behind his pelvis pretty much the entire gait cycle, but it's not as easy to spot as a forward lean. It often gets confused with 'good posture' so the root cause of the chronic pain pattern can get missed. Military folk (no matter how long ago they left the services) often find themselves here through a mixture of mechanical parade drills and the choice words hurled at them from the Flight or Staff Sergeant, embedded deeply into their psyche. Even now - over 30 years later - if I hear the "tenn-hut!!" bark on the television, my shoulders want to reflex to 'pinned back and pulled together'!

All the injuries previously listed in the sagittal plane still apply to this postural alignment, with lower back pain and plantar-fasciitis being particularly common. Michael shared his story of surfing passion as a youngster when he realised his 'backward lean' was probably connected with the many hours he'd enjoyed paddling to catch the next wave, endlessly lifting his torso off his surfboard. Masja, a keen skier, gym-owner and repetitively injured runner, could trace the onset of her lower back pain to her teenage years and gave a wonderfully intuitive description when she said it was "like there's something really heavy on it and I want someone to take it off". That 'heavy something' was her ribcage leaning backwards and once she understood the problem, she did indeed take it off! She instinctively connected her posture with the phrases drilled into her as she grew up, words we can all relate to hearing from our well-meaning guardians, be they family or school tutors: "stand up straight", "shoulders back", "sit up straight, no slouching". Understanding 'why' you've adopted any alignment that isn't 'on axis', or effortlessly balanced, is a powerful piece of the jigsaw puzzle. After all, if you know why you got there, once you've unravelled, you can relax knowing you won't go back.

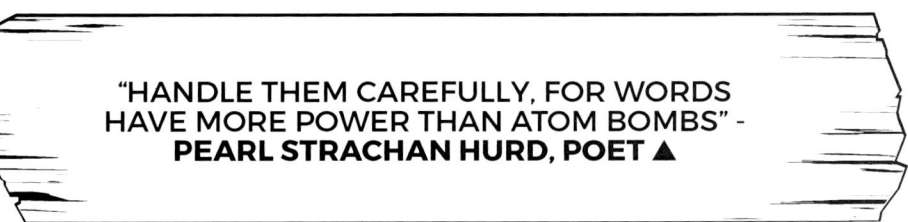

"HANDLE THEM CAREFULLY, FOR WORDS HAVE MORE POWER THAN ATOM BOMBS" - **PEARL STRACHAN HURD, POET** ▲

What about the dude running away from the bottom of the pyramid? As Dom's artistic skills clearly show, he's stacked his body *vertically*.

WHERE YOU STAND

Before we find out more, let's find out where you stand, literally! Taking your book with you, stand with your bum, mid-back and head touching a wall (close a door if you're struggling to find clear wall space. And - yes - I *did* have to mention that. Improbable as it sounds, I've heard "I couldn't find any uncluttered walls in the house - there's furniture everywhere" being used as a reason for 'not being able' to do this as a daily movement practice). Place your heels comfortably close to the wall without actually touching it - we all have backsides of differing sizes to accommodate, after all - avoiding a 'lean against the wall' by checking they're not too far away either.

You're now standing with your pelvis stacked over your feet, your ribcage stacked above your pelvis and your head stacked on top of everything. Does this alignment feel 'natural' to you? Don't worry if it doesn't; you're amongst the majority, which is why we start here. Remember the 'Intention Marker': the first level of the pyramid is about you first finding your body's vertical alignment, followed by discovering for yourself all the benefits it offers.

When using a tangible point of reference for vertical - such as a wall or a fence - many remark on the first occasion that it seems too far back! Certainly, 'on axis' is often further back than most folk think. To make sense of this, it's helpful to imagine the fluid in the inner ear as being 'sticky'; for many who habitually lean forward, the immediate sense when upright is that of falling backwards because the 'sticky' fluid moves more slowly than they have just done. In due course, if 'on axis' is adopted as the habitual alignment, the 'sticky' fluid will settle to give appropriate feedback.

Once a vertical surface has aligned your body for you, we can explore how resistant your habitual posture has become to that alignment. So relax in this space if you can, taking a few breaths to help you. Some bodies are positively mutinous initially, and that's fine too. It's all information we need to do the work necessary to reclaim 'comfortable when upright';

we're laying fabulous foundations for a *stable, monumental structure.* Stay there long enough for you to get a good sense of how it feels in your body. Explore your structure with heightening awareness. Are you looking straight ahead or upwards? Is your neck straining in order for your head to keep contact? Is the pressure in both feet the same? Is the pressure between the front and the back of each foot the same? Are you standing relaxed in your bones, or is muscular tension having to hold you in position? Is muscle tension screaming at you to release it? Does standing with 'head over ribcage, over pelvis, over feet' hurt? If it does, stand with your body markers as close to the wall as you can *without any pain* and just notice how big the gap is today. As you make progress, it will get smaller ...

> **"THINGS DO NOT CHANGE; WE CHANGE"** - **HENRY DAVID THOREAU, AMERICAN ESSAYIST** ▲

For many who can stand against the wall fairly comfortably to begin with, within a short time a body part - or two - feels bothered enough to want to peel off. If that's you, let the most aggravated part of you come off the wall. Was it your head? Heads are the bits of us most likely to resist being aligned in this modern 'civilised' world of sitting at desks and burying our heads in our mobile phones as we walk around. Was it your pelvis? If so, it probably prefers being ahead of your ribcage. Maybe it was your head *and* your pelvis, because you have a tendency to crane your neck forward whilst 'standing to attention'. Was it your ribcage? Some folk have a strongly-developed lower back curve and aligning the ribcage over the top increases the pressure there. There's no right or wrong, there is only what there is. Notice it. Were you surprised? Was this new information to you? Scribble down whatever you noticed. It could be your first 'marker' for change.

WHY DOES 'VERTICAL' MATTER?

Prior to that mini experiment, you probably thought you already stood vertically; isn't that what humans have evolved to do according to the specialists who've studied our predecessors? Aren't we all upright Homo sapiens, arguably evolved into bipedalism from knuckle-walking quadruped ancestors? Well, look around you. I get the feeling that there are off-axis, unstacked folk milling around in abundance, with the elegant, upright movers noticeable by their rarity, *especially* within the context of runners. Almost daily I observe that whatever walking alignment and movement patterns are being used by someone, running magnifies them.

Anatomy Dog-Leg: At PFM HQ we like to refer to the state of vertical as being 'biomechanically well-stacked': head over rib-cage over pelvis over feet, with reference to bone position. Getting clear on where the bones are helps us figure out more easily what the muscles and soft tissue might be getting up to. This is the prevalent paradigm of 'Structure determines Function'. It makes sense then that if we get the bones in 'better' places, we could be rewarded with 'better' muscle combinations firing up automatically. Some consider it the evolutionary destiny of predetermined and calculable biomechanics. I consider it important enough to be the primary subject of exploration at Level One.

This trail being all about You discovering what's best for You - rather than being told what to do - I invite you to decide for yourself. As **considerations**, let's look at a few factors that might spur you on to explore your current concept of 'vertical alignment'. I'll keep the anatomy and anatomical language to a minimum, as flowing through these ideas is as important as the flow I feel they create in your body; I wouldn't want you to miss any of it by sounding tedious.

In many branches of healthcare, practitioners learn that **vertical alignment is considered to be the position from where the circulatory, breathing and musculoskeletal systems are able to perform most efficiently.** If you look at any basic anatomy book, you can see the major vessels leading to the major organs resembling the main pipes of an upright irrigation system, with smaller branches travelling at a variety of vectors to the rest of the body. It's not difficult to imagine that kinks in the main pathways would disrupt delivery of blood, lymph, air and even nerve information along the sub-branches. We can test one aspect of this theory now: stand in alignment against your wall again, and take a lovely breath in to fill both lungs, and exhale. Then stand off the wall, adjusting your alignment to bring more pressure towards your toes - just enough to know you're 'unstacked' but not so much you're having to claw with your toes to stop yourself face-planting! Breathe in again to compare the quality and size of this inhale. You might need to do this several times, not because you weren't able to sense the difference, but because the difference was so significant you might not have trusted your own initial findings!

This is a seminal moment for umpteen of the runners I've worked with. Breathing is at the top of the Totem Pole of Life, and even with such a simple exploration, many connect that they've probably - unwittingly - been inhibiting the aerobic capacity they've been training so hard to improve. On the upside, just imagine what you might achieve now, with all that training and improved air flow! There's more on breathing at the oxygenating-altitude of Level 4, but it will be more productive if you cover the landscape of the lower levels first.

Continuing the story of alignment, vertical seems to optimise the **load distribution** through the body, all the way from the feet to the head. Don't forget, you haven't just got your bodyweight to consider; gravity and the forces of three-dimensional movement also have to be managed without you toppling. As Phillip Beach describes beautifully in his engrossing book 'Muscles and Meridians':

"It is no accident that worldwide, simple baskets with a forehead strap have been employed to carry ... Nepalese porters regularly carry their body weight in produce using this simple harnessing technique ... If 20kg is placed on the shoulders and back [the Western backpack] the body will attempt to move 20kg forward, thus placing a shear strain on the junction between the neck and thorax [ribcage] ...

"Load carrying on the head is another way of carrying loads very efficiently when the terrain will allow it. Up to 40% of one's body weight can be placed on the head basket with almost no metabolic cost to the carrier. This remarkable efficiency is probably due to a smoother gait pattern that the added weight seems to encourage."

Notice the effect your backpack has on your mobile mass management next time you put it on. Did the pressure through your feet change? Did your bone positions shift? If they did, the work of the muscles modified too. Did your movements become more awkward or 'lumpier'? It's not about dumping your backpack, but rather recalibrating your thought processes around how you transport yourself ... and maybe your gear too.

Vertical alignment shows every sign of offering the most effective position from which to gain access to the biggest muscles of forward propulsion - the **gluteus** muscle group. Those wonderful buttocks strapped behind you seem *designed* for the job of forward propulsion at running speeds.

Given more time to test and interrogate your systems, you might find that vertical alignment is **more comfortable, more efficient and more sustainable**, and if you do, it makes sense that it'll be in part *because* it accesses the biggest muscles AND tendons.

Being biomechanically well-stacked consistently gives the feeling of **less strain** on the quadricep muscles at the front of the thigh, **less strain** on the hamstrings at the back of the thigh, **less strain** on the lower leg muscles and **less strain** through the muscles of the feet - in comparison to a forward lean. Although that sentence sounded 'absolute', I believe every element is perceptible if you're attentive enough.

Vertical is alignment in the sagittal plane. It seems to provide the potential for easier joint rotations in the frontal (left to right) and transverse (rotational/twisting) planes. Try this - hang your head forward a bit and look from side to side; now stack your head as if it's the 'pointy bit' on the top of an umbrella (the brolly represents your ribcage over your pelvis) and repeat the action. Did you notice the difference in the range of motion? For some, the improvement in rotations when their 'head is on right' is dramatic, and frequently correlates to a known limitation in rotating to a particular direction. It wasn't that they couldn't rotate left (or right), but rather that they couldn't when their head wasn't sitting sweetly on its perch. When they can for the first time in a long time, it's a potent moment of empowering discovery.

In conversation, the phrase 'vertical alignment' is a mouthful and 'upright' tends to promote a 'soldier-stood-to-attention' reaction, especially in the initial stages of exploration. So I'll continue using 'vertical' as easy-speak short-hand for the rest of this 'considerations' list.

Muck about with being vertical and 'not'. By exploring the differences between 'on' and 'off' the vertical axis you'll both improve your internal awareness skills by 'noticing changes' and simultaneously discover 'changes that matter to you':

- You'll probably find that vertical gifts even pressure between the forefoot and the heels, and enables the toes to be 'free to play the piano' without the need to claw or grip to prevent you face-planting. Nice.

- It's where ankles tend to feel more relaxed; where the ankle joint is more 'open' compared with a forward lean.

- Vertical is where neck muscles can feel more relaxed because their job is now merely to move the head, rather than 'hang onto it'.

- Vertical is where shoulders can drop and muscles relax, now that they no longer have to assist the neck muscles that were hanging onto the head (how many times have you seen runners rub their aching shoulders? Maybe that was you, too?).

- With less strain through the quadriceps muscles at the front of the thigh, vertical is where knee joints seem better protected in their motions, situated as they are between the pelvis and feet, and therefore at the mercy of the relative actions of those bony structures.

Initial sensations of being 'biomechanically well-stacked' may have felt odd, but do you see how relaxed 'vertical' is sounding now?

- This one always grabs everyone's attention: vertical fires abdominals! We shouldn't need to hold our tummies in; our tummies get held in by the activation of our abdominal wall when upright. Every step could - and perhaps should - be a 'core activation'. Try it for yourself: stand away from the wall in your 'habitual' vertical. Without holding your tummy in, if you poke your abdominal wall you might find it feels quite soft (harsh, but often fair!). Now stand in vertical alignment (against the wall again is perfect) and notice the difference in the tension of the abdominal wall. If you feel your ribs are thrusting out under tension, add a thought of "let go of your lower ribs"; they'll drop a millimetre or two, and the hardness of the bony ribcage will continue seamlessly into the firmness of the support girdle that is a now-activated abdominal wall. Enjoy it being there - with you every propulsive step of the rest of your life - and stop wasting precious time with sit-ups and crunches. If you're the 'stick-man' on the far left of the pyramid, you're flexed enough as it is!

- (PS. You're welcome).

- Vertical is where many use an imaginary plumb-line to great effect: drop one from each cheekbone to your pubic bone and your alignment will likely travel back a bit. In my experience, this happens every time - maybe not to 'perfectly vertical' initially, if the sense of falling back is creating a battle within your central nervous system, but to probably 'more upright than you were'. Don't Forget: Progress not Perfection!

Vertical could be considered as the absolute domain of bipedal posture and answers the question of "Why?", with a resounding "Why Not?" If you try it, I'll bet you'll like it.

That's a LOT of 'Sagittal Plane Data' and we haven't even passed the first pyramid checkpoint; feel your way around it steadily, noticing elements bit by bit and in time you'll probably be able to tune into all its benefits. We learn by doing and exploring ... and by following this path, we discover 'stuff'. Patience ... and progress ... and Time ...

CHECKPOINT ONE
NOTICEBOARD

▲ ▲ ▲

TERRAIN: FENCE OR WALL AND A SLOPE
RUNNER STATUS: TTF 2
KIT LIST: LAYERS, COMFORTABLE FOOTWEAR

This being an outdoor activity, we start with the practicalities, the first of which has to be trail terrain: to replicate it, you need a wall or a fence to stand up against and a nearby slope to perform hill drills. Yes, hill drills on Level One; don't worry, they won't bite!

And as far as personal requirements are concerned, whilst I wouldn't suggest anyone attempt any kind of running with TTF 1, you could start with just the drills in this session and see if they help your pain or restriction issues, whilst simultaneously seeking appropriate help. TTF 2 is the absolute minimum to qualify to play with the whole of this section.

 **TTF 1:** you aren't able to walk without feeling restricted or in pain through tension in soft tissue (not just tight muscles, muscles so tight you feel restricted).

TTF 2: You can walk without tension restriction/pain, but notice its restriction as soon as you run; it's less noticeable first thing in the morning.

Layers. Remember the stiles? You're not going to be running continuously. Taking on the mantle of being your own Perpetual Forward Motion Efficient Running *Form Explorer* means a whole heap of stopping, starting, sensing, feeling, noticing, performing brilliant - but *on the spot* - drills and comparing their after-effects. You need to give yourself *time* to discover how to sense things happening in your body whilst it's moving. *Especially* at Level 1, you're unlikely to break sweat. 'Layers', please! There is nothing more impossible than feeling for alignment when your posture is reflexively flexing to maintain core temperature! And there is nothing less fun than shivering!

Many runners ask what they should wear on their feet when they start to explore their running movement. The question often comes embellished with a self-deprecating "I know it's a silly question", but actually, it's an important question as it shows an awareness of relevance to the task. My answer is always the same. "Wear nothing new and whatever is your most loved, most used and most comfortable." It'll be much easier for you to notice change within your body if you're not distracted with new sensations wrapped around your feet. There will of course be times when you can't follow the guidance, such as when the only trainers you have are brand-new, or if you've decided to combine this journey with a simultaneous foray into the world of minimal footwear. If the latter, please head straight for Appendix 2, page 366, for further assistance.

Right - you're dressed appropriately and as keen as mustard, so, let's get going for a ...

... walk.

Have you noticed how sometimes the first mile of running feels *awful* and then something seems to wake up inside you, and the 'deadness' just seems to disappear? Yup! The science boffins have long known that sitting or 'being still' depresses all bodily functions, so it would seem logical that to get your running kit on, get out the front door, and just start running would be harsh on your body. Some time is required to get your muscular and cellular systems activated. Apart from great movement patterns, *time* is the gift I'll keep reminding you to give yourself as you progress up the Pyramid.

There's quite a bit of 'easy read' information about being in one position for too long on bookshelves and on the internet (a link to one is in Appendix 3). Manufacturers have responded with all sorts of standing desk configurations - with the result that many are swapping one mode of stillness for another! The Industrial Revolution has already taught us that standing all day isn't a great idea. Let's move forward ... by moving!

'Science' can't seem to agree whether the time required to wake up sleepy systems is 7 or 15 minutes - so 'something in between' would seem reasonable, erring on the side of caution if you know the state of your muscular and/or cellular systems is 'on the sad side of sorry'.

So, walk briskly for let's say, 10 minutes. This mobilises joints in a weight-bearing gait pattern, and diverts the blood to the newly-active muscles. If we carried enough blood for all our needs at any given moment, we'd be a balloon. Instead, we cleverly carry just enough blood for all our systems to use as they need it. When we're busy being active, we're not repairing or growing or digesting, so the working muscles draw blood from the non-vital organs, the glands producing hormones and the intestines ... super efficient, eh? *So now you know, wait until that's happened before you start running.*

Following Level One, this walking warm-up will include postural sensing in preparation for great biomechanics when running. Skipping ahead, the walking gait provides the perfect cool-down too, with the strong venous return through the heel-to-toe roll, in addition to a gradual reduction in heart rate and sweating rate, creating a kind return to homeostasis.

TOUCHDOWN AND OUR ACHILLES TENDONS

10 minutes later, you've either arrived at your chosen location for your first self-exploratory lesson or you've walked around the block to return to where you started. We kick off with a few questions - and for some, these are BIG ones; we're talking about the running touchdown ...

WHERE ON YOUR FOOT IS YOUR FIRST CONTACT WITH THE GROUND?
> ON THE HEEL?
> SOMEWHERE IN FRONT OF THE HEEL?
> DOES THE HEEL TOUCH THE GROUND AT ANY POINT?
> ARE YOU 'NOT SURE?'
> IF THE LATTER, HAVE YOU EVER BEEN AN INJURED RUNNER?

View them simply as a consideration of this: if you don't know what you're doing with your body as you move (you might have just admitted to not even knowing which part of the foot you land on - again and again and again and again), then self-preservation via *sensing* is currently not your strong point. As 'luck' would have it, it's an innate skill you can unearth and hone.

Anatomy Dog-Leg: To be accurate, replace the word 'luck' here with: wisdom woven into our brainstem, relaying information between the peripheral nerves and spinal cord to the upper parts of the brain. Cool, huh?

Discovery through the feel of doing something (kinaesthetic learning) is one of four learning styles. We have a preference to learn by either doing it, seeing it, listening to information about it or writing and reading about it. Apparently, less than 15% of the population have a strong lean towards 'sensing whilst doing' or kinaesthetic learning.

Did you see that?

Potentially, as few as 15% of folk lean into themselves and elect to find about *how* they move by noticing stuff! BOOM!! That - right there. Let's rewrite that gargantuan statistic. 85% of us might be moving around without any kind of conscious sense of what our bodies are doing at any given moment. Is it *really* any wonder there are so many injured runners?

Anatomy Dog-Leg: These definitions might prove useful:
Proprioception: the body's awareness of itself when in motion.
Somatics: awareness of one's own bodily sensations & movement from within, ie in the first person.
Kinaesthetic Learning: this occurs as we engage in a physical activity; we learn by doing it, exploring it, discovering it. Kinaesthesia - the ability to feel movements of the limbs and body; it is the sense that detects bodily position, weight, or movement of the muscles, tendons, and joints. The sensation of moving in space. You are going to discover Efficient Running by helping yourself sense and feel it, kinaesthetically/proprioceptively and somatically!

So with those truly eye-opening figures in mind, connections between enquiring minds and moving bodies need to be made. There'll be an audio journey to partner the map-book you're already reading, so how about rallying the visual element (the optic nerve *being* part of the brain, rather than something that leads to the brain) and observing how others move? Start noticing movement patterns in your fellow runners - once you've started, it's hard to stop. It can become a new, endlessly fascinating game. So many times, runners have returned for their next session with me, enthusiastically recounting the 'travesties' they've witnessed during their practice sessions. They become alive to observation, which then helps them recognise what they themselves might have become somatically insensitive to. You don't need to get picky; it's not about being critical or judgmental; simply observe, starting with the single most obvious element of each person's running style. Keep it simple. Things like a really obvious forward lean; pokey elbows (I call them 'unfriendly'); s-m-o-o-t-h (not everything you see will be a negative - some might be instinctively efficient runners, or have already experienced the PFM magic!!) or lumpy.

If you find you struggle to see things, ask yourself questions; for example, do they look smooth? Can you see any movement of the pelvis or shoulders, or both? Does it look effortless or effort-full? Where does their lead leg seem to land - in front of their body, or under their body? Which bit of their body moves the most? (the often surprising answer to this is not the legs, but the arms!). Do they looked relaxed, no matter the speed?

Back to you. As Ben so beautifully phrased it, let's go and

"EXPERIENCE NEW MOVEMENT PATTERNS AND RUNNING SENSATIONS AND BOLT KNOWLEDGE TO THAT EXPERIENCE".

Jump up and down on the spot. Just enough to get your feet off the ground. Where do you land? Where's your 'first contact'? In my experience, it's always on the 'sweet spot', somewhere *between* the heel bone and the toes. OK - now try to land on your heel bones. Tricky, eh? In just a few aborted attempts (instinct will most likely take over and stop you at the last moment!), you'll find your body firmly informing you of its position on this endlessly and hotly-debated subject.

Even With Your Shoes On.

(P-leease - totally intentional).

Whilst it's even *likely* that someone, somewhere within our 7 billion population, will lie outside the bell-curve of 'average' and happily have their heel bones as first contact with the ground when jumping, even with no shoes on, I've coached hundreds of runners one2one (I might even have reached into 4 figures if you count those who've followed the *Barefoot Audio* downloads) and my experience remains a statistically significant one: 100% react in a 'no thanks, not on my heels, about there, just forward of the heel; that 'sweet spot' feels safe, I'm relaxed again, thanks' kind-of-a-way.

> "INTUITION IS ALWAYS RIGHT IN AT LEAST TWO IMPORTANT WAYS: IT IS ALWAYS IN RESPONSE TO SOMETHING; IT ALWAYS HAS YOUR BEST INTEREST AT HEART"
> **GAVIN DE BECKER, AUTHOR** ▲

And if we then put this discussion *into the context of capturing all the ingenious ways the human body can move in gait more efficiently,* I feel the 'first contact' debate simply fizzles out. Let's hear it for our two wonderful Achilles tendons. Are you aware that they're the largest tendons in the human body? Did you know they transfer the most stored potential energy into the kinetic *and free energy* of the stretch recoil? Think 'catapults'. We're talking up to 90% versus about 50% for all other tendons. Must be useful for something then ...

You can choose to be more efficient or less efficient; you can choose to have 'first contact' on the heel bone or not; but to argue the rights and wrongs is a waste of energy, inherently inefficient in and of itself, and in practice, a damp squib. If you're looking for efficiencies of movement, you're looking for catapults.

Anatomy Dog-Leg: Humans are the only bipedal mammal with Achilles tendons; with strong enough feet, a human can walk but CANNOT run with a ruptured achilles. We're considered to be the best endurance athletes on the planet, able to out-run all other mammals due to the many mechanisms associated with being upright, and whilst I can't personally prove any connection and the anthropologists can only theorise, I have a hunch that two Achilles tendons are useful equipment to fulfill that status.

There is minimal 'lengthening under load' of the Achilles tendon when first contact is on the heel bone; the Achilles lengthens and becomes taut via the preparatory lifting toes and flexing ankle, but the foot is unloaded and swinging through the air at the time. If you reap what you sow, proportionately less free energy becomes available through elastic recoil; just *one* line of reasoning for suggesting that first contact on the heel bone is probably not as efficient as a 'sweet spot' touchdown - somewhere forward of the heel - when in running mode ...

I'm skipping a bit here, but if I recall every "Lesson One" I've ever coached where the runner began with first contact on the heel bone, that touchdown position had simply 'gone' by half-way through the session. They hadn't made it go away, and neither had I. It just went away of its own accord whilst the runner was exploring better, more comfortable body spaces to use. I'll always mention it at the end of the session, asking "when was the last time you landed on your heels when running?" because watching faces change as they realise what's happened never fails to thrill me. Their body had already answered the question. Bodies are always answering the questions. You'll see. Which - of course - is the point. You will come to your own conclusions, driven by what you perceive to be more enjoyable and less effortful; you'll smoke out your preconceptions and replace them with your empirical successes.

You'll test for yourself the 'three' human gait patterns:

1. walking: probably heel-to-toe (few debate this one), with first contact on the heel bone being perfectly comfortable when you still have one foot on the ground. Unless you're Forest Gump, we all spend more time walking than running, so having a big, dense bone to take our body weight and the force of a walking ground impact makes evolutionary sense.

2. running: probably first contact on the 'sweet spot' somewhere in front of the heel, with the force of impact dissipating through the movement of the many foot joints, which in turn loads the tissues; the heel descends to 'kiss' a nano-moment later, followed by a roll through to the front of the foot. It sounds more long-winded, but it all happens in milliseconds and you gain access to more catapults. If first contact from being totally airborne was on the big, dense heel bone, the impact forces would probably be uncomfortable without cushioned shoes, but its size still serves a positive evolutionary running purpose, when you consider that the extending-under-load enormous Achilles tendon requires something substantial to attach to in order to return the forces involved.

3. sprinting: probably forefoot contact only; the heel descends but forward speed is such that there isn't time for the heel bone to actually make it to the ground. Interestingly, few debate this one either - ever seen a runner with first contact on their heel bones during the 100m sprint event?

Before we leave this gentle probe into the different movement behaviours observed at various 'gears', one final consideration: have you come across any defining parameters for first contact on the heel bone in the running context? I'm widely 'running-read', and I haven't. Is it *anywhere* on the (huge) heel bone? With *any* force? If you're wearing shoes, can you pin-point which bit of the heel you touch down on first? Maybe it's a bit of your shoe that isn't even under your actual heel bone, which could more accurately be labelled a 'crash-pad-of-shoe-first-contact'? Do the research studies give us 'the answer'? I don't think they do. I don't think anyone knows *exactly* where first contact is meant to be. And when opinions abound with the strength of conviction, but without meaningful delineation, it's confusing, isn't it?

This isn't about being vague and standing on the fence; this is about being cool about what *your body tells you*, and being OK with wherever your foot decides first contact feels 'safe and responsive'. Wouldn't it feel more amicable if we had many different ways to explore and talk about movement behaviours? I'm on a mission to help nurture exactly that, and I hope you'll join me ...

STRETCHING

So you've walked, you've had a bit of internal discourse whilst jumping up and down, now let's get moving forward again.

Ah-ha! Did you think I'd forgotten something? Would you like to stretch first? Have you noticed it helping your running? It's true that many runners swear by their stretch routine, but it's also true that there are plenty of you for whom stretching not only doesn't help, but appears to make things worse. I don't know about you, but I fit into the latter category. And does it matter? To stretch, or not to stretch? Well, instinctively I feel the first thing to decide is what we might be stretching *for*.

Perhaps it's for mobility? We all want to be fully mobile, don't we? If all our bones move in all the directions they have the ability to, giving us the capacity to move in all the ways we were designed to access, I get the sense it would feel like a body 'at ease' with itself. It's tempting to add superlatives like 'great' when discussing how optimum mobility might feel, but I think that would only accurately fit if it was in comparison with sub-optimal mobility. After all, when everything 'works', it's easy *not* to notice, isn't it? And perhaps for many of us (that 85% figure springs to mind as being relevant here), our powers of sensing seem to light up only once we're plagued with problems; I've listened to pain being described using near-poetic language in terms of volume of adjectives, whereas a 'no pain' status tends to come across more succinctly.

If a joint can move well, the soft tissue crossing it will be stimulated according to the design of the meeting bone surfaces, nourishing the area and helping to create pliability where it should exist. Let's hear it for the tissue elasticity that rocks up with joint mobility!

Maybe the purpose of stretching is for flexibility? If tissue elasticity offers 'flexibility' then being flexible would certainly seem to matter, but to what degree? With the body's innate ability to create balance *whilst in motion*, an overly-mobile joint in one area can have the effect of locking down movement in a joint elsewhere. You could say it's a genius way of staying 'safe' and staying upright with more than 200 joints in play at any given moment.

Scott, a personal trainer and martial artist with chronic neck issues and self-confessed "awful flexibility", was gutted to hear his party piece at yoga - the one thing he was able to manage with some flair - was down to an off-axis alignment and worse, significantly contributing to his ongoing pains. His stance - influenced by Muay Thai and a background in bodybuilding - had sent his ribcage behind his pelvis, lengthening the hip flexors. Needless to say, the thrusting pelvis had done more than keep the hip flexors long; the structural coupling of the pelvis and the skull had pulled his head forward to match, compressing the neck bones, held - as they were - in a position of extension. For many, the inflexible areas stay inflexible *because* of the mighty fine party tricks they carry around with them.

Sticking to the brief of making your running journey productive and enjoyable, let's avoid the Pandora's box that is the musculoskeletal system in its entirety. All that's necessary here - even if it's considered to be over-simplification - is to question what might have been happening without question (if you see what I mean). Here are a few thoughts worthy of attention when Efficient and Joyous Running are the goals:

- Stretching areas that seem tight compared to others, without understanding *why* the tightness is present, may well interfere with your central nervous system's current adaptation, causing it to work hard to adapt some more.

- Stretching areas as part of a mechanical 'routine' could also prove detrimental in terms of challenging an existing harmonious structure if those areas were already 'long enough'.

- Stretching areas that feel tight can become a self-fulfilling prophecy *if they are tight because they are continually being held 'long'*; you pull and groan in appreciation but the good feeling doesn't last and before you know it you're pulling again; like an itch you want to scratch but you just can't find it. Just to be clear, you could be lengthening that which is already 'too long'.

On the upside, noticing movement restrictions is information; stretches that feel different from one side of the body to the other are calling you to the imbalance. If your right hip flexor feels tighter than your left, the answer to the issue comes in the form of a question: 'why?' If your left calf resists you pulling it more than your right, your solution lies in finding out 'why?' If you're always needing to - or feeling the need to - stretch the same area, you guessed it ... 'why?'

Maybe that's why stretching works for some (the tissue really wasn't long enough due to a joint restriction, and the movement you used freed up space in the joint capsule?) and not for others (the tissue was already too long)? I don't know, I'm just musing.

My remit is not to get tedious about anatomy or declare absolutes; I want to help you seek answers from within your own systems, and you don't have to look far or get overly complicated, so hang in there with me if this is new to you. We'll just dip toes into this complex, fascinating subject.

Soft tissue (which includes muscles, tendons which attach muscles to bones, and all the other white, connective stuff you see if you chop up raw meat) crosses joints. Sometimes it crosses one joint, sometimes multiple joints. Some joints, like the hip and the shoulder move in three dimensions; for instance, your leg flexes and extends when it moves forward and backward (that's movement in the sagittal plane; remember, side-view action?); it can move outwards which is known as abduction, and in towards the middle, called adduction (all frontal plane movements which we'll cover in more detail in the next section); your leg can also rotate inwards and outwards (internal and external rotation respectively, in the transverse plane of movement). Some joints, like the knee, move in two dimensions, whilst your ankle only moves in one dimension. The soft tissue shortens or lengthens, in however many planes the bones are moving, on either side of the joint.

OK. Press pause.

Socks are a kerfuffle aren't they? But there's a lovely story of avoided hip replacement surgery that redeems them. A wonderful Finnish family had developed technology to create Feelmax toe socks that were both seamless, and used the latest fibres to enhance the wicking of moisture away from the skin. Each member of the family had a role to play in the business and of course wanted to wear them, but 'Dad' couldn't get them on because of his arthritic hips and his 3 year old grandson struggled with the co-ordination of tiny toes into tiny pockets. Together - with daily kerfuffles - they succeeded; toddler dexterity became impressive and Grandad created so much pain-free movement, both at the hip joint and within each foot, that the need for surgery was simply forgotten.

Back to your leg. When it moves forward (hip flexion) does it *just* move forward? Do you *want it to* just move forward? When you're putting your socks on, do you bend your knee and hip in a dead straight line, or is it actually quite handy for your hip joint to move outwards (abduct) to create a little more space for the kerfuffle? Flexed, abducted with a touch of outward rotation (external rotation) is even more helpful, isn't it? Especially for us 'unbendy' runners!

When you reach to the top shelf, do you line yourself up perfectly and reach your arm straight forward? No, of course you don't. A robot might need to, but we don't. We can reach forward, up, move closer or further away from the midline and turn our palm up or down according to what we require, in order to grasp the object of our desire.

The concept I'm attempting to illustrate here is that if there are three dimensions of movement available at a joint, they aren't 'either this or that or the other' ... they should be 'this *and* that *and* the other'.

Nearly there.

Having established that soft tissue crosses the joint (or maybe two) and that the joint might have one, two or three planes of movement, we should now consider where the soft tissue begins and ends. Given it has to be on two different bones (see - I told you it was simple), the next consideration must be *how many planes of motion is EACH bone moving in, and therefore torquing the attached soft tissue in?*

Maybe muscles that work hard with forces travelling along three different planes *sometimes at both ends,* don't particularly enjoy being pulled in a straight line, from end to end? Again, I don't know, but I'm just thinking about how I'd feel if I was a muscle being pulled from one end to the other. When I stretch lazily in the morning I seem to do it in halves; my arms reach up and straighten, my back straightens and my legs curl; then, if I stretch my legs out my body flexes and my arms curl. I'm not saying this means anything, but when you start thinking about these things it can become quite intriguing. It gets all the more curious when you look at joint mechanics in the greatest detail and discover that at no point in the gait cycle does any muscle seem to get lengthened at both ends simultaneously.

And then there's the timing debate; perhaps you've already questioned what a 10, or 20 or even 30 second stretch is designed to achieve? My 'get up after being still' stretches are like luxurious yawns, lasting a couple of seconds, maybe three at most. And they're always delicious; you know what I mean? When I watch my dogs stretch, they seem to behave similarly; front legs out, bottom in the air, hold for the time it takes to feel 'grrrr, that's good', followed by back legs out, chest up for a few moments, and finishing off with a good whole body shimmy. Ever noticed that?

I'm not suggesting for a moment that stretching is bad and we must leave any imbalances where they are. That would be silly. There are big 'pre-exercise' plans awaiting you further along the trail, but for now - at the beginning of your movement investigation - you could simply swear allegiance to your internal friend 'Sensory Feedback'; continue with any pre-existing 'warm-up' routine you feel better for doing and give yourself permission to drop anything you feel instinctively hasn't served you. *Adding* the pre-run walk of course!

> **"YOU KNOW THE TRUTH BY THE WAY IT FEELS"**
> **INDIA ARIE, 'THE TRUTH' ▲**

I find it all thoroughly engrossing and thought-provoking. If we just keep asking better questions, there's a good chance we'll get better answers. I love how the late, great, theoretical physicist Richard P. Feynman put it in his wonderful book *The Meaning Of It All* (lectures from 1963):

"... IF WE WERE NOT ABLE OR DID NOT DESIRE TO LOOK IN ANY NEW DIRECTION, IF WE DID NOT HAVE A DOUBT OR RECOGNISE IGNORANCE, WE WOULD NOT GET ANY NEW IDEAS. THERE WOULD BE NOTHING WORTH CHECKING, BECAUSE WE WOULD KNOW WHAT IS TRUE. SO WHAT WE CALL SCIENTIFIC KNOWLEDGE TODAY IS A BODY OF STATEMENTS OF VARYING DEGREES OF UNCERTAINTY. SOME OF THEM ARE MOST UNSURE; SOME OF THEM ARE NEARLY SURE; BUT NONE IS ABSOLUTELY CERTAIN. SCIENTISTS ARE USED TO THIS. WE KNOW THAT IT IS CONSISTENT TO BE ABLE TO LIVE AND NOT KNOW. SOME PEOPLE SAY, "HOW CAN YOU LIVE WITHOUT KNOWING?" I DO NOT KNOW WHAT THEY MEAN. I ALWAYS LIVE WITHOUT KNOWING. THAT IS EASY. HOW YOU GET TO KNOW IS WHAT I WANT TO KNOW."

GETTING YOUR HEAD ON RIGHT

Back to the subject of forward motion. Run up and down - say the length of a swimming pool and back - so you can focus on yourself and how your running feels to you (somatic kinaesthesia). Identify the most obvious _negative_ you notice; just one. This could be tension in the groin, above the knees, in the calves, in your toes, between the shoulder blades, in your shoulders or neck - invariably it's tension _somewhere_!

Now, let's stack our bodies _vertically_ by standing up against the wall or fence on your trail. You might be getting more used to it already. Is that body part you initially noted as wanting to be anywhere except on axis calmer now? Relax as much as you can as you stand against the wall.

With the sense of a more accurate representation of upright still fresh within your body, use an imaginary **'plumb-line from cheekbone to pubic bone'** as an internal cue to help you maintain your new stacking and run the same length of your venue as before, comparing sensations. To clarify, the goal isn't to 'hold' a position; you are running, so everything _should_ be moving.

By _thinking about_ a new alignment you're creating an opportunity for the bone positions to maintain their stacked relationship _whilst you're moving_. Is anything different? Has your 'most obvious negative' changed? Then return to your 'old' form without any attention to alignment and compare once again. Do you notice any other changes? Any positives shining through? Any negatives?

Avoid comparing yourself with others; only compare the 'before' you with the 'after' you. Many find themselves distrusting the feedback from their senses because it feels _so much better_ from a disproportionately small change of input.

This is common and nothing to worry about - repetition of the same results will breed confidence in your ability to trust your senses.

Now to our first drill, always with grateful thanks to Gary Ward's *Flow Motion Model™, **vimeo.com/244972301***

- Sagittal Cog Against the Wall ... or ...
- Knock-Kneed Amazonian meets Bow-Legged Hunchback:

Take 1 - Bit by Bit:
- Stand relaxed against the wall, with head, mid-back and bum against it; heels as close as is comfortable to the wall without touching it.
- Knees straight but not locked, nose roughly horizontal to the ground, ribs as relaxed as possible rather than thrusting skywards (this isn't Baywatch). Notice where any lines of tension exist. Do they need to be there? You're resting against a wall after all - so you can probably relax a little more ...
- Slowly arch your lower back by tipping the front of your pelvis down, towards your feet. Think about letting your pubic bone be heavy and letting whatever movement wants to happen elsewhere in your body, happen.
- Keeping your head in contact with the wall at all times, you might quickly notice your chin is being pulled down towards your chest, which in turn seems to be simultaneously lifting.
- Your bottom might feel as if it's being pushed into the wall - which it is through your lower back being more arched.

Does it all add up to feeling a bit 'Amazonian Warrior'?

- Reverse the movement of the pelvis so it tilts backwards towards the wall, creating a tucking of the tail-bone between your legs. Imagine your tail-bone is really heavy and let it pull your pubic bone up.
- Notice now that your chest wants to cave inwards, and if your head has remained in contact with the wall (which is the goal!) it will have fallen backwards so your chin is tilting upwards.

You're now slouching in 'Hunchback' mode.

Repeat a couple of times, then run 'out and back'. What's different? There are no right or wrong answers. There is only what you feel. Is what you feel better or worse? More or less comfortable? More or less fluid? Just notice.

- Repeat Amazonian meets Hunchback, this time adding a lovely breath into the belly, so the belly softens and swells as the pelvis tips forwards (heavy pubic bone, light tailbone), and an exhale as the pelvis tips backwards (heavy tailbone, light pubic bone).
- Notice that if you allow your abdominal muscles to lengthen with the in-breath, the lower back seems to more effortlessly contract to create its arch and the pelvis tilts forward more easily; by contrast, the range of motion of the pelvis will be less and/or the lower back won't feel as comfortable if the abdominal wall is held short and tight.

Please note: I'm not encouraging full belly breaths, or full range of motion of the pelvis, with every step. This is a drill! I'm simply showing you in a practical way the Principles of how your body moves and functions. You're exploring by moving towards your limits of motion, and by doing so, you're both nudging the boundaries of your motion range and discovering limitations you may not have known were there. It's a win-win-win thing.

Repeat a couple of times. Run out and back again. What's different? What your body enjoys will be what it's more likely to adopt or seek once again.

- Repeat Amazonian meets Hunchback, this time adding arm movement to the previously added breath:
- as the pelvis tips forward (heavy pubic bone), lower back arches, bum sticks into the wall, chest lifts with the filling breath and chin drops - add an external or outward rotation of your arms and feel the shoulder blades drive both towards the spine and down your back;

- as the pelvis tips backwards (heavy tailbone), lower back flattens, chest caves with the emptying breath and chin lifts - add an internal or inward rotation of your arms, allowing them to travel in front of your body, and feel the shoulder blades get dragged apart, noticing that they also slide upwards towards the backward tilting head; only move within a comfortable range of motion.

Repeat a couple of times. Run out and back again. What's different? When you can cope with more sensory input (which probably won't be the first time you try this), rotate through another round of 'Amazonian meets Hunchback' sagittal cogs, bringing awareness of the affect of the skull and pelvis on your feet. In the sagittal plane (remember, this is simply what's happening in the view from the side), whatever the skull and pelvis are doing e.g. tipping back, so are the heel bones. In summary:

- arms are straightening and externally rotating when the pelvis is tipping forwards (heavy pubic bone); a tipping forwards pelvis creates internal rotation of the thighs, and unlocks the knees; softening knees create a slight bend in the ankles which tips the heel bones forward; heel bones tipping forward push the rest of the foot ahead, and flatten the arches (pronating feet): Knock-Kneed Amazonian.
- arms are bending and internally rotating when the pelvis is tipping backwards (heavy tail-bone); a tipping backwards pelvis creates external rotation of the thighs and locks the knees; straight knees tip the heel bones backward; heel bones tipping backward pull the rest of the foot backwards, and raise the arches (supinating feet): Bow-Legged Hunchback.

Put another way:
- your feet are supinating (heels tipping back, pressure on the outside edge) on the exhale;
- your feet are pronating (heels tipping forward, pressure on the inside edge) on the inhale.

 In the context of joint mechanics, we could say that movement patterns are The 3 F's: **Fluid, Fluent & Forecastable**

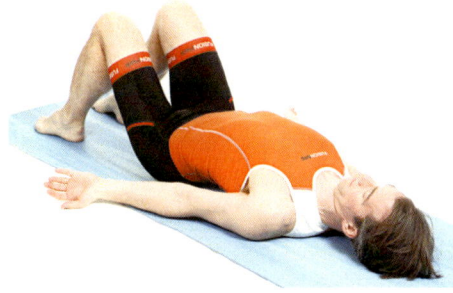 

If you're on dry grass and the weather is mild enough to remain comfortable, you can perform this drill lying on the ground; if it's winter, and you're struggling with these connections in the upright position, try it in the comfort of your home; folk often find it much easier when they're horizontal and out of the field of gravity, because counterproductive, habitual muscle activity gets 'switched off'.
vimeo.com/244972690

▲ ▲ ▲

HELPFUL HILLS

Remember this marker? This is our "Why Am I Here?" reminder. This segment is about alignment in the sagittal plane, fondly known as *Getting your head on right!* and so far, it's been about noticing where upright *actually* is and discovering what can happen when you're there. By now, your body may well have made at least one internal adjustment that you're able to sense. You might be able to hear a difference in your footfall, or see a different part of the ground as you run or notice a change in effort in a particular muscle group. If you're still struggling to notice anything, it's not a failing on your part, but simply a reflection of the fact you probably haven't ever *thought* to tune into what your body is doing. You've been used to 'just doing, without thought' and therefore without 'sense' - in the nicest possible way! Don't worry. Head over to your niftily located slope - remember the one that was part of your pre-session planning? The next drills will either embed what you *have* discovered, or send pennies from heaven if you're currently in sensory deficit.

Whilst you're trotting over to said slope, let's introduce the concept of "Axial Extension", which has two advantages: firstly, when newly introduced to the concept of being an effortlessly-stacked, vertical human being, many folk seem to want to stand to attention. That kind of 'forced upright' generates both stiffness (read immobility: the exact opposite of what I'm seeking to encourage!) and thrusting ribs (read: horrible for your lower back). Secondly, some get transfixed by the concept of being a plumb-line to the world, and work only on 'stacking' without 'spacing', forgetting that the fluid, fluent and forecastable nature of our joint motions require being both aligned *and*, rather critically, not being crushed by the gravitational forces we exist in.

The in-built imagery of **"float your head off your neck"** is often enough to generate both a lovely upright *and* 'the height the skeleton was meant to be, inclusive of the gaps between the bones', allowing for *freedom* of joint motions and the soft tissue reactions they provoke. Neck tension floats away and, oh, everyone grows a millimetre or two! Enjoy occupying your full height in this world ...

Start at the top of your 40-50 metre slope; it doesn't need to be long and it shouldn't be particularly steep (say a maximum gradient of 6%) as with repetitive drills, you'll either fatigue or (worse) lose focus. If your hill is longer, just use a part of it. Less is most definitely more at this level.

Trot downhill without allowing the hill to gift you speed; what I mean by that is you maintain the same trotting speed throughout the descent, rather than yield to the momentum the hill can create. This is to avoid the need to brake which would shift the focus from what we're seeking: great 'form', adroitly shaped by the slope.

So far, without fail, every single runner I've ever coached has trotted down the hill in PERFECTLY VERTICAL mode!! Without even trying to. I don't like to use the word 'perfect' but it's appropriate here - it's like watching a human Y-axis in motion. I haven't personally seen a runner lean forwards down a slope, ever; so the chances are, you won't either. Self-preservation is a great learning tool! Some tell me they feel like they're leaning back when they run downhill ... not only is the ground falling away from you, but of course, vertical can feel like a backwards lean when the inner ear balance thinks 'habitually upright' is actually the Leaning Tower of Pisa!

Now, **walk** back up the hill, using as little effort as possible, elevating your heart rate as little as possible and with whatever your 'usual' walking hill form is. Did you lean into the hill? Do you even *know* if you leaned into the hill? Do you know *how* to know? If you noticed 'work' - in the form of extra muscle tension - in the muscle just above the knee, towards the inside of the leg (the tear-drop shaped vastus medialis oblique - sometimes referred to as the VMO) or in the calves, you were almost certainly leaning forwards. Whether or not you think you should or shouldn't lean into the hill is not at question at the moment - we're simply working on discovering what it is that you habitually do ...

Trot back down the hill (you're always controlling the speed unless instructed otherwise - which won't be until Level 9 - Cat's getting excited already!) and notice the most obvious difference you feel inside yourself with your newly-refined sensations of 'vertical'; tune into your abdominal wall - those muscles WILL be firing, and if you can't somatically sense them, then *actually* touch them! And then walk back up the hill using your new wall-free reference of 'vertical' - probably the activity of your abs, or the newly-lengthened space between the base of your ribcage and your pubic bone, or perhaps your relaxed neck. What did you notice? If you noticed 'knees' the first time, did you notice them the second?

Anatomy Dog-Leg: Shout-Out to all those who're starting to stress about not getting enough of a 'work-out' yet. Whilst you've only reached Level One, and knowing only too well the nature of many runners, let me reassure you that **intensity of effort** has already been introduced; the downhill trot is an effective method of eccentrically loading (muscle lengthens under load) the quadriceps muscle group at the front of the thigh - with evidence to powerfully suggest that this type of muscle action is up to 40% stronger than a concentric contraction (muscle shortens under load) and although the uphill is at walking pace, it's against gravity. Hill training safely, productively, cleverly.

Another 'hill-drill tune-in' is the landing position; nowhere is it more obvious what first contact on the heel bone does to your speed as on a downhill; it brakes you. My absolute favourite running story - after Christopher McDougall's fabulous book *'Born to Run'* - is the 2013 Great North Run 'battle' between Mo Farah and Kenenisa Bekele. Use the QR code here, or search on YouTube for BUPA Great North Run 2013 (Part 2 of 2) and fast forward to the only hill descent at 'minute 55' of the race; watch Mo and Haile using their heel bones as first contact whilst flailing their arms around ... and enjoy Bekele's running masterclass as he floats past effortlessly. I've just watched it *again* and honestly, it's thrilling action, all the way to the finish.

For any runner who was a "not sure" for the "where do you land?" question, the impact (physically and metaphorically) of using the heel bone as first contact on a downhill will give you the internal feedback you might have missed. And easily the simplest method I've found to unravel first contact on the heel when running and find the 'sweet spot' - for those who've decided they want to - is via downhill trotting. If you'd like to give it a go, follow this order:

- Jump (gently) up and down on the spot; keep your calves relaxed and your heels *will* descend and touch the ground, just not first. Notice where your 'first contact' is, your 'sweet spot'; it'll be where it was when you were first exploring it, you're simply fine-tuning your perception of where 'that' is.

- Then shift your weight from right to left, as if you're running on the spot but barely bothering to lift your feet; you'll have the same touchdown points, 'somewhere in front of the heel'. You're not 'planning' your touchdown point, it's just happening because you're relaxed and *letting it*. Be mindful that relaxed calves are enabling the natural descent of your heels via bodyweight plus gravity, so you feel the heels 'kiss' the ground on each landing. If you're not sure this is happening, keep your calves tense and you'll instantly feel the difference, generally in the hardness of the impact on the balls of your feet and the extra work in your calves. Once you're sure of what constitutes negative feedback inside your body, you have the potential to replace it with positive.

- Follow that by running down the hill with as short a stride as you need to maintain the 'somewhere in front of the heel' landing area, plus the heel-to-ground 'kiss' you had when you were running on the spot.

- If you're a habitual heel-striker it will feel like a 'flat landing' because the down slope means the heel doesn't have far to travel before it makes ground contact, but it's <u>always</u> a nano-moment after the initial touchdown of the forefoot.
  - *Imagining your insoles are made of bubblewrap and thinking about 'squishing the bubbles' as you run can be a useful story to play with.*

- If you take too long a stride and find yourself back in your habit - landing on your heel - press pause, 'reset' by running on the spot for a few moments, and then carry on. It may take you a few 'on-the-spot resets' to get the hang of it, but stay relaxed and let it come; in my experience, it always does ... on day one ...

- ... and yes ... it really is that simple, if you'd like it to be.

Repeat the trot downhill and walk uphill rhythm several times and probably no more than ten. Each downhill reinforces your upright position, abdominal activity and your somewhere-forward-of-the-heel 'sweet spot' first contact position. Each uphill can be used to reference different body parts from the list coming up. Home in on each area of your body individually until you glean a really strong sense of what's going on there. Focusing on an area will clear a 'motorway of attention'; trying to feel everything all at once will probably result in you losing focus and diverting onto a slow, winding B-road with potholes, soaking up your 'kinesthetic' sensing energy! The goal isn't to get through everything in your first 'discovery session'. A kinder plan would be to repeat the session several times, gathering more and more information from your body, mastering the art of listening to its feedback.

You could start with paying attention to the **glutes**. (Buttocks, if you'd forgotten). If you are a 'plumb-line to the world', you'll feel your glutes pushing you up the hill, in lieu of any stress just above your knees or in your calves. Remember, if in doubt, tension in the VMO (almost certainly) *means* you're leaning forwards. (I didn't want to caveat that, as in my experience, it's a 'no-exceptions' result ... but there will always be one ... somewhere in the world).

Another area of your body to take notice of is your **lower legs**. If the slope is steep enough, on the uphill walk you might observe that there comes a point where your heel doesn't *land first* unless the body leans into the slope (heaven forbid!); with 'vertical' being the default position, foot touchdown will always be under the body, and on a hill, this can mean that the touchdown point becomes 'somewhere in front of the heel' ... the same as in running mode. Bodyweight + gravity will cause the heel to descend, but it might not reach the ground if that's falling away too steeply; this will have already happened to you (probably, every time you climb a flight of steps), but this might be the first time you really *appreciated it*! This 'present or missing' heel contact is an important calf-preservation aspect in the chapters to come, so becoming aware of their position as early as possible will pay dividends later.

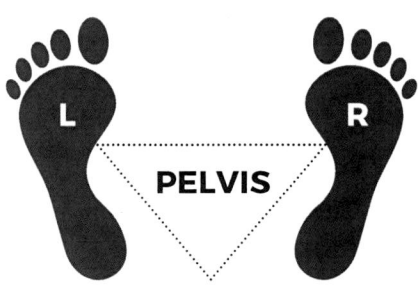

Sticking with the concept of calf-preservation, draw your attention up to the pelvis. Imagine your feet are attached to your hips, and watch what happens to your stride length and/or your effort level as you drop your hips down (with gravity!) 'onto' the ground; **'walking with the pelvis'** up a hill gives an intensity of effort that makes things easier to notice than when you're on the flat. Did you feel the work being eased away from

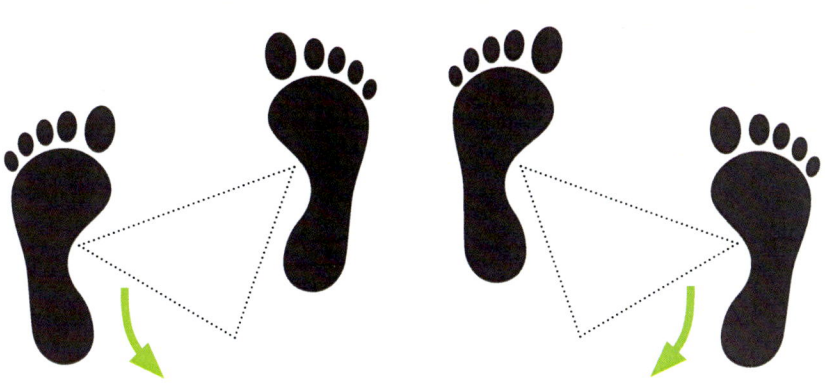

the calves, and transferred to the big power houses of the buttocks - our running muscles? Or maybe you felt that ascending the hill was simply less effort than before? In a short time, you'll probably notice both.

Whether noting 'upright' versus 'forward lean', or 'still pelvis' versus 'see-sawing' pelvis, there's a running theme here (yes - that'll be my wit at play again!) of **bones**. It's one thing noticing certain muscles e*ngage*, but it's quite another to make them work deliberately, whilst in motion. I have a hunch that your findings will match mine, and all those I've worked with ... that unless the bone is in the appropriate place *and* free to move, there's going to be a disappointing result in terms of the soft tissue response you're looking for.

Let's take the glutes as an example. Whilst 'upright' seems to trigger their activity, 'walking with the pelvis' gets them much more involved. Put another way, if the bone (in the 'right' place) doesn't move, it's not reasonable to expect an empowered response from the soft tissue attached to it!

How about a little more fun to further help your biomechanical referencing? Using the ubiquitous, throw-away, in-vogue phrase of 'switching on' (read: contracting) muscles, let's try 'switching on your glutes' whilst you're running. Right now. Either at the bottom or the top of your slope, along a flattish section, forget your bones and work on applying your attention to the buttocks. Not whilst fast running, just easy trotting. Alternately squeeze them. Now if I could see you in action, I'd put money on your movements looking as if someone has stuck a pole up your backside. At best, it'll look decidedly lumpy. On the upside, you'll probably be bolt upright ... but lumpy is *not* efficient. We don't run by 'switching on' our glutes; they *get* switched on as we stretch them under load during the hip flexion phase of pronation when each foot takes our full body-weight, and then they contract without effort - or 'doing' - through *elastic recoil*. They are our biggest *catapults*.

The best use of 'switching on your glutes' is in stopping ... I'm just going to leave that one hanging right there for now. There's no fun in knowing everything all in one go.

FEET

I've been asking you to sense for changes, to notice if things feel better or worse, easier or harder. There's no 'right or wrong' but there IS more or less efficient; more efficient is the *Absolute Right* for you.

 "Absolute Right" was the legitimizing phrase gifted to me by my wonderful friend and 'Tippie-Toe Maecenas', Chris Sritharan - just those two words in the right context offer helpful clarity when sharing my message.

YOUR BONES IN THE 'BEST' PLACES TRIGGER YOUR 'BEST' MUSCLES TO PERFORM THEIR MOST ADVANTAGEOUS ACTIONS; THE SAME 'ACTION' THEN FEELS EASIER. THE SAME SPEED FOR LESS EFFORT IS THE BEGINNING OF YOUR RUNNING EFFICIENCY!

Scan to watch

the ink blotter

Precede your final trot back to base with a 'sagittal plane' mobilisation of your feet - a simple, heel-toe-heel, ink-blotter rocker action that mobilises the ankle joint (a wholly one-dimensional joint in the sagittal plane) and the myriad of joints in the feet, and best accessed by **taking your shoes off**. Don't worry, you don't even need to get dirty socks - you can roll backwards and forwards on the top of your trainers if you really feel the need to! *vimeo.com/244976843*

- Roll s-l-o-w-l-y from heel to toe whilst bending ankles and knees and thinking *'soft sole';* really *feel* for the lengthening of the foot and the flattening of the arches as the heel tips forward and inwards, gently sending the rest of the foot bones into the space ahead. This is the 'closed' ankle joint part of the drill, which 'opens' the foot and provides an adaptive response to the ground surface.

- Having reached the ball of foot and toes, lift your heels off the ground and drive up with straightening knees as high as you can whilst staying balanced. This 'opening' of your ankle joint 'closes' or locks your foot joints into a rigid lever, shortening your foot.

- As you return your heels to the ground, bend your ankles and soften your knees to allow more 'squish' of the sole of the foot as you move your weight back towards your heel.

- Roll back towards your heels, this time lifting your toes, and feel for your legs straightening and the ankles opening again. This is a very simple drill to create movement at the ankle and an alternating lengthening and shortening of the foot.

Please note that I refrained from the mention of shoes - the removing of them that is - until *right at the end of the first level!* And I've held back deliberately as the point is made in the aftermath of the mobilisation ... your feet will probably feel different on the trot home ... more mobile? Perhaps? Better? Maybe ...

A productive habit to establish as you evolve your running efficiency is to have earmarked your most obvious 'nemesis' by the end of each run; by that I mean an aspect of your running form exploration that comes under 'Principles' and needs more of your somatic awareness in order to improve. Given this is Level One, which is all about elements of movement in the sagittal plane, it's likely to be something about your head position, or first contact position, or maybe allowing bones to move more than you're used to.

This information is not for you to get demoralized about - this is *exciting stuff!!* Without awareness, you'll continue to move as efficiently as you can whilst fettered by those invisible lines of tension you didn't even know existed until today's session. Now, you perhaps understand why your neck and shoulders get tense, given those muscles were hanging onto a head that wasn't perched effortlessly on the top of your spine. Maybe you've discovered that your pelvis didn't move and that was probably *why* your glutes have been disappointing in their productivity *in spite* of all the buttock muscle isolation exercises you've been doing. **We're not talking about you changing the way you run; this is all about your body changing the way it <u>can</u> run by creating 'access to all areas' and generating greater running economy as a result of that accessibility.**

QUESTIONS

Your trot home should allow for at least a five minute walking cool-down, and at both running and walking speeds the focus should continue to be on the relaxed alignment in the sagittal plane; those plumb lines from cheekbone to pubic bone and axial extension (head floating off neck) thoughts can be your helpful cues for somatically-sensed, self-propelled, movement efficiency.

Which brings me to an important - because it's common - 'disconnect'. When bones are encouraged to stack on top of each other - with space - we become however tall we're meant to be, with no unnecessary muscular tension, allowing for whatever movement that wants to happen, happen. The most common mistake at this juncture is to limit that which you've **re**-created ('re' because you had it before the invisible lines of tension developed!) because it feels too ... mobile.

Throw habitual tension, constraints and the comfort of familiarity to the wind and "Just. Let. It. Happen."

My suggestion at this point, is to ask your mate to film you running. All you need is a few seconds of a side view and a few more of a rear view. Then you can see for yourself that whilst that new mobility feels as if you're swaggering - as if you own the place - it simply looks ... relaxed. Efficient Running is all about your *entire body moving* ... not just your legs and arms.

Let Movement Happen. Please. 'Swagger' *is* human gait!

Right then. The end of your first session is likely to trigger a barrage of questions, and when working directly with runners, I find the most frequent are the following four: firstly, the transition process from first contact on the heel bone to first contact on the 'sweet spot', somewhere forward of the heel bone - it felt so good, you want to do it? Go to the Appendix NOW for information on how to proceed with this in comfort (page 363). Right now. Don't go any further in the Pyramid until you have this information *and you've acted upon it*. To rush further into the Principles before you've done the necessary ground-work is to be unkind to your body and the most likely result is it'll growl at you. Short-term reins for long-term freedom.

Perhaps because of what folk see on my feet whilst I'm with them, the next most common line of enquiry is the transition process from wearing standard trainers to more minimal footwear or 'simulated' barefoot - you're starting to feel the restriction by the shoe of the 33 joints in each foot, and you want freedom for your feet? Bravo! It's all in the Appendix.

Then comes stretching - again! Did you do any? More of this in later sections, but as a starter, you took your joints close to their range of motion limits whilst maintaining harmonious joint exchange in the sagittal plane, which would have sympathetically lengthened the muscles around that joint close to *their* limits in the sagittal plane ... lengthening is a much *kinder* word than stretching, don't you think?

And finally, injuries. Thinking about and feeling 'stuff', and relating it to joint mechanics using day-to-day language, often sparks connections in relation to injury histories. As I've already mentioned, common running injuries lie in the sagittal plane of motion; examples are foot pain, metatarsal stress fractures, shin splints, Achilles tendonitis, calf issues, runner's knee, hamstring strains, neck & shoulder pain and headaches. Maybe you've already made the connection to some of your issues or restrictions? Perhaps you've newly discovered that you were *in poor sagittal alignment*?

No judgement is necessary. Open your mind and body to new information - the most important of which is coming from within, not from outside. Nobody can tell your body what it should be doing. Your body *always and already* knows best. Even now it is Efficiently Running to the degree it currently can. Just to be very clear (in case you glossed over The Beginning), there is no 'way' we should run. No 'method'. Your body determines its movement efficiency around the invisible lines of joint restrictions and muscular tensions that develop through life; bumps and bruises, knocks and set-backs, held postures and mannerisms are all part of life. The goal of this book is to map the route to *improvement* of your running efficiency by rooting out those limiting restrictions; to give back to your moving body the freedom it *can have* by easing the 100s of joints towards their maximal range of motion. Once the bones can move more freely, the soft tissue can respond in kind.

The real - and bigger - question for <u>today</u> is: "Why do you move *'like that'*, and can you help yourself move *more comfortably*?"

LEVEL ONE SUMMARY CHECK LIST ▲

✔ You re-read The Beginning!
✔ You discover where <u>Vertical Actually</u> Is.
✔ You walk and know the reasons why.
✔ You discover 'how' you currently run.
✔ You explore self-preservation and instinct with a bit of jumping up and down.
✔ You watch others run to help your own 'sense' of what might be happening internally.
✔ You focus inwardly whilst running to find your most 'obvious' negative.
✔ You play with Sagittal Cogs Against the Wall, meet Amazonian and Hunchback, and discover you've got them both in you!
✔ You add Axial Extension as you head over to a slope.
✔ You thank the Running Gods that slopes down 'gift' upright ...
✔ ... slopes up 'gift' glutes ...
✔ ... and that downhill running effortlessly demonstrates the benefits of sweet spot landing!
✔ You repeat probably no more than 10 or so times, discovering that drill repetition keeps the focus on form, and sensible numbers limit fatigue or overusing newly awakened muscles!
✔ You introduce the concept that when the 33 joints in the feet are able to move, it feels G-O-O-D and great things start happening in the body above.
✔ You finish the session aware of your particular form 'nemesis'; that aspect of a habitual motor programme that needs special attention in order to gradually replace it with something more helpful; motor neurones that fire together, wire together. Patience and internal scanning over Time will work wonders.
✔ You walk to cool off - and you know why.
✔ Your first session generates a barrage of questions ... so now I'm excited ... because it means you're engaged.

Thank YOU ...

LEVEL ONE CLOCK-IN/ CLOCK OUT ▲

Stay a while with the first level of your pyramid. Give this one some *time*. That word again! Honestly - time spent here is *always* time well spent. Nothing wonderful will happen if you don't own the right to stack your bones effortlessly. Not a single Leaning Tower of Pisa masquerading as a runner has ever achieved the hip extension he or she has the potential to express. Nor have they optimized their aerobic capacity - no matter how many 'VO2 max training sessions' they've punished their bodies with. Running efficiency starts in the sagittal plane - '**s**' is for '**s**tart with **s**ide view **s**tacking'!

Repeat the session a good handful of times if you've ever had one of the injuries listed on page 108. A really good indication of when you're ready to progress is when you *know* there's no change in your body alignment as you move from your uphill walk to your downhill trot; that when you start the down hill you don't find yourself drifting backwards from the forward lean you hadn't realized you'd adopted ... the 'reset' between drills is a handy button to keep with you. If you find yourself pressing it, then stay with those drills longer until your stacking remains seamlessly continuous.

And don't feel you need to reserve the use of walls as reference points for vertical just when you're running either. Embrace 'vertical' as often as you can. The more you expose your body - upright in the field of gravity - to the more balanced loads when all your bones are stacked on top of each other, the more your central nervous system will adopt it as default, via the neural changes that undoubtedly follow positive repetition.

Delicious.

CONNECT THE ACTION WITH THE THOUGHT WITH THE FEELING ▲

A final point of note. Have this one in your back pocket to return to periodically. As you 'unravel your ravellings', you'll be constantly changing. Life gets in the way, and messes with your gains. What felt like 'x' before you went on holiday, perhaps now feels like 'y'. You need to know if that's a loss of efficiency or just familiarity. Even experienced efficient runners slide into inefficiencies when circumstances are challenging. James returned from the epic UTMB CCC event - a 100km ultramarathon in the Alps, involving three countries and 5950m of climb - having successfully completed without so much as a blister. However, training and competing for many hours in the dark staring at a patch of ground immediately in front of his feet, running with a pack, running and walking up endless inclines becoming increasingly fatigued, and then hours of travel followed by work-life, involving desks and commutes had all conspired to off-balance his sense of where vertical was. At his two week post event check-up, he displayed all the signs of 'horror of horrors' a forward lean!

After a good deal of sagittal cogging - checking in with Misters Amazonian Warrior and Hunchback both on the floor and against the wall, adding arm movement and great breathing as the skull, ribcage and pelvis began tilting more cohesively, and noticing the changes in his body after each set - he was ready to put the new spaces he'd created into gait. Because his inner ear balance was still slightly 'skew', he tapped into the same sensations he'd noticed whilst vertical against the wall; he sensed his pubic bone felt heavy, as if weighted and the base of his sternum seemed light, as if attached to a balloon. As he walked and noted and let bones settle into a place that seemed at once unfamiliar and yet ever-so-much-more comfortable, his body seemed to relax and everywhere *moved*. There wasn't a stuck area of non-movement anywhere. He described it as feeling **'erect-at-ease'**, a phrase I instantly pinched, promising to credit him!

Things change. And thank goodness, otherwise why would we bother? As Remy wisely retorted in response to his father, Django's comment "You can't change nature":

" CHANGE *IS* NATURE, DAD."
RATATOUILLE, PIXAR ANIMATION STUDIOS

DEPARTING LEVEL ONE ▲▲▲

RUNNER STATUS: TTF 2 AND RISING

✔ HEAD ON RIGHT

✔ FOUND VERTICAL

✔ BODY DELIGHTED TO BE THERE

LEVEL TWO
IS THERE POO ON MY SHOE?

LEVEL TWO CONTENTS

Marking the second layer of foundations 115
What is tracking width? 120
Why does tracking width matter? 123
Checkpoint Two 126
Is there poo on my shoe? 130
Effortlessly hanging onto your non-urgent wee 137
Checkpoint Two Noticeboards:
    Checkpoint Two Summary 142
    Leaving Level Two 143

PRINCIPLE 2: CONTINUING THE STORY OF EFFICIENT RUNNING & GENERATING AWARENESS IN THE FRONTAL PLANE

Have you found yourself joining the league of running 'self-massagers, prodders and pokers', using all manner of implements varying from 'somewhat mean' to 'downright torture' to (ironically) alleviate pain? You probably haven't considered absent movement patterns...

 This segment is where you'll explore the space between your feet and the benefits of shifting your weight from left to right ...

The foundational element of the pyramid took you on an exploratory journey to find the alignment that gifted 'bones stacked effortlessly', to notice what that felt like in your body and discover for yourself the myriad of benefits being graciously 'erect at ease' brought. Now, we're off again, in search of the tracking width that offers best 'bang for your buck' in terms of ease of motion and running propulsion. You're going to discover the incredible gains on offer simply by noticing the left-to-right ground-breadth you take ownership of, and how you move from one side to the other.

MARKING THE SECOND LAYER OF FOUNDATIONS

'When' to leave the first and move onto the second level of the pyramid and its second Principle is an important question, and one that *should* be asked. Whilst you already know there's no schedule to follow, the variability in those I've coached is fairly minimal. There might be the odd runner for whom 'Amazonian meets Hunchback' remains a mystery long after everyone else's body has started knitting the joint rotations together seamlessly, but generally, I'd suggest getting on with Principle 2 as soon as you feel relaxed and comfortable with the majority of the content in Principle 1 (as I've described at the end of the last chapter).

The reason you needn't wait until you've nailed every last sagittal plane detail is because the second Principle is inextricably linked to it. I *have* tried coaching the two planes of motion together and the experiences showed me that better results came when they were separated. With so much new information to grapple with during the session - both physical and mental - most folk get overwhelmed and end up trying too hard. That word 'try' sounds like way too much effort for an efficient runner, and if you remember from *The Beginning*, you've thesaurus'd it out of your running vocabulary!

The reality is that whilst the three planes of motion are inseparable in gait, they are better separated (but not by much) in their discovery. The process is that of 'unravelling', with a small 'u'. (*'Unravelling'* with a capital 'U' being the title of a fabulous book by Philip M Greenfield - my copy being dog-eared and much loved).

Without getting bogged down in the myriad of rabbit holes surrounding the generic topic of biomechanics, perhaps this is the right moment to explain a little bit about the clinic work that underpins the PFM run coaching philosophy you're reading about here. It's so much easier to 'get' concepts if the subject is wrapped up in context, offering flavour through storytelling, isn't it?

Let's continue with the not-unreasonable hypothesis that a body is a complete, communicative unit with a skeletal framework linked together by joints, which when fully functional enable effective, efficient, fluid movement. In the context of movement and pain,

> "THE PURPOSE OF A STORYTELLER IS NOT TO TELL YOU HOW TO THINK, BUT TO GIVE YOU QUESTIONS TO THINK UPON."
> - BRANDON SANDERSON, THE WAY OF KINGS

my feeling is that the notion of a foot, a knee, a back or a shoulder specialist separates that which is inseparable. All joints are influenced by at *least* what happens below and above them, to the left and to the right of them, not to mention the influence of brain activity, local air pressure, footwear impacts ... you can see the minefield we're trampling around! Now, remembering the 'joints are doors' analogy from The Beginning (page 53), when movement doesn't look or feel elegant, effortless or fluid (and equally when chronic pain persists), it's often productive to look structurally to see where some doors have had to stay ajar continually in exchange for others that have locked tight.

My work, analysing posture and movement and developing the PFM Efficient Running School standard, is all about looking at the structural dance of the 'doors', sleuthing to find the 'endlessly open versus endlessly closed doors' which can tell the story of why folk are moving in 'that way', or got injured seemingly inexplicably, or keep getting injured, or are in chronic pain.

> "There are known knowns. These are things we know that we know. There are known unknowns. That is to say, there are things that we know we don't know. But there are also unknown unknowns. There are things we don't know we don't know."
> **Donald Rumsfeld, American Politician**

I saw the truth in Aristotle's quote: *"The more you know, the more you know you don't know"* as the more I learned, the more I realized I had yet to discover. And one of my favourite quotes is the now-famous soundbite from Donald Rumsfeld, about *"known unknowns"*;

despite the historical context it was uttered from, the words fill me with wonder that there is so much left to unearth in our world. So with an insatiable thirst for endless learning, and with Paul Chek's words ringing in my ears *"If you're not assessing, you're guessing"*, I invested everything I had (and then some) in the most advanced gait and motion technology available in Europe; as I write it's still the only one of its kind in the UK. I wanted to know more. Here are a couple of brief videos showing you the fun and games of a 4D scan assessment with me. The scanner like an enormous toy that I get to play with daily, whilst objectively measuring with great precision how well each of the 'doors' in a spine move, relative to the pelvis, relative to feet, in all of their (mostly) three dimensions, simultaneously and whilst the person is moving.

Then, armed with all this fabulous information - with the goal being to re-connect effective, efficient, comfortable movement by sharing the work load throughout all doors/joints - I use:

> **"MOVEMENT TO INSPIRE CHANGE FROM WITHIN, RATHER THAN INFLICT CHANGE FROM THE OUTSIDE" - GARY WARD (SUCH A GOOD STORY IT HAD TO BE QUOTED TWICE!)**

The movements used in clinic can be very similar to the 'stiles' dotted throughout this trail, the differences lying in the customized detail for each person, simply because I can see them. Translating those new potential joint rotations into better running enjoyment and efficiency - and if desired, speed - is the next step (nope - no pun intended that time - didn't even see that one coming!).

So what I'm sharing in this map book is my running experience interwoven with the joint rotations of the gait cycle, and backed up with accurate information I've been gathering using incredibly advanced technology: running anatomy in motion - literally, and in the contextual light of the Flow Motion Model™.

> **RUNNING ALONG A TIGHT-ROPE?**
> **SHUFFLING ALONG A CENTRAL LINE?**
> **AWARE OF SPACE BETWEEN YOUR FEET?**
> **FOLLOW THE ▲ TO RECEIVE THE BOUNTIES**
> **OF OPTIMISED TRACKING ▲**

Back to the development of *your* running and movement efficiency and the ideal timing of progress along the trail. In the absence of a clinic session with you, I'm ethically - and I feel morally - bound to tread carefully with you, whilst joining up the dots as swiftly as Nature allows. Your forward lean might be as a *result* of your narrow tracking, or co-operatively connected to it, so you might find the 'upright stacking' easier as soon as you've combined it with the ideal tracking width (the left-to-right gap between each landing foot) - one that's absolutely right *for you*. That said, don't rush straight from Level 1 to 2, as the movement of the spine in the sagittal plane is critical for the use of the primary respiratory muscles, which would seem to be right up at the top of the totem pole of 'Life'!

To realise your full efficient running potential, of course you need 'everything' ... but you can't have it all ... at least not all at once!

On a practical level, there are a few other reasons for beginning with the focus on the 'upright' and the sagittal plane, quite apart from the need to start *somewhere* (after all, whilst human gait is cyclical by nature, even drawing a circle starts with a point on the paper!). Primarily, I'm driven by the sense that it's logically safer. This is an experiential book about movement, and I'm talking to you but can't see you. If I caveat every 'play with this drill, see how you feel' with disclaimers, it's going to dampen the spirit of the enterprise. However, by applying common sense, we can infer that the pervasiveness of the human 'forward lean' exists not through the majority of the western world *needing* to hold that posture, but more from folk unconsciously adopting that posture through their dominant environment; sitting at desks, walking with their head leaning towards mobile phone screens, computers on laps, etc; creating lines of tension that really don't need to be there - that arguably shouldn't be there - and therefore can be eased first, without harm.

The second reason is Google. Ahhh - if I had a pound coin for every injured runner who told me they 'got it from Google' ... or from their mate who 'got it from Google' ... referring to running methods that seem to promote a forward lean. Perhaps because they thought it might be a quick route to their next personal best time, they took the snippets of information they remembered most clearly, leant forward with gusto (probably not what the authors had in mind) and their bodies protested.

For me, and every runner I've ever worked with, having a head perched effortlessly on top of an 'on axis', vertical spine, stacked without any unnecessary muscle tension, is where the magic starts.

I propose it's *impossible* to run as efficiently as *is* possible when muscles are expending energy and sinews are being held tight to literally hang onto your 'off axis' head and stop you face-planting!

WHAT IS TRACKING WIDTH?

This is all about investigation in the frontal plane, which is left to right movement, as if along the baseline of a tennis court.

Anatomy Dog-Leg: For our purposes, just think of movement in the **frontal plane** as **sideways movement visible from the back or front of the body**. For instance, leaning the upper body sideways, bending the spine to the left or right; reaching an arm out to the side (abduction) or pulling one leg closer to the other (adduction).

Before we start sensing internally, you can get a head start by observing externally. With the focus of Level 2 being on shifting weight from the left to the right foot efficiently and effectively ... who around you isn't? Next time you're out and about, you'll now be alert to this variable. What you're looking for is anyone 'running along a tightrope'. Even reading that might alter perception of your own tracking width, especially if this is a new consideration for you. Whilst everyone instantly knows what I mean when I say 'running along a tightrope', a few examples of what it tends to look like might help:

- Toes turned out, heels turned in to the extent the heels almost touch as they pass each other; in fact, sometimes they do! Having watched a few tightrope runners in my time, I can spot the ones who kick their own ankles even before the tell-tale dirt streaks give the game away. Its significance to ease of running through symmetrical movement patterns, hits home to a runner when they realise I can even predict *which* foot kicks which ankle.

- Toes turned in, heels turned out (it's rarely symmetrical), lower legs 'dishing around' with knees close to knocking. If the run is long enough, these runners can report bruising or redness to the inside of their knees.

- One foot tracking straight and the other foot crossing the mid-line; sometimes both feet crossing in front of each other. These folk tend to recount stories of hours spent on their wobble boards doing extra balancing homework because they feel unstable. They can end up being able to do party tricks on the wobble board, but the challenge when running remains the same.

- Some foot turn-out but with less emphasis on close heels and more on the fact they look like they're only making ground contact with the outsides of their feet - they 'look' bandy-legged even if their shins are straight. The outsides of their feet can track so closely together that you wonder how they don't tread on their own big toes. They don't, and *that's* their challenge ... forward motion without ever bothering to use their mighty Hallux (read: big toe!).

- From the front or the back, if you see no light between their thighs, this means no space between their legs; at the very least this is a chafing issue but from an efficiency perspective, 'no space' is a number of joint restrictions *somewhere*. Weight shuffles close to the mid-line rather than shifts laterally, elastically and effortlessly through repetitiously-loaded-and-released catapults.

Anatomy Dog-Leg: Did you realise that those ITBs (ilio-tibial bands) you might be endlessly massaging, connect to the tensor fascia lata (TFL) muscles on the anterior side of each hip? You can feel them 'pop up' into your hand if you make the movement as if to stub out a cigarette on the floor. The TFL muscles get involved in 'catching' your weight as you transfer it from one side to the other, stretching like a catapult and throwing you back the other way? Gloriously effective ...

- Perhaps the least noticed form is ... simply no weight being shifted!! I call it a 'trit-trot' run because as well as hardly any movement it's almost as if they're barely touching down. I know it well. I used to be proud of leaving no mark on the ground - as if I was trying to be a bird! Until that is, I discovered I was missing out on a tonne of plantar fascia load and sling system usage. I have done many things in my time, and one of them is run inefficiently. But without that experience, I probably wouldn't be writing this now. All part of the journey ...

Before we go on, I'd just like to emphasise that these gait patterns aren't 'wrong'. You see them everywhere, even in elite runners. But just because you *do* see them everywhere, doesn't mean to say the shapes they make are either efficient or non-injurious. Remember, this is a trail leading to running *efficiency*; there's no dog-leg to a kiosk disseminating information on how you should or shouldn't run. The invitation is to observe others to help draw your attention to your own movement patterns. The question we're asking is:

"IS 'HOW YOU RUN', COMPROMISING, LIMITING OR RESTRICTING YOUR RUNNING EFFICIENCY?"

If you've never thought of it before, how will you know? Just think '**Donald Rumsfeld**'!

Even the term 'tracking width' is an unknown for some, so let's shine a light on it. With reference to efficiency of gait at all speeds, I'm suggesting that your ideal tracking width is **the width apart your feet need to land to** *'access ground contact with the whole breadth of each forefoot'*. Logically, that should improve the chances of optimal movement *in all 33 joints of each foo*t, and in turn, generate more productive reactions in the rest of the body above. We'll find out ... soon ...

Not a single runner I've coached has ever considered whether or not they use the entire breadth of their forefoot, walking or running, until I asked them. Those that walked and ran 'along a tightrope', had no idea they were doing that, habitually and consistently. A few knew they were kicking their own ankles; many more had noticed that the mud was always on the same inner calf, but hadn't thought any more about it. I have seen redness and inflammation on the insides of knees, and then discovered that the runner hadn't noticed it. 100% of those I've watched walk along it, maintained the same tightrope tracking as soon as they geared up into a run. And given none with a narrow tracking width knew of it, none had any reason to connect its possible relevance to their repetitive injuries, until after this session. This lack of attention and awareness is common in 'us'. It's 'human'. And it's the reason I'm intent on guiding you along this path with as much hand-holding as I reasonably can. If I can't see you, then I need to take care of you somehow, otherwise I'll worry about you!

WHY DOES TRACKING WIDTH MATTER?

Common injury patterns associated with 'tightrope runners' seem to be repetitive ankle sprains, the so-called 'dreaded' runners' ToFP (Top of Foot Pain), repetitive calf issues, repetitive Achilles tendon issues, Iliotibial (IT) band syndrome, endless knee issues, groin strains, lower back issues when running, neck and shoulder pain when running, headaches during or after running …

Did you notice how many match the sagittal plane list? It's misguided to focus on one thing when solving problems; with so many joint combinations at play, 'x' does not necessarily equal 'y' within bodies. For instance, one runner's sprained ankle could lead to knee pain on the same side, and another runner could have the same injury but end up with chronic pain in the opposite hip and neck. Your injury *might* be to do with something in its location, but it *might* be to do with something elsewhere, related to a restriction far away from the pain. Treatment for a repetitively-bothered knee for example, can't be the same for everyone, as the cause can't possibly be the same for everyone. I don't believe there are any formulaic solutions to pain and injury situations, only better questions. American psychologist Abraham Maslow called it out: *"I suppose it is tempting, if the only tool you have is a hammer, to treat everything as if it were a nail".*

Interestingly, at my first bike-fitting course in 2011 with the Godfather of triathlon innovation, Dan Empfield, I googled the most common running and cycling injuries. Apart from broken wrists and broken collarbones which were specific to cycling crashes, the rest of the list was *the same*. Cycling isn't even fully weight-bearing! It would appear it's less about 'what' you're doing, and more about 'how' you're doing it … and then even more importantly, 'why' you're doing it 'like that'.

"Why" is such a great question.

Without getting too technical, let's look at why those common injuries might be related to the relative landing position of each foot.

1. When the body's base of support becomes very narrow, it would be reasonable to assume there's more of a challenge on all the soft tissue below the knee:

- calf tissue, both along the back and the side of the lower leg, probably has to work harder than if the body had a wider base of support;
- ligaments around the ankle are likely to be more at risk of strain when less of each foot is available to spread and balance the load above;
- the position of the foot relative to the hip could make the ankle more vulnerable to the classic inversion sprain injury (ankle falls outwards, sole of foot inwards);
- and with less of each foot making ground contact, there's likely to be too much work for some of the foot and not enough work for the rest - what hurts tends to be what's doing the most work, not the areas that have gone to sleep!

2. An excessive angle inwards - towards the midline - from the hip to the foot also influences knee mechanics; the TFL muscle (remember, the tensor fascia lata?) in the anterior hip attaches to the IT (iliotibial) band which in turn attaches onto the outside of the shin bone, below the knee. With narrow tracking, tension is held through the TFL and the IT band. No amount of rolling - or the agony of deeply massaging it - is going to solve its over-tensioned unhappiness. Letting go of any needless tension probably will though ...

3. Thigh bones angling close to the mid-line have inner thigh muscles working under more constant shortening tension, which could feasibly reduce free movement in the hip joint, have a knock-on effect on the mobility of the pelvis as a whole and then influence the work-load of the lower back.

4. Remembering the 'doors closed means others will need to stay open' analogy, with a restricted pelvis, the shoulder girdle might need to help out to keep the running movement going. Quite a few tightrope runners I see have a disproportionate amount of awkward arm activity compared to what their legs are managing, and these are the ones who tend to suffer with upper back, shoulder and neck grief.

5. Trouble-shooting running-related headaches is a wonderful theoretical journey into the integrated nature of our amazingly clever bodies. Even though I have no proof of the following hypothesis, I've had empirical success with eliminating running headaches using the thoughts and actions at Level 2 of the pyramid. So I invite you to follow my suppositional thought processes on how one thing might lead to another, and 'narrower than your body would like' tracking width just might be at the route of the seemingly incurable:

- A narrow tracking width is a balance challenger.
- A challenged balance is a survival switch left 'on'.
- Survival is 'fight or flight', a veritable cortisol-fest of muscular readiness.
- Ever-ready muscles fighting for balance are under a lot of tension.
- Muscular tension is 'stiff'.
- Stiffness limits 'give', pliability and cushioning.

And then:

- Narrow tracking means less side shift from one foot to the other.
- Less weight shift means less elastic recoil, which reduces natural spring.
- Less cushioning coupled with less spring means more impact.
- Impact is jarring.
- Brains don't enjoy repetitive jarring.

Even if you consider that a fairy tale, requiring whopping leaps of faith to get from one anecdote to the other, I still find it's a narrative that resonates helpfully enough for folk to willingly apply themselves to the improvement of their joint mechanics. As the American mythologist Joseph Campbell puts it: *"if you're going to have a story, have a big story, or none at all"*.

So if you are running a narrow path, can you safely broaden it?

Time for some fun.

As every runner knows, establishing whether that squelch was mud or poo is important, sometimes tricky and to an onlooker, often comical. The contortions we get ourselves into ...

Comedy aside, what's important here is continuing the theme I mentioned in *The Beginning:* using evocative language to embed memorable movement patterns. You probably have an image of this level's title in your head already, it'll no doubt be spot on, and as we continue along the trail its relevance will be unveiled.

CHECKPOINT TWO
NOTICEBOARD

▲ ▲ ▲

TERRAIN: FENCE OR WALL
RUNNER STATUS: TTF 2 (WITH CARE)
KIT LIST: LAYERS, COMFORTABLE FOOTWEAR, GROUND MARKERS, SENSE OF HUMOUR

On arrival at the next checkpoint, it's all about the practicalities. This section of the trail covers slightly different terrain to the first layer of the pyramid; your venue requires a big enough vertical surface somewhere so you can remind yourself where 'sagittal alignment' is, and whilst you don't need a nearby slope, you DO need props ... a stack of the 20cm diameter football 'sports saucer markers' is ideal, but you could equally use a collection of 20-odd gathered sticks and stones. If it's windy, make sure your markers aren't feather-light!

TTF 2: You can walk without tension restriction/pain, but notice its restriction as soon as you run; it's less noticeable first thing in the morning.
TTF 3: You notice the restriction/pain after a couple of kilometres; it may or may not be noticeable on waking.

In terms of *Tissue Tolerance Factor* (see page **48**), there's an argument to having the personal requirements here at TTF 3, but actually, your problems may well be related to what we're about to cover, so **with caution** if you're at TTF 2, give it a gentle go and see what happens.

Right then - going up - Pyramid Level 2: TTF 2 or over; you're dressed appropriately (layers, runners, layers!) and waiting, so let's get going ...

... for your 10 minute walking warm-up! No short-cuts - this is important, with no-one but you getting to reap the rewards: joint mobilisation in a weight-bearing gait pattern; diversion of blood from the non-vital organs, the glands producing hormones and the intestines to the working muscles; and, as a result of Level 1, postural self-cueing in preparation for great biomechanics when running. Bones get aligned, soft tissue warms, neurones start firing together - all good stuff with no negatives. What's not to love?

'Feeling' for your vertical, what are you noticing today? Do your abs feel engaged? Are your ankles more relaxed, with your ankle angles more open? Is there pretty even pressure through the fronts of your feet and your heels? Are your neck and shoulder areas more relaxed because you're 'floating your head off your neck'? And do you still feel 'odd' here, or are you perhaps already wondering how on earth you managed to get around in your previous, more effortful, slanted posture?

Following your warm-up walk, your joints should feel somewhat lubricated and your muscles warmed and ready. But just before you start running, check your 'sagittal side-view stack' by lining up against your wall prop. With bum and mid-back against the wall, can your head touch without your neck having to extend, which would force your gaze upward? Remember: *we're seeking Progress not Perfection.*

Whilst you're there, let's revisit **Sagittal Cog Against The Wall.** It's your 'bread and butter' movement pattern until vertical feels normal and leaning forward feels ... well, forward! This time we'll look at it through another lens; I need a library of words to express the same thing as different words resonate with different folk:

Amazonian Meets Hunchback: Take 2 - the Innies and the Outies: *vimeo.com/244972509*

- Head, mid-back and bum against the wall (heels will touch only if you have a flat backside - which hopefully won't be for long now you've started using it!)

- Nostrils are roughly horizontal to the ground and your ribs are relaxed/dropped - nothing is thrusting skyward.

- Breathing **in/in**haling marks all the '**in**s' ...
  - weight moves to **in**side of heels (pronation)
  - legs **in**ternally rotate
  - knees turn **in**
  - bum/tailbone pushes **in**to the wall
  - lower back arches **in**wards
  - shoulder blades move **in**, towards the spine
  - chin moves **in**wards, as neck flexes and head tips forward.
- Breathing **out**/exhaling marks all the '**out**s' ...
  - weight moves to the **out**side of the heels (supination)
  - legs **out**wardly (externally) rotate
  - knees turn **out**
  - lower back curves **out**wards
  - bum/tailbone pulls **out** from the wall
  - shoulder blades move **out**, away from the spine
  - chin moves **out**wards, as neck extends and head tips back.

Scan to watch

the Innies and the Outies

- And whatever your legs and feet are doing, your arms and hands are doing the opposite:
  - If your legs are internally rotating and feet pronating, your arms are externally rotating and hands supinating (palms out).
  - If your legs are externally rotating and feet supinating, your arms are internally rotating and hands pronating (palms in).

Lastly, 'wake-up' your feet in the sagittal plane with slow 'ink-blotter' rocks from the heel to toes and back, really feeling for the squish of the sole-flesh as the bones move to accommodate your bodyweight pressing down onto them, and not forgetting the all-important opening and closing of your ankle joints.

OK - you're walked and sagittally cogged, so now run 'easy' for a good 10 minutes. You need to give yourself enough time to feel loosened up and comfortable, gathering information from your senses to find your 'best' upright stacking alignment and be ready to advance into a further dimension - literally!!

Once you feel relaxed and ready and you're at the venue you're using for the session, run a 'swimming pool length and back' focusing internally to identify the single most obvious _negative_ you now notice; this could be tension around the hips, the knees, in the lower legs or ankles.

IS THERE POO ON MY SHOE?

Grab one of your cones (or substitute prop) and jump up and down on the spot a few times. Stop in the exact foot position you landed in and see if your cone (or 20cm-ish diameter stick) can sit between your feet, albeit with the sides squashed a bit. You might be surprised to find your feet too close together for that to happen. If so, don't worry - you're not alone, and you're in the right place; this session is all about giving personal space back to each of your feet!

Back to jumping up and down, this time thinking thoughts such as, **letting your thigh bone just fall with gravity** from the outside of your pelvis ... or ... **dangling your legs** from the outside of your hip socket ... or ... **dropping an imaginary plumb-line from your outer hip to your outer ankle bone** ... it might *feel* like you're John Wayne, having just dismounted your horse (or some modern-day cowboy if you're of a later era than me!) but I promise it won't look like that.

Now run again, and this time we'll add some lovely 'weight-shifting' thoughts. You'll get used to this, with the emphasis always being on 'thinking a thought' rather than 'doing an action'. You can start with thinking "left side, right side, left side, right side" with each footfall, and then trim that down to "left, right, left, right". I'm not kidding - just *thinking* about having a right and left side is a revelation for many!!! As you run, you can ask yourself "what do I need to let happen in order to feel the *entire breadth of the front of each foot?*" Or even more simply, if you think about relaxed feet ... you'll get 'relaxed feet'. Do you get a sense of your body weight shifting from one whole foot to the other foot? If you don't feel it straight away, *think it* and keep playing ... your weight shift is waiting to be noticed. A favourite game with those I work directly with is to forget about their legs (whilst being forever grateful for them), and *stick their feet on the outside of their pelvis and run from there ...*

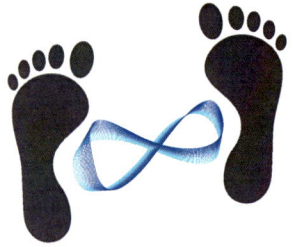

... this is often an 'ah-ha' moment ... if you let whatever movement wants to happen, happen, it's as if your pelvis rolls like a figure of 8 on its side ...
... the sign of infinity
... the PFM logo :)

Jump up and down again on the spot; now how much space is there for the cone? Has it improved? Is your stance wider?

Let the unravelling continue with more 'Before & After' games. There is a sequence to follow and whilst I prefer writing stories, this will be easier to follow if I lay it out as more of a list:

- Run up and down your venue, and simply 'sense'. Given we're only on the second level of *principles*, keep the sensing 'big'; by that I mean, use your internal friend 'Sensory Feedback' to find *obvious* things to attach your attention to. Rubbing upper thighs is an easy one, as is feeling air move on the inside of each knee if the swing leg is passing perilously close; noticing something on one side of your body rather than both; tuning into the most conspicuous tension. No need for the magnifying glass just yet ...

- Now, run up and down with the intent to have 'dangling legs'. An important point of clarity here is that the thought is *only* that of 'dangling'. You're dangling within the context of 'no held tension'. You let go of any tension that might have been previously taking them towards a tightrope. You're not directing your legs out, and you're not directing them in. You're not holding them vertically either - that's called standing still. And you're not adding any adjectives. No 'heavily' dangling. That sounds mighty effortful. Just 'dangling': **does anything feel different? Do you feel 'wider'?**

Scan to watch

Frontal Plane Foot Mobilisation

- Stop and mobilise your feet s-l-o-w-l-y in the frontal plane by rolling from one long edge to the other, repeatedly. It's such a simple movement, but powerful if you luxuriate in it, allowing yourself the unrushed time to feel for movement in the bones as you pass over them: *frontal-plane-foot-mobilisation.*

- **Run again: does anything feel different? A sense of wider, more pliable feet, perhaps?**

- Open your body in the frontal plane with **Frontal Cog aka I'm a Little Tea-Pot**: *vimeo.com/244972923*

- Stand upright (if there's a wall handy, even better - make use of it, with mid-back and buttocks staying in contact with the wall).
- With the palm of one hand in contact with the side wall of your lower ribs, exhale and side bend away using only the weight of the opposite arm as 'ballast'.
- Just as the amount of natural movement from the weight of the hanging arm stops, breathe in deeply with the aim to swell the ribs under the hand resting on your rib wall; notice the side bend continue further, without effort or strain.
- Next, allow your pelvis to shift laterally, away from the ballast arm, to further increase the side bend; the goal is to allow the outside of the hip to be outside the edge of the foot, challenging the right-left base of support.

- You'll hopefully find you've 'edged' each heel - you should have obvious pressure on the outside of the outside heel, and probably less obvious pressure on the inside of the inside heel; maintain ground contact across the whole breadth of each foot, so from the base of the big toe all the way across to the base of the little toe.
- Finally, bring the ballast arm up to be parallel with the ground and reach through its fingertips to maximise the lateral movement of the pelvis whilst working a side flexion of your neck towards the bent arm to get your nose vertical.
- Whilst doing a pretty good imitation of a long and lean teapot, you are eccentrically loading (stretching under load) the hip and lateral buttock muscles, the same side waist muscles and the opposite side inner thigh muscles or adductors.
- Repeat a couple or 3 times, and then repeat to the other side.

- **Run again: does anything feel different? 'Bigger', 'wider', 'freer' are common adjectives used to describe the new running sensations.**

- Open your body further by adding the joint rotations that occur when inverting (pulling the sole to the inside) and everting (pushing the sole to the outside) the feet - otherwise known as **"Is There Poo On My Shoe?"** Admit it, you've been waiting for this, haven't you? *vimeo.com/245649047*
    - Stand upright. If your wall is handy, it makes sense to use it, especially initially; try

not to lean on it, but rather use it to stop you sending your foot behind you (which would be cheating!).
- Lift one foot, rotate your knee outwards and make as if to check your sole for poo, looking from the big toe side. No other instruction is normally required! You will drop the same side shoulder as the leg you're standing on, whilst opening the outside of your lifted ankle in order to turn your foot enough to see the sole. This is inversion of the whole foot. You're side-bending away from the foot you're trying to view.
- Stand back upright, then rotate your knee inwards, and try to view the sole of your shoe from the little toe side; this lifts the shoulder above the leg you're standing on, whilst you 'close' the outside of the airborne ankle to see the sole. This is eversion of the whole foot. You're side-bending towards the foot you're trying to view.
- Repeat a few times, smoothly and within a comfortable range of motion. You might really struggle with this, and push for success because you'll feel as if you *should* be able to do it. After all, how difficult can checking the sole of your shoe for poo be? Actually - for many - really quite tricky when focusing on clean frontal plane joint rotations! So don't worry, but *keep e-a-s-i-n-g the movement bigger, whilst staying strain-free*!! Meet resistance and don't push past it.
- Work the lateral (outside) and medial (inside) lower leg muscles as much as you can to rotate the foot and bring the sole into view from both directions.
- Repeat both movements to the other leg. Many find they can easily evert one foot and invert the other, but not the other way around. It's not the eversion/inversion necessarily that's the restriction here, but often the side-bend in whichever direction is required for that combination. Revelatory poo on shoe! Who knew?

- **Run again: does anything feel different? Many report tangible weight shifting after this drill.**

- Now get the next drill ready. Line all your cones, sticks or stones up in one long row, spreading them roughly a running stride length apart. You need at least 20 or so markers to provide enough steps to generate feedback and differences. I tend to use enough to cover the length of the local cricket wicket - keeping outside the boundaries of the hallowed turf, obviously.

- Run the length of the cones, consciously landing with a wide enough tracking width for the cones to remain inside each footfall.

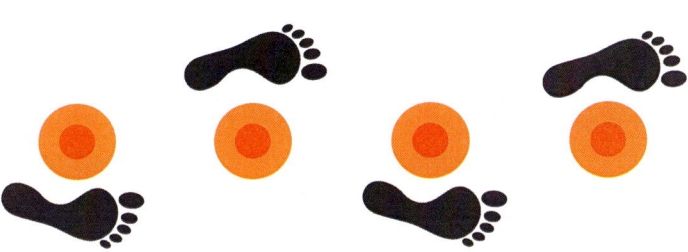

- How does it feel? Too wide? Mad wide? Just a bit wide?

- *Run without the cones: does anything feel any different?*

- Next, zig-zag the cones to create a 'one-cone-for-each-footfall' overly-wide channel.

- Bound laterally from just inside one cone to the next, feeling for the 'weight shift' of left foot to right foot and back again. Zig-zag left and right as far as you can comfortably. And if you don't want to bother repositioning the cones, simply use the line you have as one boundary and leap laterally away from it on alternate steps.

- **Run without the cones: is there any change? Generally, the chatter of unexpectedly *big* change comes here!**

- Return to the 'lateral bounding' with the additional focus of feeling for your outer hips 'catching you' and throwing your travelling weight back in the opposite direction.

- **Run without the cones: does anything feel any different? Groans of appreciation as *weight effortlessly shifts left and right* are heard here. 'Springy' and 'elastic' are words commonly used.**

In summary, you've got 7 drills plus the verbal cueing to play with to start to feel the whole breadth of each foot and the shifting weight of your body between them. This has always been enough for even the most rigid (body and mindset) runners to become excitable, with their awakening sense of new running potential:

1. Jumping up and down with the cone between your feet.
2. Running with thoughts of 'feet on pelvis', etc.
3. Running after mobilising the feet joints from long foot edge to long foot edge.
4. Running after executing 'I'm a Little Teapot' several times to each side.
5. Running after executing 'Is There Poo On My Shoe?' several times to each side.
6. Running with feet landing either side of the lined-up cones.
7. Running with lateral bounds inside an exaggeratedly-wide channel of cones.
8. Running with lateral bounds and with the sense of the hips catching the travelling pelvis and throwing it back to centre.

Keeping playing with whichever drills and cues elicit the most tangible differences in your tracking width and enable you to feel the whole breadth of your squishing foot. Even without being with you, I would put money on these being the drills your body is enjoying the most.

And in the unlikely event that you *don't* feel change straight away, don't worry. Everyone is different (and yet so so similar). It might be that your adjustments are more subtle than others, making them more challenging to tune into; maybe you're still learning the skill of 'noticing stuff' because you habitually turn away from your discomforts to block them out. At the end of the day, if you change the input for long enough, you're going to get a different output; after all, 'input' is how we all get ravelled up in the first place …

EFFORTLESSLY HANGING ONTO YOUR NON-URGENT WEE

This new width to your gait can feel very odd for many; 'odd' means change and if you wanted to change because you knew you were inefficiently 'running along a tightrope', then it's OK to feel odd! The next question is always "Well how wide *should* it be?" And the answer is always the same: "Wide enough *for you*". If you think of 'too narrow' as legs forming a capital V, then 'too wide' is legs forming a capital A (without the bar across, of course), which is challenging in a different way: now you have thigh bones 'jamming' inwards into the hip sockets, only the inside edges of your feet to play with and a penguin-waddle for a gait pattern. Not a great swap.

I used the word 'chafe' earlier; just the once (the second time I referred to it, I said 'rubbing'; you just can't be too careful with words). It's such an easy cue to think about, but I've seen folk take the concept of 'running without chafe' to the extreme. And it's happened enough times for me to decide it wasn't helpful in a book. What *would* be helpful though is to flip it, and mention that finding your ideal tracking width will mean you have little or no chafe at the top of your thighs. So it's better used as a confirmer, rather than a cue. Running to avoid chafe is a whole world of different to running *without* chafe.

In summary, if the tracking width is right for you, it'll feel like a 'good odd' because whilst it's wider than you're used to, it feels balanced and stable with feet landing under your hips, gifting access to their entire width. Just right. It's the Goldilocks of tracking widths. Another sweet spot! I think the American author Dakota Cassidy must have sneaked into one of my workshops without me noticing just before she came out with this beauty: ***"Life is messy, relationships are messy, but sometimes you have to keep jumping in the mud to find the sweet spot. Or you can give up."***

That 'sweet spot' is also the gift of a pelvic floor that seems to wake up naturally. That might sound a touch far-fetched, so let's explore (if you're sitting reading this, I'll bet you don't stay there for long!). Start by running with narrow tracking (if you're a tight-rope runner, this bit will be easy); as you run, pull up on your pelvic floor as if you're "hanging onto a non-urgent wee" (girls) or "pull up your scrotum" (boys - I had to get a lad to describe what it felt like to him as 'my' version didn't seem to be getting through to the opposite sex. This is the only time so far in my career that my coaching cues have needed to be gender-specific!). Notice how far the pelvic floor 'travels up'. Let it go again - back down to wherever it was. Repeat a couple of times so you get really familiar with the movement.

Imagine me behind you, coaching this, yelling exactly these words as we run along the road, and be thankful you can do this in anonymity. For those who were with me as we ran through the jam-packed Christmas Market, under the London Eye ... honestly, it was necessary! Hopefully, all around us were non-English-speaking tourists, and didn't understand ...

Now find your Goldilocks tracking width - that wonderful structural shape which seems to 'dangle' your thigh bones, accesses the whole breadth of each forefoot, enables the pelvis to move freely and generally feels more balanced. As you continue to run, pull up on your pelvic floor hanging onto that 'non-urgent wee', or 'pulling up your scrotum'. Did anything happen this time? Give it a few goes.

Most distrust their initial findings (aren't we all such cynics?!), but sensing and comparing is a skill that can and should be honed, and in the process, who knows what information will pop out? So, let's repeat from the top: run with narrow tracking and notice the movement of the pelvic floor as you 'hang onto your non-urgent wee'; keep running and let it go; then allow your feet to find their 'Goldilocks' tracking width, and search for the movement of your pelvic floor as you hang onto that wee again. Anything this time? *Really* focus internally. OK - that wee is really urgent now. Get anything that time? If you did, did you need to pull so hard you nearly halted in your tracks?

My experience with all the runners I've coached is the same every single time. Compared to narrow tracking, with 'Goldilocks in place', they can't feel as much movement of the pelvic floor when they try to hang onto their non-urgent wee ... *because it was already holding! The activity was already there!* Even when folk are too shy to admit to it, their faces tell me everything.

Anatomy Dog-Leg: The 'figure of 8' spiral of pelvic floor perineal musculature is already in place just 12 weeks after you were conceived (to give that contextual importance, you're about 5cm long - or the size of a lime at this stage - with no ears, tongue or external genitals), and continues to develop to support your uprightness and everything that comes with it: gravitational forces, pressures within the abdominal cavity, giving birth to large-brained babies. You get the feeling it's evolved with tensile strength in mind.

It seems to me that when walking and running along tightropes, the pelvic floor can go to sleep. As far as I can tell, reaffirmed by all those I've worked with, the balanced tracking width of legs falling from the outside of the pelvis, offering the frontal plane SPACE to enable the use of the entire breadth of each foot, gifts us a natural ability to hang onto our non-urgent wees - to fire up appropriate tension in the pelvic floor - effortlessly, as a normal function of human gait. *So walking and running more efficiently maintains muscle tone that should never be lost if efficient gait continues throughout life. We continue to hone and tone that which is already there. We use it, therefore we don't lose it.*

And did you notice the earlier reference to the Goldilocks tracking width and it enabling "the pelvis to move"? If bones move, soft stuff changes shape, right? If the pelvis moves freely as you walk and run, its 'bowl' is in constant motion; it tilts forward and back, hikes up and drops down, and it shifts and rotates to the right and left. In short, there is multi-directional stimulation to the nine muscles that converge and fuse with the central tendon of the perineum (the bit between your 'bits' at the base of your 'bowl'), forming a *substantial* pelvic floor. If the pelvis doesn't move (and have you noticed yet how many *don't?*), is it any wonder incontinence is considered an inevitable part of ageing ... apparently, from about the mid-forties? We have an amazing 'use it or lose it body'; so let's hear it for hearty bladder control.

*Find your **F**rontally **F**it **F**anny **F**loor through Efficient Running* (sorry - couldn't find anything unisex that began with an F!).

Anatomy Dog-Leg: endlessly deliberately contracting the pelvic floor, raises the abdominal compartmental pressure. Hernias form where perpetually raised pressures seek a release valve and find a weak spot. It's either that or a leak from a sphincter. No laughing matter ...

Oh, and did you salute that little spurt of speed that came with the 'Full Flush' of pelvic muscle action? Yup. If you ever feel tired, check in with your tracking width; had it shrunk? Find your sweet spot, let it re-engage your pelvic floor muscles, and you'll go faster for no more effort. Turns out, that sagging pelvic floor is another brake. Isn't that brilliant? We are sooooo brilliant!!

And finally, it's always good to feel progress, so let's have a bit of 'pennies from heaven' fun. Re-position your cones into a narrow corridor - allowing only the tracking width that you had originally, even if it was as close as 'running along a tightrope' - and run landing *between the cones*. Most - if not all - are amazed that they ever ran like that! And if that wee has become urgent through the course of the session, you'll be in trouble!

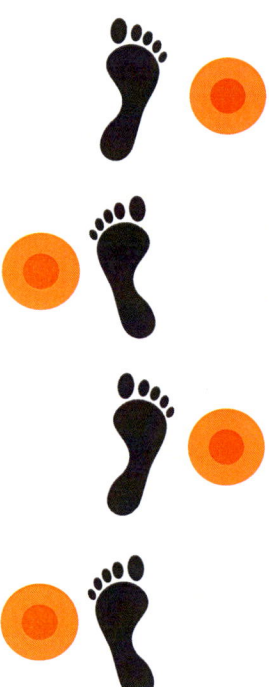

This session is a wonderful reminder that your body can instantly adopt 'better' if it's exposed to planes of motion in context, in safety and with reference to global biomechanics. And quite apart from the increased challenge of staying upright when you're flying through the air and landing on that tightrope on an itsy-bitsy bit of one foot ... did you notice how your pelvis seemed to stop moving when your feet came closer together? If not, try again and see what grabs your attention.

Back to that nemesis you identified right at the beginning of the session. Run up and down the 'drill area' one last time and feel whether today's earlier 'single most obvious negative' ... has changed ... and ...

... to that information, add your *current* 'nemesis' ... that aspect of your running form you're noticing right now, which needs your somatic awareness i.e. your personal 'homework'. Given this is Level Two, and it's all about elements of movement in the frontal plane, it's likely to be something about your foot position ... or it might even still be your head position! And it's probably taking the form of tension. Whatever it is, make sure you finish knowing it, so you can focus on *thoughts creating actions and actions wiring thoughts* to improve it.

The trot home should allow for a final 5 minute walking cool-down, and at both running and walking speeds the focus needs to continue to be on alignment in BOTH the sagittal plane (are your ankles, neck, shoulders relaxed and abs under a lovely 'viscera-containing' tension?) and frontal plane (is your weight shifting from right to left and back again? Do you have easy 'spring'? Are you tracking along a sweet-spot width, which now has unexpected added value?) ... not forgetting 'axial extension' through the thought process of 'head floating off neck'.

> **LEVEL TWO SUMMARY CHECK LIST ▲**

- ✔ You walk briskly to warm-up, adding the sagittal plane biomechanics from Level 1.
- ✔ You run for long enough to be fully warmed-up by the time you reach your venue, being mindful of all the principles from Level 1, staying alert to learning opportunities by observing other runners' form as they pass you.
- ✔ You revise Amazonian Meets Hunchback (bread and butter for modern man).
- ✔ You use 7 drills plus the verbal cues to find Frontal Plane efficiency and effectiveness i.e. the 'Goldilocks' tracking width that allows you to access the entire breadth of each foot, which in turn enables you to effortlessly shift body weight from one side to the other, with a natural spring to your step and much less danger of bladder-failure.
- ✔ You use drill-run-&-compare repetition to keep the focus on form, limit fatigue and avoid overusing newly awakened muscles!
- ✔ You finish the session aware of your particular form 'nemesis'; that aspect of your habitual motor programmes that needs special attention in order to gradually replace it with something more helpful; motor neurones that fire together, wire together. Patience and internal scanning over Time will work wonders.
- ✔ You walk to cool off - and can explain to your friends why!
- ✔ Your brain fires off a barrage of questions ... because you're still engaged.

Marvellous!

LEVEL TWO CLOCK-IN/ CLOCK OUT ▲

With two planes of joint rotations on your radar - and with a good number of drills to play with - you can now have some fun, combining them and exploring your body's responses. As ever, listen carefully to what your body is saying; don't 'try' or 'push', rather 'let' and 'challenge kindly'.

Keep hold of your 'reset button'. Regularly moving from a run into a walk gives you important information about how your alignment has held up and whether ranges of joint movement have changed in certain areas. Shifting into walking gear is not about waiting until you're tired; it's about taking control long before fatigue sets in. And I'm referring more to brain - rather than body - fatigue here; being able to maintain awareness of the form you *think* you have, and being able to compare it to what your body is *actually* up to. As your ability to accurately scan your body as you run improves, you'll naturally and gradually increase your 'running lengths' before shifting into walking gear to confirm your senses. At this stage, if I was running with you, the 'running lengths' would probably be no more than a few hundred metres. You might still be moving for an hour or so, just not continually running.

Combine your internal sensings with external visuals by observing other walkers and runners around you. Appreciate easy movement and when you see awkwardness, lumpiness or slow but effortful movement, consider 'why?' Ask yourself 'why' it seems so; you might even notice in others what you can feel but not see in yourself. Runner-watching - without judgement, only curiosity - can be such a great learning tool; it offers a framework for problem-solving simply by stimulating you to think about what you're noticing around you.

Remember our intention marker? This segment being about exploring the space between your feet and the benefits of weight shifting from left to right? Languishing around this level is a great idea. Play with it. Find creative ways to sense everything within it.

So many runners grasp one element of it quickly and then forget the other. The sweet spot of tracking width is the easy bit. Once found, the idea is to *use it* effectively; shifting your weight effortlessly from one lovely, relaxed, broad foot - having all five of its long bones and toes in contact with the insole of your shoe (or the ground!) - to the other. Put another way, to have a great tracking width - one that's Absolutely Right for you - but without weight shift, would be to akin to cross-country skiing (or 'langlauf'). For great tracking width with bonkers weight shift, just watch the very beginnings of the long jump run-up or as the sprinters first come out of the starting blocks; they need all the leverage from the elastic recoil of lengthened hip musculature they can if they're to 'wind up' their speed most productively.

Those are examples of the two ends of the scale; when volume of repetition is required, somewhere less 'end range' will serve you better. Easy, efficient running uses a Goldilocks tracking width in combination with a left to right weight shift without any obvious exaggeration, even if it feels like an excessive amount initially ... it only *feels* like 'more' in comparison to 'less than ideal'.

I'm a fan of anything that helps folk sense more. Props can work wonders to enhance awareness. For example, if you're walking or running with your dog off-lead, you can tie the lead around your waist with the metal clasp dropped like a pendulum between your legs (not too low - it hurts if it bangs your knees!). As you walk and run, you'll receive clear feedback on your weight shift: if you have none, the lead will most likely end up wedged between your legs driving you mad; if you have an asymmetrical weight shift, the lead will end up knocking the thigh of your dominant leg; if you have a balanced weight shift, and just the right length dangling from knot to clip, you'll find your lead bounces satisfyingly from one thigh to another. I suppose even then it could become irritating after a while ... but I have yet to feel anything other than quiet satisfaction. You don't *make* it *swing* (it's not 'keepie-uppie'!), it just swings with the easy rhythm of your shifting weight. The idea is similar to the swimming belt that has a small contraption housing a weight that slides to the downside of a pelvic rotation; it palpably 'tick-tocks' if each stroke creates an alternating pelvic see-saw.

Any body part can be used as an ever-present prop, offering clues as to what's happening above the ground. Elbows are versatile, can be used in a variety of ways, and seem to work well for many, being both close to the Sensing HQ (your head) and also within most runners' peripheral vision. Here's an idea to get you started. An imaginary light-beam, shining down from the underside of your bent elbow as you run, is more likely to form straight lines if you have no weight shift (the lines will be back and forth or crossways, dependent on whether your torso is counter-rotating or not), and *will* draw little circles if you do weight shift. Let your mind wander around your moving body parts and play with noticing both what the movements are when they feel good, and what those good movements feel like. Give what you find words; name what you feel and you'll be able to find it again.

CONNECT THE ACTION WITH THE THOUGHT WITH THE FEELING

If running efficiency starts in the sagittal plane, it finds freedom in the frontal plane ... 'f' is for 'fully fanned-feet fun'! Be thoughtful as you run, but avoid being over-critical; we're still on *principles* remember, so let your sensory awareness land on the 'big and obvious' rather than diving down the rabbit hole of finer detail ... that will come, it's just not appropriate at this stage.

Continue to embrace 'vertical' as often as you can whilst adding a tangible 'left & right' to your life. The more often you stack your bones and give them space to move *either side of centre*, the more your central nervous system will adopt it as default, via the neural changes that undoubtedly follow positive repetition.

... MAKING FRIENDS WITH YOUR MATE, SENSORY FEEDBACK ...

Now we're cooking ...

Before we turn the heat up, let's take one last look at why we're here.

Chris came to claim the Christmas present his wife had given him: a clinic session to look at improving running efficiency and to reduce injury risks as his training volume ramped up. With a long history of knee issues going back to childhood, 'lazy VMOs' and a surgical reconstruction of a partially torn left knee ligament which appeared to have no known mechanism of injury, the session was always going to be interesting and it didn't disappoint either of us. We had some joint restrictions to unravel of course, with his lower body determined to rotate left, whilst his torso seemed in charge of rotations to the right, but what was staggering was his tracking width. 8 centimetres. To offer some context, this lovely guy was 6 feet tall ... with just 8 centimetres between his feet as a base of support. He was 'leaking' running energy just trying to stay upright, and with no space to perform any function, the VMOs hadn't had a chance of developing to any helpful extent.

 Anatomy Dog-Leg: VMOs ... vastus medialis oblique; one of the four quadriceps muscles on the front of the thigh; the teardrop shaped muscle just above the knee on the inside, often highly developed in footballers' legs.

Chris was wonderfully enthusiastic and committed to do his part. Drills were performed, missing space in joints was generated, through mindful movements his 'sweet spot' tracking width was found and the clear 'left and right' it established was happily alternated via weight shift. In his words, old running habits were named "Thumper" following his new awareness of bouncy running and inner groin discomfort, and his new sense of self was dubbed "Poiser" as he felt poised, but quite self-aware with his "rotatey buttocks and dangly thighs"!

Four months later, he wrote:

Morning Helen, hope you're well,

Success! I completed the Milton Keynes Half this Bank holiday Monday and managed a 1:47! Very pleased with that, and I know there are at least an easy 2 minutes I can gain through consistent application of mindful running as my natural pace now is around 8.00 miles. I'm very, very pleased!

I have also started to figure out the pace of 5 k runs and took a further 1 minute off of my previous PB, now down to 21.20. With more application of the techniques you have shown me and more miles under the belt, I know I can achieve 1:45 and a sub 20 minute 5k this season.

The raw figures:
Half marathon - **Pre** – 1.58.59 **Post** - 1.47.26
5k - **Pre** – 24.00 **Post** – 21.25
10k - **Pre** – 50.12 **Post** – 47.00

The only injuries I have sustained in this period have been shin splits through walking with my son on my back in a rucksack in formal shoes! I can say without a doubt that the sessions with you have been the best investment I have made in any of the triathlon disciplines and will certainly be back for some running coaching in the near future.

All the best

Chris

"THE SECRET OF CHANGE IS TO FOCUS ALL OF YOUR ENERGY, NOT ON FIGHTING THE OLD, BUT ON BUILDING THE NEW." **- SOCRATES**

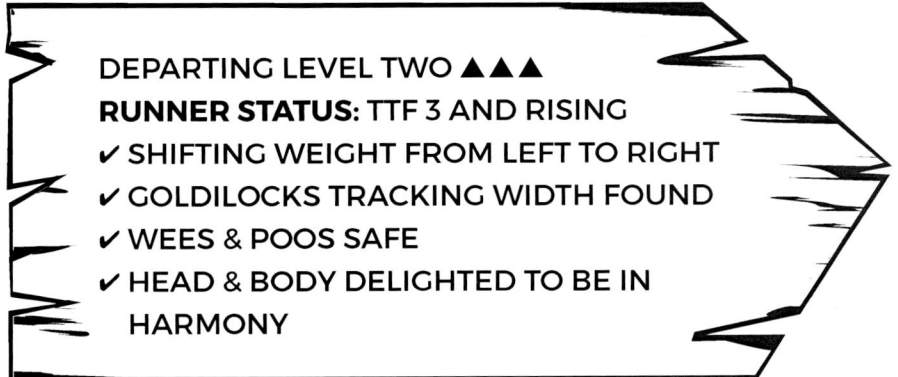

LEVEL THREE
OH, *THAT* PELVIS!

LEVEL THREE CONTENTS

Picking up *The Lemni*	151
Checkpoint Three	153
Oiling the running machine	155
Hills ... from behind!	161
Hills with ease via stiles	167
Checkpoint Three Noticeboards:	
Checkpoint Three Summary	173
Leaving Level Three	174

PRINCIPLE 3: HILLS... FROM BEHIND!
(YOU'LL LOVE THEM WHEN YOU RUN THEM EFFICIENTLY)

The next section of the trail takes a distinct upward turn, which means there must be hard work looming ... or does it?

A BIG WARM WELCOME to HILLS! Don't be nervous - so many of you tell me you dread hills and hate them with a vengeance. But if you do, you've almost certainly been running them inefficiently and ineffectively, making them either unpleasantly hard and/or painful!

Time to change that ...

 Whilst firming down ground already covered, this segment is where you'll appreciate the power you carry everywhere; it's behind you ...

I love watching runners build their stable, monumental foundations as they pass along Level One of the trail; the recognition that, simply by tuning into their head position, so much of their tension could be dispelled, is always wonderful to watch. I'm particularly partial to following their steps along the second level, especially when novel 'full loading' of the soles of feet generates an easy, effortless, spring recoil-effect that never ceases to induce happy faces. I *adore* the time spent playing at the third level:

DISRUPTING ALL PRECONCEPTIONS REGARDING HILL RUNNING?
MY FORTE.

SHIFTING MINDSETS AS FOLK DISCOVER HOW EASY IT IS TO RUN HILLS WHEN THEY USE THEIR BODIES EFFECTIVELY?
BRING IT ON.

And my party-piece ...

Here's where we pick up my invention, the runners' magic wand, your real-life running spanner which helps fix just about everything and in my opinion, is the only external piece of running kit that actually adds value to your running form. Let's hear it for...

PICKING UP THE LEMNI

The Lemni is your secret to Perpetual Forward Motion, your personal efficient running coaching tool, your portable soft tissue massager should you need it to be, *and* quadruples as your 'anti-evil cow' protector. Tested in the field, it came in very handy for me on my first 50 miler - those scary white cows (they looked like ghosts in the dark) didn't dare come near me with my *Lemni* shielding me from the stampede I could see they were planning. Its potential is only limited by your creativity, as Mat discovered whilst in training for his challenge to run across the breadth of the UK: *"I've been out with the Lemni each day which is great for form and also very helpful for reaching blackberries :)"*

It may look like a chair spindle to you, or even a tai chi ruler if you're a CHEK practitioner, but it's neither. It's simply genius taking the form of light, unvarnished, warm wood of a particular shape and length. I thank Paul Chek for introducing me to its cousin, I take some credit for its contextual transformation, and give the rest to Gary Ward who held it in his hands as I stood watching; I was on the edge of a biomechanical

abyss, thinking I'd got it all completely wrong, when he shrugged his shoulders, rotated it as a figure of 8, and pronounced "Yup, that'll work". I will never forget that moment. Thanks Gary.

Cup each end into your palm, closing your fingers around the end without gripping, and with your elbows bent so that the centre of The *Lemni* hovers just below the base of the sternum (your central breastbone); now roll your shoulders alternately as if you're shrugging a light pack-strap into place and watch its 'lemniscate' (a figure-eight shaped curve) action.

Doesn't this remind you of the 'stick your feet on the outside of your pelvis and run from there' movement?

... like your pelvis is a figure of 8 on its side
... the sign of infinity ... the PFM logo

from the last session? This innocuous little tool has transformed runners. Not just their form, but their ability to hold form for more miles than anyone thought possible. Great movement patterns feed themselves energy. You can be your own Newton's Cradle - all you need is know-how and your own self-oiled *Lemni*.

"I've found the boxing thoughts really good for keeping my hands going and getting the shoulders moving.

If I keep my hands rolling like Muhammad Ali, then I'll float like a butterfly on my trot from St Bees! Sorry, I like cheese :)

Yours sassily,

Mat"

Checkpoint 3 is in sight …

▲ ▲ ▲

CHECKPOINT THREE
NOTICEBOARD

TERRAIN: FENCE OR WALL AND A SLOPE
RUNNER STATUS: TTF 5 - THOROUGHLY WARMED-UP
KIT LIST: LAYERS, COMFORTABLE FOOTWEAR

The next section of the trail towards running efficiency - the third level of the pyramid - is guaranteed to animate both me as well as the runner, or group of runners, I'm working with. BUT. Please. Rein understandable enthusiasm in, and replace with a good old-fashioned dose of common sense. You'll be running up the hill now, which is much more of a challenge to the smaller muscles of the lower legs than walking an incline.

It's not that running hills efficiently is injurious. Of course not. But running hills efficiently beyond the existing soft tissue tolerance certainly is. So employ some patience, be kind to your lower leg compartments and wait until they've developed some resilience and pliability through great movement patterns over a couple of months. Yes, months. Not my rules. Speak to Nature - she's in charge (remember the three 'reminders' in bold on pages 60 & 61?). If you've been repetitively injured below the knee, the inflamed tissue needs healing *time* to catch up with everything surrounding it. Not feeling the discomfort any more because you're not stressing it in the same way is NOT the same as it being healed. ***Changing symptoms does not equate to 'healed'.*** And when you are ready, take your first jaunt along Level 3 gently. Better to do less the first time, and be able to return to it a few days later, than do too much in one go and risk your calves growling at you for being over-zealous.

The boundary between soft tissue being relaxed about the work-load and being decidedly put out, is unique to each person. You can't hurry soft-tissue endurance along - that control is in the domain of the cellular and repair systems - but you *can* control 'you'. Calves, Achilles tendons, ankle ligaments and feet muscles are NOT soft-hearted. After all, they're the small ones doing more of the bodyweight + gravity + impact work with each step, compared to the big, propulsive muscles. Proportionately, they are MIGHTY - when you use them fairly. A bit of consideration goes a long way. Just saying.

So in terms of your personal status, take a Paddington 'hard stare' at your Tissue Tolerance Factor. Perhaps you haven't got injury history to consider, but instead you've been enjoying transitioning to the 'sweet spot' as your first contact, or you've been kicking the 'Prancy-Pony' habit? Or maybe you've chucked your high-heeled trainers in the bin for something 'less' (following the guidelines in the Appendix, of course)? If so, please delay progressing onto this level until you've had another couple of weeks running without noticing your calves 'talking to you' at *all*, especially when you get out of bed in the morning.

All this carefully-phrased, hand-holding, attentiveness is my way of saying I'd put a TTF of at least 5 on this one, meaning you notice any previous restriction only towards an hour of running, with any pain now being rare. You don't want to over-cook things just when they're about to get really interesting ...

 TTF 5 You notice the restriction only towards an hour of running; pain is now rare and it's only a memory on rising.

Trail conditions at this level take you from a flattish warm-up area to a nearby slope to perform the hill drills; the same 40-50 metre slope you used for the first level will be perfect for this, or a section of a longer hill. And layers are more important than ever today! We continue with 'Before & After' games, and with the work between the drills being more intense, the chances of chilling off *during* the drills is greater, so wear easily-adjustable layers to be sure your working muscles are kept warmed and ever-ready.

OILING THE RUNNING MACHINE

Let's get going ... for the ubiquitous 10 minute walking warm-up! Is this your new best running habit yet? Given I ask people on a daily basis how much they walk, and the average responses I get range from 'not much' to 'hardly any', I've got a strong sense that folk don't walk *enough* these days.

If you *have* been walking before you run, how many differences have you noticed *when* you run? Here's the spiel again - you'll know this off-by-heart very soon, and because it's important I'm happy to repeat until you do. You're lubricating your joints by mobilising them in a weight-bearing gait pattern, and diverting blood from your non-vital organs, the glands producing hormones and the digestive system to your working muscles. And whilst you're at it, you're sorting out plumb-lines to effect great dynamic alignment. You now have four of them if you enjoyed employing them: one descending from each cheekbone to the pubic bone and one from each outer hip to the same side outer ankle bone, together gifting active abs, active lateral glutes (most sense this where the hamstrings meet the bottom of the outside butt cheeks), relaxed ankles, relaxed toes and relaxed neck and shoulders ... do you still feel 'odd' here?

If you're still resisting because it feels odd, visual comparisons always help; get a mate to film you moving or give yourself permission to be vain and clock yourself moving (walking or running) in a big reflective surface like a shop window. Honestly, it's NEVER looked like it seems to feel in the early stages of change, and once you realise you *don't* look 'as if you own the place', the willingness to relax with it and adopt it is almost always immediate. Because it's *natural*.

Having arrived at your venue, you should be more-or-less upright. I can't state this often enough - in my experience ***Efficiency Begins With Upright!*** Until 'heads are on better', energy will almost certainly be wasted - even just through the muscular tension hanging onto said head sitting forward of where it could. The more you practise *Amazonian Meets Hunchback,* the more it will flow as it becomes familiar to both your body and your brain; it was already wired into your system ... you're simply reconnecting it.

With *Progress not Perfection* in mind, let's use that wall you find yourself next to and get your bum and mid-back against it; can your head touch yet without your neck having to extend, forcing your gaze upward? We'll cue the movement using different words once again:

Sagittal Cog Against The Wall:
Amazonian Meets Hunchback: Take 3 - Top To Toe:
vimeo.com/244977015

- Head, mid-back and bum against a wall.

- Is your head still tilting backwards to reach the wall? Feeling the contact point of your skull slide downwards towards your hairline, let the weight of your head slowly relax forward until the back of the neck is lengthened. Stay there for just a few seconds. Return to the start position. Can your head now rest against the wall with less backwards tilt?

- Now slip your head backwards so your contact point moves towards the crown of your head, then slide it fully forwards again, moving the contact point back down towards your hairline.

- Slowly repeat the exaggerated nodding movement maintaining contact between the wall and your head throughout, allowing whatever movement wants to happen in your ribcage, happen. Are you noticing yet that with the backwards tilt of the head and short back-of-neck comes a sunken chest; and with the forwards tilt of the head and long back-of-neck comes a lifted chest?

- Next, deliberately lift the chest and then cave it. Notice that a lifted chest tips the top of the ribcage backwards, and the bottom of the ribcage forwards. On the flip-side, a caved chest is synonymous with the top of the ribcage tipping forward and the bottom of the ribcage tipping backwards.

- Repeat, and notice that with the lifted chest comes the forward tilt of the head AND shoulder blades moving towards the spine (retraction); conversely, with the caved chest comes a backwards tilt of the head and shoulder blades moving away from the spine (protraction).

- Next stop, the arms: turn your arms inwards - driving the movement through your thumbs - and then twist your arms outwards.

- Repeat, and notice that with the inward rotation comes the caving chest, the protracting shoulder blades and the tilting backwards head; with the outward rotation of the arm, comes the lifting chest, the retracting shoulder blades and the dropping chin as your head tilts forwards.

- Moving down, deliberately arch your lower back - think about the lower back curve leaning towards your belly button (pelvis tilts forward, bum untucks), then flatten that same arch as you send your belly button back towards the wall (pelvis tilts backwards, bum tucks).

- Repeat, and notice that with the arched lower back comes the forward tilting pelvis, lifting chest, retracting shoulder blades and dropping chin; with the flattened lower back comes the pelvis tilting backward, the chest sinking, protracting shoulder blades and lifting chin.

- Do that again and take the movement a little further, or a little slower - dig deep into your somatic awareness. Did you notice this time that when you arched your back, your pubic bone dropped down (or your tail bone lifted) and your thigh bone rotated inwards a little? And when you flattened your lower back, your tail bone dropped down (or your pubic bone lifted) and your thigh bones rotated outwards?

- Bring all that together and notice that with the arching of your lower back comes a lifting chest, retracting shoulder blades, externally rotating arms, a dropping chin AND internally rotating legs with the forward tilting pelvis.

- Then, the tucking under of the bum and backward tilting pelvis brings a sunken chest, protracting shoulder blades, internally rotating arms, a tilting back of the head and externally rotating legs.

- Bring more attention to your legs; from the hip joint, deliberately internally rotate them and then externally rotate them.

- Repeat, and notice that with the internal rotation of your legs comes an awareness of the inside of your heels and with the external rotation of your legs comes an awareness of the outside of your heels.

- The dropping of your chin is co-operatively married to:
  - The tilting forward of your head.
  - The lifting of your chest.
  - The tilting backwards of the top of the ribcage.
  - The retraction of your shoulder blades.
  - The external rotation of your arms.
  - The arching of your lower back.
  - The tipping forward of your pelvis.
  - The internal rotation of your legs.
  - Pronation of your feet.

- The lifting of your chin is harmonious with:
  - The tilting backwards of your head.
  - The sinking of your chest.
  - The tilting forwards of the top of the ribcage.
  - The protraction of your shoulder blades.
  - The internal rotation of your arms.
  - The flattening of your lower back.
  - The tipping backwards of your pelvis.
  - The external rotation of your legs.
  - Supination of your feet.

Have you noticed that whatever your head is doing, so is your pelvis? And that whatever *they* are up to, the ribcage in between is doing the opposite? Isn't that cool?

As you notice more and more within your own body, it might occur to you that I could have described the connections happening through calculable joint mechanics, the *4* Fs:

FLUID, FLUENT & <u>FORTUNATELY</u> FORCASTABLE!

You've been warming your body into great movement patterns. You've diverted the blood to the about-to-be-running muscles. You've set yourself up for success, now let's get running.

The key to a great hill-drills session is being thoroughly 'running warm' before you add any intensity. You need a good 20 minutes or so of relaxed trotting on flat, unchallenging ground. Relax and get into your now-familiar, upright and mobile running form.

Maybe you're doing a couple of 'blocks' around your wall prop. Folk learn very easily when they feel *differences*. So after a good 10 minutes or so, you could introduce a 'stile' and have a brief drill-stop to revisit the frontal plane … with **Frontal Cog: I'm a Little Teapot: vimeo.com/244972923**

- Feet under hips, toes facing front (or as close to 'forward' as your body allows with reasonable comfort; we don't want to incur pain, but performing a drill to create joint space with your feet turned out like Charlie Chaplin, isn't going to help its potential productivity).
- Allow the weight of a hanging arm to side-bend your body.
- Breathe into the opposite ribs (a hand can rest here for enhanced 'sensing') and allow your body to side bend further.
- Ease your bodyweight laterally, so your outer hip is now outside the base of support.
- Your dangling arm can now extend along the wall in the opposite direction to the travelling hip.
- Pressure will be on the outside of your weighted heel, the inside of your non-weighted heel, but maintained across the breadth of each foot (read: focus to keep both the balls of each foot and the base of the little toe in contact with the ground).
- Head stays upright, with nose vertical.
- Repeat a few times to each side.

By running again, and comparing form 'before and after', you'll continue to learn *somatically*, sensing and absorbing any benefits you notice.

Add the 'wake-up' of feet in the sagittal plane with slow 'ink-blotter' rocks from the heel to toes and back, really feeling for the squish of the sole-flesh as the bones move to accommodate the bodyweight pressing down onto them. Don't forget to notice your ankles; they should be changing shape in the sagittal plane too - opening as you tip onto your toes and closing as you spread your body load from the heels to the balls of the feet. Finally, open your feet in the frontal plane with a side-edge to side-edge mobilisation action. If your shoes aren't too restrictive, you can even keep them on!

HILLS ... FROM BEHIND!

And so to the hill! There's *always* a lot of cueing, revision and preparation before actually getting to the meat of your session ...

Start at the bottom of the hill you're going to be using for your drills, and walk to the top, with the challenge being to use your lower legs as *little as possible* ... use 𝑇ℎ𝑒 𝐿𝑒𝑚𝑛𝑖 to connect your hands, and see if you can 'let your body roll'; the sense is of your shoulders rolling in synchronicity with your pelvis ... with your calves staying (probably remarkably - as in - noticeably) relaxed.

From the top of the slope, we start our 10 descents and 10 ascents. To be practical and give everything clarity, the substance of the session needs to be listed. Please forgive the headings and bullet points.

Descent 1: trot down, controlling the hill just as you did at Level One. Every descent will be the same as this, so by the end you should be able to sense everything in the list below:

- Vertical - just as you have been since the middle of the first session.

- With your 'Goldilocks' tracking width! It was always there - also from the first session - but we were busy sensing 'side view' balance then. I have never, EVER, come across a downhill tightrope runner. Self-preservation wins every time.

- With hands connected, now you could add, 'with feet under hands' which often helps cement new tracking widths.

- With abs firing... are pennies falling from the sky as you realise how busy your abs can and perhaps *should* be when your arms aren't free to fly all over the place to maintain running balance?

Oh how we love 𝑇ℎ𝑒 (Magical) 𝐿𝑒𝑚𝑛𝑖 for effortlessly sorting out wild, non-balanced running form! It is the epitome of efficient self-coaching!

Ascent 1: The Control.
With the goal being to gather sensory information to be able to compare 'before & after', the first uphill is a simple trot up at a comfortable effort level, with *The Lemni* held in one hand (or in a pocket); you're running the incline as you would habitually, focusing on identifying where you can feel the effort. Did you lean into the hill, feeling the work in, or just above, your knees? Did you notice yourself push with your toes? Were your calves busy? Was everything moving? Was anything still? Get good at noticing by being *curious rather than critical* ...

Descent 2:
The Lemni is back between your palms. Over the next nine descents, consider the following and see how many you notice:

- If the ground is falling away, unless the pelvis moves, the landing seems to jar more.
- The hip drops as the (relaxed) lead foot heads down slope, which of course must lift the other side of the pelvis. On downhills, the most common 'sense' is that of the up-swing side of the pelvis as the movement squeezes the 'love handles'.
- The pelvis 'see-saws'; as one side hikes up, the other side drops down.
- With the body remaining a plumb-line to the world, the pelvis can only see-saw (hike/drop) so far.
- Too long a stride takes the foot lower down the slope, further than the pelvis can tilt, risking a more impactful landing.
- Controlling the speed of the descent and keeping landings non-jarring, seems to shorten the stride and increase the cadence (steps per minute). Put another way, if momentum (read: speed) is to be maintained, a shorter stride will generate a higher cadence.
- It's actually really hard to land on your heel if you want to run smoothly, maintain a downhill speed, reduce impact and stay relaxed.
- The 'core' muscles appear more noticeable. The obliques have no choice but to be active when the pelvis is in motion; they attach to the pelvis so if the pelvis is moving, they're awake!

You don't need to try to feel this all on Descent 2. You have 8 more in this session alone, so just enjoy the process and whatever you notice is a great beginning.

Ascent 2:

Another trot up, this time with hands connected by *The Lemni*. Remember to curl your fingers without gripping. The ends nestle securely in each palm, and if you shake like a maraca, *The Lemni* should 'rattle' in your 'caged' fingers. What did you notice? It might be one or more of these:

- Did you find yourself 'dishing' or 'arcing' your feet around instead of slicing a straight swing through the air? This tends to result from a forward lean, which limits pelvic movement and can drive a knee inwards.
- Did you grip *The Lemni* causing your neck to disappear as your shoulders crept towards your ears, blocking the upper body counter-rotation?
- Did you get bowled over by the noticeable 'ab work' that tends to increase when your hands are unable to flail around?
- Or maybe you simply noticed *different stuff?* Differences are more appreciable because *The Lemni* becomes a mechanism of instant biofeedback, and on the first ascent with this tool, that's all you want ... to notice that which you might have been previously inured to.

Descent 3-10:

Same again, and again, and again!

Repetition: Like a chorus, it breeds familiarity; familiarity develops more relaxation; a relaxed body yields both more information and more movement; more information creates neuronal connections; more movement delivers more soft tissue conditioning ... and you've got gravity's help.

It's just a wonderful win-win scenario - enjoy yourself!

Ascent 3:
Efficiency against gravity begins ... with the sensory awareness generated by processing thoughts of *"Upright!"*

You can either use the imaginary plumb-lines from cheekbones to pubic bone here, or use the upright running posture you'll have towards the end of your last descent; turn around at the bottom without changing the angle of your torso on top of your pelvis, aka, you *remain upright as you go back up the hill ... what do you notice?* More glute action? Leading to ... less knee stress, perhaps?

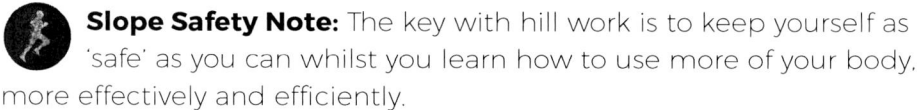

Slope Safety Note: The key with hill work is to keep yourself as 'safe' as you can whilst you learn how to use more of your body, more effectively and efficiently.

As you run up a hill, after touchdown 'somewhere in front of your heel', your heel descends with the force of your bodyweight plus gravity, because you're not actively holding it off the ground (which would seriously stress your calves and probably hurt your feet too). If the slope is shallow, your heel will 'kiss' the ground briefly before your travelling-forward body peels it back off again for the next swing through. If the slope is steep enough, there comes a point on that incline where the heel doesn't make it to the ground - it will have descended but the travelling body pulled it into the swing phase before it touched down. In this case, if the descending heel had touched the ground, the calf will have overstretched.

From now on, make it a point of 'good form' to notice whenever your heel no longer makes ground contact on any ascent. You should become instinctively aware of when it's appropriate (and therefore safe) for a heel to touch down, and when it isn't.

Ascent 4:

 Remembering our intention marker of discovering the power you carry everywhere ... behind you ...

Using gravity to help you defy gravity - yes, you did read that correctly. I'm excited already!

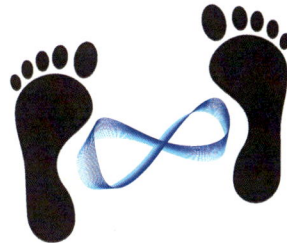

As you run up the hill, *'drop your pelvis into the step'* by imagining your feet are stuck to the outside edges of it. Put another way, stick your feet onto the outside edges of your pelvis and run from there. (Yes, it's the same, but some folk respond better to the former, and some to the latter. Not sure why. It'll be some fabulous brain-thing - I'm sure one of you reading this will know).

On the uphill, we tend to notice more the <u>down</u>-swing of the pelvis on the side making ground contact. Remember that on the downhill, we tend to notice more the up-swing of the pelvis. Essentially, it appears we're more aware of the side that's in contact with the ground, rather than the swing leg side, which makes sense as contact offers tactile feedback.

Get a few strides under your belt whilst noticing the pelvis' drop as you roll over the foot that's on the floor, and then **add a gentle 'nudge' of the pelvis in a downward direction** - *yes, that'll be in the same direction as gravity.*

It really is that easy to get a 'shove up the *Hills ... From Behind'*. Be sure you let your body respond to the changing input of a little downward nudge of each hip ... it knows what to do, and you need do nothing more than allow it to happen and not get in the way. Hint: don't restrict the stride length! Don't make anything happen. Just *'Let Your Body Run You'* up that hill.

Ah, the joys of uphill when you use your body cleverly! It's not easy to find the words that properly describe the towering waves of disbelief I see *every time a runner feels this for the first time*. It really is the head-holding, eyes-popping, jaw-dropping look of "What Just Happened? Did I Just Do That? How the? Whoa!! W.O.W." Closely followed by delight as they instantly recalibrate their mindset on hill work. Makes me want to get off my writing backside and go and play ...

Ascent 5:
"2 points of contact, trail leg ..."

Literally grounded in 'if you think it, you'll have it'.

'Think' *Base of Big Toe to Base of Little Toe Contact, Trail Leg*. Don't 'do it', just 'think it'. Less is more ...

In time, you might make the connection to 'poo on your shoe'; the two points of contact in the forefoot should create the same heel inversion you felt when you turned your knee out to view your sole from the big toe side. Ground contact from the 1st to the 5th metatarsal heads is required for optimum foot supination and the most effective forward propulsion.

The full breadth of foot contact at 'push-off' created by the thought of ground contact all the way from the base of the big toe to the base of the little toe, drives an external rotation up the leg to the pelvis. Lose the external rotation and you lose the base of the little toe. Lose the base of the pinkie and you lose the external rotation. One without the other is like coffee without butter ... soooo disappointing and simply doesn't hit the spot. Remembering the little things is what makes all the difference.

When added to the 'nudge' down of the pelvis *with* gravity and coupled to the rear leg position in extension, this external rotation adds full 3D eccentric loading through the hip flexor. This 'stretch under load' precedes the elastic recoil which creates the next stride - with very little energy cost attached to it.

A 'swing leg' is only that if it's breezing through the air under its own steam ... and it only gets to do that effortlessly with *"2 points of contact, trail leg"* ...

HILLS WITH EASE VIA 'STILES'

Ascents 6-10 are all performed following a **3D Glute Load drill**.

Let's wake up every inch of the glutes with the extraordinary power of full 3D eccentric loading, which some of us at PFM HQ like to refer to as *strorquing*: 'stretch + torque'.

> The drills come from Anatomy in Motion, and credit for the made-up-word (quite 'portmanteau-esque' I thought) goes to Bryn Green, my first of two, wonderful, apprentice 'Grasshopper' coaches; Bryn and Pip Haylett put their trust in me, honed their skills as they followed the map-book of the full Pyramid not once, but twice under my watchful eye, patiently keeping step with me as I repeatedly refined and groomed the trail ... and have since out-run me on numerous occasions. I couldn't be prouder.

A 3D eccentric load (strorque) on a muscle is a lengthening under load in all three of the directions it can move in; as opposed to the more common 'stretching' actions, which tend to pull along a linear path of muscle or muscle fibres.

According to many bodyworkers, the glutes are public enemy number one in terms of being 'sleepy' - and as you now know, it's pretty hard to use them comprehensively if the pelvis doesn't move. As you'll discover very shortly, it's also pretty hard to wake them up if you don't allow pronation of your foot and gain access to your big toe.

When glutes shorten, they extend your leg backwards, abduct your leg pulling it away from the midline, and externally rotate your leg turning it outwards. So to achieve the 3D stretch-under-load needed for them to elastically recoil into an almost *free* propulsive contraction, you need to do the opposite; you need to flex at the hip, adduct your thigh bone towards the midline and internally rotate it.

In this first hill running session, I offer three different 3D drills. You don't have to use them all, and it's perfectly acceptable to focus on one, and return to the others at a later date. There are no rules; be directed by how you feel you initially grasp each movement.

Ascents 6 & 7:
3D Glute Load #1: "Please pass on my lunging side"
vimeo.com/244973290

- With feet hip distance apart, step one foot forward up the slope into a split stance (you can see we used a step for James and Karen, given we were in the studio).

- Load your front foot by pushing your weight forward from behind, and then flexing (bending) your ankle, knee and hip joints. This puts you into a classic static lunge position.

- Heavy pubic bone - or light tail-bone - tips your pelvis forward (bum sticks out).

- Now where is that bent knee? Looking down from your 'bird's eye vantage point', is it hovering over *the inside edge of your big toe*?

- If it's where I think it is, and you've directed it over your second toe - or towards the outside of your foot - then you're going to struggle to make ground contact with the base and pad of your big toe. You might also have a nasty over-stretch through your calf and Achilles tendon; if your knee tracks straight or outwards, the foot remains supinated and the heel bone stays tipped back, pulling the Achilles insertion down with it. This needs immediate attention.

- Let's go through a checklist:
  - You're bent at the hip? Tick: hip flexed.
  - Now, on the same side as your flexed, front leg, lift a straight arm to shoulder height and rotate it backwards.
  - This rotates your body towards your front leg, adducting the thigh bone and gifting a great big glute load. Feel it? Tick: thigh adducted.

- Finally, give yourself 2 points of ground contact in your rear forefoot - base of big toe and base of little toe in your back foot want to join in the fun. Did you feel what just happened? Accessing the full breadth of your forefoot dragged the pelvis towards it and away from the front leg. That final adjustment added the rotational element, putting the weight firmly through the inside of the front heel bone and through the front big toe. Check you've still got ground contact with the base of your little toe. Front foot is now pronated. You don't force the knee inward, you simply let it travel with the pelvis travelling away. Tick - thigh bone internally rotated.
- You should now feel your glutes working even harder.
- As you get familiar with this, really let the front foot 'splat'. Let all the tension go in the sole of your foot and allow your bodyweight to 'collapse' through your bending hip, knee and ankle to access full load through the entire sole of your pronated foot. From your bird's eye view above your foot, the outside of your knee joint now probably lines up just inside your big toe and your loaded lower calf is comfortable. Sweet.

● Check you're not over-stretching your rear calf; if your body has travelled forward your rear heel should be lifted, with only the breadth of your forefoot pushing into the ground. Only the front heel should be in contact with the ground during the 'work' part of the drill.

- Keeping your front foot where it is, straighten the front leg to push yourself back and redistribute your weight evenly between both heels to rest.
- Repeat no more than a handful of times, each time travelling slowly as you reach the limits of each joint rotation. Challenge strongly but kindly.
- Now load the other glute a few times.

Directly after the "Please pass on my lunging side" drill, run the hill using all the cues you've developed through Ascents 2-5; upright, with *The Lemni*, nudging the pelvis down and thinking about two points of contact in the trail leg. What did you notice? **Did an enormous invisible hand grab your backside and shove you up the hill without you having to do much?** Welcome to the PFM world of hill *fun*!

Repeat the same drill to each glute, and run the hill again provided you don't yet feel fatigued; what did you notice this time? Even bigger invisible hands helping you? Each hill repetition can feel different - more powerful or easier - compared to the previous, through the increasing activity of the roused glutes. If you notice fatigue after 7 ascents, consider it a triumph and start heading home.

Ascents 8 & 9: 3D Glute Load #2: "I'm lunging, but I really want to be a ballerina" *vimeo.com/245611058*

- Split stance once again, lead leg up the slope.

- Load the front foot by 'splatting' the sole, folding at the ankle, knee and hip with a forward-tilting pelvis (bum out).
- Just the same as before, your lead foot is pronated (pressure across the whole breadth of the forefoot and the inside of heel), your knee travels slightly inwards and your rear foot has 2 points of contact, base of big toe and base of little toe.
- You're going to adduct the hip differently this time by easing your pelvis sideways (lateral pelvis shift) towards the bent front leg; this also adds more load to the piriformis muscle (an external hip rotator) so it can feel a bit more intense, especially for those who tend to turn their feet out.
- Raise the same side arm up and arc it overhead to generate torso side bend to add to your pelvic shift; this will give you an even bigger glute load.
- In full 'ballerina-mode', repeat just a few times and then swap legs.

Run the hill again, practising letting *The Lemni* roll, the pelvis drop with gravity and thinking about your '2 points of contact, trail leg', not forgetting your bread and butter for forward propulsion: uprightness! If you preferred glute load #1 to drill #2, and still have some energy left, repeat the first before Ascent 9. There are so many ways to open your body - experiment and use the ones you feel give you most benefit.

Ascent 10 - The Finale:
3D Glute Load #3: "I can't reach; my feet are stuck" *vimeo.com/245611832*

Your split stance lunge position might be feeling nicely familiar now, but let's go through it once more to be sure:

- Lead leg up the slope, adding more flexion in knee and hip than on flat ground - bigger glute load right there!
- Further flex, adduct and internally rotate the thigh bone in the hip socket with the help of a lovely splatting, pronating front foot; a pelvis rotated away from the pronating foot enables both base of big toe and base of little toe of the supinating rear foot to remain in ground contact.
- Your bum sticks out gently as your pelvis tips forward.
- In position for the finale ...
- Now add more hip flexion by reaching forward with both arms into the space in front of you. Remember to peel the rear heel off the ground so you don't limit the potential of this peachy drill (couldn't resist!).
- As you move forward and back, in and out of this huge glute load, you can drive your arms both forward AND down to find as much load as you want. You don't need to push it to find it - it'll be right there!
- Swap lead legs and repeat to the other side.

You might have reached tissue tolerance by Ascent 6 or 7, but if you're still in the game, repeat the hill one last time. This last, and fabulous drill is the one that shoots folk up the hill when they know they'd normally be really tired. When you try it, if you weren't amazed, you probably didn't collapse your lead foot, ankle, knee, hip enough and instead focused on the reach forward. Get the glute load going with the basics and *then* add MORE with the reach. I'd be surprised if you're not *astounded* with your body's reaction.

Once back at the top of the hill, it'll be time to head home. After all the work against gravity, and the focus on the joint rotations of your feet, ankles, knees and hips, the run home on the flat will probably feel easier than you'd expect given the work you've just done. Enjoy all the new space you have to move in, and don't forget to brake into a cool-down walk at least 5 minutes away from your destination.

LEVEL THREE SUMMARY CHECK LIST ▲

Working your way through a session at Level 3, often takes a bit longer than the first two levels of the pyramid. Sessions at the first two foundational levels can be accomplished nicely within 45 minutes to an hour, whilst you need around 75 minutes for a level 3 session. It generally looks like this:

- A 10 minute walking warm-up.
- A 20 minute warm-up run where lots of sagittal and frontal plane practising can happen (upright + weight shift).
- 30-35 minutes of up to 10 hill repeats, including breaks to perform the 3D drills.
- 5-10 minutes trotting into easy walk to cool-down.
- **Ascent 1:** the control 'status quo'.
- **Ascent 2:** add *The Lemni* cupped in relaxed hands. Upper body is relaxed and detrimental arm movements subdued.
- **Ascent 3:** to *The Lemni* and relaxed hands, add plumb line cheekbone to pubic bone. Gifts upright and less or no work around knees.
- **Ascent 4:** to *The Lemni* relaxed hands and plumb lines, add 'feet on outside of pelvis' gently nudging foot/pelvis down with gravity. Wakes up glutes and feels as if you're being pushed up the hill from behind.
- **Ascent 5:** to *The Lemni* relaxed hands, plumb lines and nudging pelvis down with gravity, add 2 points of contact in trail leg. Adds pelvis rotation to pelvis drop offering more glute activity with the addition of eccentric loading of hip flexors for an improved swing phase.
- **Ascent 6 & 7:** precede with **Please Pass On My Lunging Side** and repeat with the accumulated form thoughts of Ascent 5.
- **Ascent 8 & 9:** precede with **I'm Lunging, But I Really Want To Be A Ballerina** and repeat with the accumulated form thoughts of Ascent 5.
- **Ascent 10:** precede with **I Can't Reach, My Feet Are Stuck** and enjoy the magic!

▲▲▲

Many come to Level 3 of the pyramid believing that the only use for hills is intensive work (and pain). Few realise how easy it is to use slopes to discover the effective action of your pelvis: forwards and backwards, rotation right and left, hiking up and dropping down ... together creating the figure of 8 on its side ... the sign of infinity ... a "wibbly-wobbly-on-its-hinges-see-saw" ... the PFM logo ...

Efficient running is all about **letting the pelvis roll** ... *by allowing the huge bones of the pelvis its DNA-driven motor programmes, you automatically access full co-operation of every muscle attached to it ... quadriceps, hammies, lateral hip muscles, adductors, pelvic floor* ... **AND GLUTES!!!!!**

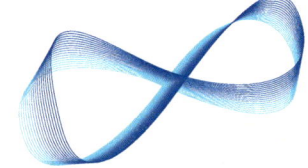

By the end of your first romp through the third level of the pyramid, you will probably have nailed Vertical - that which gifts you effortless alignment and ever-present abs - established beyond doubt your Tracking Width - that which provides weight shift and access to the full breadth of each foot - and have truly found your Pelvis!!! Yes - *that* pelvis!!! You should know enough about the Sagittal Cog and the Frontal Cog as helpful joint rotation tools to be able to give them a go whenever you want, and feel comfortable with at least one of the Glute 3D Eccentric Loadings in your toolbox so that you can play with it on your next hill lesson.

Perhaps you're already feeling more confident that this 'bigger' body movement you're discovering really *is* more efficient ... and that less body movement ('quiet' running form) is isolating the moving parts, using fewer muscles to do the job instead of sharing it out to the holistic whole. You might even be unable to wipe the grin off your face ...

Of course the next question is always, always *"How many times a week can I/should I repeat this hill session?"* And the answer is always the same, "I don't know". Unless I'm writing a training programme for you and am party to what's going on in your life, I have no idea how many stress-taps are in full flow, how much of your life is NOT under your control, how much you might be at the mercy of what's happening TO you, how (and even, if) you're sleeping at night, what your nutrition is like ... the list goes on.

Whilst it is an undeniably joyous session - it even gives me joy *thinking about it* and I've had a ball writing it! - hill running is also intense, and newly-intense to those parts of your body you might not have been moving much before. 'New' and 'intense' in the context of movement are both red-flag words that require you to wait for your body to give its response and then for you to act upon whatever that response is. There are no rules. No belief systems. There should be no expectations regarding what your body ought to be comfortable with. You just need your TTF and your honest internal awareness that always tells you when it's ready for more. Please listen to it - it's got your back, and it never lies.

With *conditioning over t-i-m-e* (read: not immediately!!), I consider it important for runners to hone their co-ordination skills, improve functional running strength and keep their bodies open with some form of hill drills at least once a week, and probably no more than twice.

As a rough guide, it takes folk two to SEVEN days to recover properly (read: gain the full benefits from!) from big hill drill sessions, especially when you're taxing muscles in a new way. If I'm pushing towards extended efforts (short efforts are much quicker to recover from), it *always* takes me a week - I'm just that kinda gal - I love them, I put everything into them and then my body wants to rest and do easy stuff for a while ... lovely pacing stuff. Pacing is probably my favourite subject after showing people how much fun hills can be - using gadgets like ... noses ...

I can smell it coming ... Principle 4 ...

Before we sniff the air further up, let's remind ourselves why we're here, talking about running, and hills, and power and the joy of it all. First up, the lovely and inimitable Ted again:

Helen

When running to the top of the Roc Noir (2475 M) this morning from our base at 1850 M, I thought it remarkable how effective a little drill & hill technique were.

Regards
Ted

And then Jesse Owens, the great American Olympian:

"I ALWAYS LOVED RUNNING ... IT WAS SOMETHING YOU COULD DO BY YOURSELF, AND UNDER YOUR OWN POWER. YOU COULD GO ANY DIRECTION, FAST OR SLOW AS YOU WANTED, FIGHTING THE WIND IF YOU FELT LIKE IT, SEEKING OUT NEW SIGHTS JUST ON THE STRENGTH OF YOUR FEET AND THE COURAGE OF YOUR LUNGS."

Ahh, I couldn't have timed that better ...

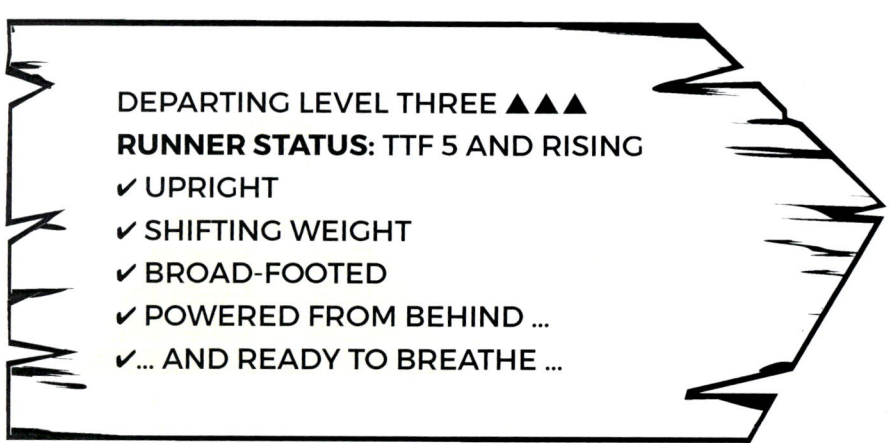

DEPARTING LEVEL THREE ▲▲▲
RUNNER STATUS: TTF 5 AND RISING
✔ UPRIGHT
✔ SHIFTING WEIGHT
✔ BROAD-FOOTED
✔ POWERED FROM BEHIND ...
✔ ... AND READY TO BREATHE ...

LEVEL FOUR
MEETING IN THE MIDDLE

LEVEL FOUR CONTENTS

Sketching real-life scenarios 179
Checkpoint Four 181
Introducing The Twist 186
What do we need to feed our muscles? 193
Nose-breathing your run 200
Checkpoint Four Noticeboards:
    Checkpoint Four Summary 202
    Leaving Level Four 203

PRINCIPLE 4: UPRIGHT + WEIGHT SHIFT -> 3D TRANSVERSE ROTATIONS THAT MEET IN THE MIDDLE

If I had a pound coin for every runner who told me it's not their legs that hold them back, but their breathing ... let's investigate and find solutions ...

 This segment completes 'planes of motion' exploration with rotations and investigates your breathing equipment

As a conservative estimate, I would suggest that the vast majority have forgotten all about one of their biggest muscles. Everyone knows of its existence, but very few seem to give it any consideration; no head-space, despite it occupying huge body-space. I've even asked a couple of surgeons which they think are the top three muscle groups in terms of size, and this muscle didn't appear in their answers. Despite wielding scalpels inside bodies, they responded similarly to the majority: glutes, quads, lats.

So, at this fourth level, we're going to give one of your biggest muscles - *the diaphragm* - a warm welcome, and make sure it never gets forgotten again. And whilst we're here, we'll introduce your in-built magic wand ...

> **Anatomy Dog-Leg:** "lats" is the commonly-used nickname for the latissimus dorsi muscles, that wing out from the lower back to the armpits when bodybuilders do the 'Incredible Hulk' pose. The word latissimus dorsi (plural: latissimi dorsi) comes from Latin and means "broadest muscle of the back". "Quads" is the short-hand for quadriceps femoris (Latin for "four-headed muscle of the femur"), the large muscle group of the front of the thigh.

SKETCHING REAL-LIFE SCENARIOS

Before we start, let's 'check-in' with how you are, where you've been and what you were doing whilst you were there.

Imagining I'd been working directly with you, we'd have stuck with Level 1 for just enough time for you to feel more relaxed as a running Jenga-Skeleton - you'd recognise one if you saw one - so well-stacked it simply oozed balance and elegance. Not just during, but between run sessions, you'd have been encouraged to embrace every vertical surface you see, make like Baloo The Bear, morphing yourself between an Amazonian Warrior and the Hunchback of Notre Dame against it, experimenting with the different ways to self-cue the movements that effortlessly feed each other.

We'd have added the principles of Level 2 as soon as possible, and then stayed there awhile, enjoying the new sensations of space and balance. The nourishing gift of *t-i-m-e* would have enabled any newly-busy muscles to catch up with the general fitness level you brought to the journey.

Meanwhile, between runs, you'd have been slipping your shoes and socks off regularly to investigate what might actually be going on down there, given half a chance. You'd have rocked and rolled through those mighty 33 joints, slid your fingers between your toes in the shower (multi-tasking opportunity right there - balance, foot mobilization, pronation of the support foot, glute load of support leg, 'pigeon'-stretch of the lifted hip rotators), seen walls in a whole new light (cleared furniture even, so I've been told!) and taken a few questioning looks at your shoe collection. How many of those eye-candy designs have the same pleasing effect on what they're covering, I wonder? I'm not judging, just saying.

Throughout, you'd have been collecting somatic data on the myriad of changes you noticed, both during your runs as well as whilst simply 'living', and added to those the visual data that you'd be increasingly-easily able to pick up on as you observed the movements of folk around you. Wikipedia describes people watching as a *"subconscious activity [we] partake in everyday without even realizing"*; the difference being you're looking at the same things you've seen day to day for years, but now that you're looking more closely, the more you're seeing. *"Observe Curiously"*, as my clear-sighted friend Chris Sritharan often ends his sagacious posts.

I keep wanting to say this out loud, so I'm going to put it right here. In the times we live in - where commuters put post-it stickers on their cover of **'50 Shades of Grey'** saying "Don't judge me" (genius, by the way), where every new block-busting box-set steams with sex, where many TV programmes are preceded with the warning to expect 'scenes of a sexual nature' - I find it **staggering** that runners - in general - hardly move that part of the body which seems to dominate somatic awareness outside of sport! Everyone knows it intimately. But if it doesn't move when you run, the muscular stuff attached to it doesn't either. I hereby give scientific permission for you all to STRUT YOUR STUFF!! It's not exactly an 'Anatomy Dog-Leg', but I'm glad to have had a chance to say it out loud.

When your body told us it was ready for more challenge - with old lines of tension ironed out and running endorphins wanting some action - we'd have introduced the 'golden bowl' of your body: the pelvis.

Principles at Level 3 would have been thoroughly enjoyed by body and soul, incorporated as many reps as was deemed prudent before fatigue set in, and *not repeated* until the intensity of work had been absorbed by your body. Challenging yourself and your body is fun; over-challenging is to be somatically-oblivious. At the same time as enjoying the new pelvic duties of 3D movement in gait at all speeds, you'd have been keeping mobile with trots and cogs reinforcing the motor neurone connections in the 's' for side view and the 'f' for 'freedom for fanned feet' planes, continuing to:

CONNECT THE ACTION WITH THE THOUGHT WITH THE FEELING

by ... *making friends with your mate, Sensory Feedback* ...

Waiting for no longer than your body waking up 'ready' for a more continuous run section - so with a TTF of 5 or above - we'd launch into the principles along the trail at Level 4. To fully oxygenate your body is to drive nutrition to - and waste away from - the extremities, which would seem to be a pretty good reason for putting off the chores and taking your body off for its next experience. Don't forget your layers - always layers, runners! *With pockets ... for stashing a handful of tissues; you're likely to need them ...*

CHECKPOINT FOUR
NOTICEBOARD

▲ ▲ ▲

TERRAIN: FLATTISH ROUTE, FENCE OR WALL OPTIONAL
RUNNER STATUS: TTF 5
KIT LIST: LAYERS, COMFORTABLE FOOTWEAR, YOUR LEMNI, TISSUES

This part of the trail takes us along flatter terrain. I love hills for informing as well as strengthening, but the flat road has benefits in allowing you spare somatic capacity to focus on different things. If your route can take in a drill area with a vertical surface to lean up against, so much the better, but it's not a strict requirement for this level. Right … all set for the now-familiar 10 minute walking warm-up! How many of you have been telling your friends off for not warming up 'properly'? Converted folk can get quite evangelical …

Given I talk a lot about **Efficiency Beginning With Upright!** how about establishing it before the walking warm-up even begins? There's no 'right or wrong' don't forget, 'many ways to skin a cat' and 'variety is the spice of life' (I'm sure I'll have thought of some more metaphors before writing the next level). There's nothing more boring than rigidity, especially in the world of movement! Play with the way you self-cue the same information; the more ways you can find to express the same thing - the more words you can use to describe the same action or response - the better and more fine-tuned your internal awareness will be. Connect with yourself rather than perform by rote.

So, here's Sagittal Cog presented yet another way:
Sagittal Cog Against The Wall:
Amazonian Meets Hunchback: Take 4 - Cog Popping
vimeo.com/245649810

- Head, mid-back and bum against a wall.
- Roll your feet so there's more pressure along the inside of the heel, without losing full breadth of forefoot contact; your feet are pronating.
- Feel your pronating feet turn your knees in and bend them slightly.
- Feel your turning-in knees internally rotate your thigh bones.
- Feel your internally rotating thigh bones tilt your pelvis forward so your bum pushes into the wall.
- Feel the pelvis pushing forwards lift the ribcage.

- Feel the lifting ribcage pull your shoulder blades towards your straightening spine *and* pull your chin down towards it, tipping your head forward.
- Feel your retracting shoulder blades externally rotate your arms.
- Feel your externally rotating arms straighten.
- Relax back to where you were.
- Now roll your feet so there's more pressure along the outside of the heel, without losing full breadth forefoot contact; your feet are supinating.
- Feel your supinating feet turn your knees out and straighten them.
- Feel your turning-out knees externally rotate your thigh bones.
- Feel your externally rotating thigh bones tilt your pelvis back, tucking your bum under.
- Feel the pelvis tilting back pull the ribcage forward.
- Feel the sinking ribcage push your shoulder blades away from your flexing spine *and* push your chin away from it, tipping your head back.
- Feel your protracting shoulder blades internally rotate your arms.
- Feel your internally rotating arms bend a little.
- Body pop along the cog lines in both directions a couple of times, feeling the movement become more fluid, more sequential, more integrated.

Scan to watch

Holding and Using The Lemni

Let's get walking ... upright ... whilst mastering the art of using *The Lemni* to help create and maintain the rolling action of both your pelvis and shoulder girdle. We could even call this movement "Hot Potatoes", which should be self-explanatory, but given my vocabulary is both military and Yorkshire-influenced, here's the QR code again. The quick video offers clarification; it's definitely a 3D 'Hawaiian Hoola Dance', rather than a one-dimensional carriage return on an old-fashioned typewriter!

The walking warm-up should see you feeling more-or-less upright and with an effortless lack of upper thighs rubbing together. Remember *Progress NOT Perfection*. A 15 minute warm-up run immediately after should give you time to focus on encouraging smoothness of weight shift through a rolling pelvis and co-operative upper and lower bodies. **Don't 'do' ... only 'think' and 'let'. Your body already knows how to do all this; you 'doing' will just get in the way. Your job is let your body get on with it. Let your body run you.** Things will only get better from here ...

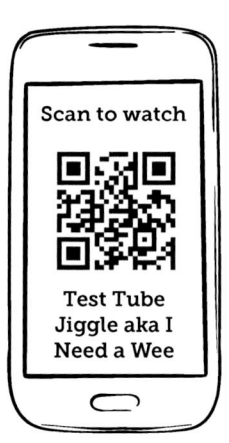

Scan to watch

Test Tube Jiggle aka I Need a Wee

A quick review of the Frontal Cog before moving on might help concrete the idea of shifting weight from the right foot to the left foot and back, avoiding the pervasive tendency for runners to trot along that invisible tight-rope (so challenging to the lateral hips, knees, lower leg fascia, ankles and dismissing the potential action of parts of their feet - and yet most hadn't even noticed ...), but equally, we could introduce another way of cogging in the frontal plane. It's a simple one, but effective, and I call it: **Frontal Cog: I need a wee** (not 'my' move of course - Gary Ward is to be given full credit - I just call them names to help me remember them ... so the titles probably say more about me than I'd realized. Ah well ... too late now!).
vimeo.com/244974374

- Start with an easy balanced posture, with your feet under your hips.
- Imagining you're in a human-sized test tube with your shoulders touching the glass walls, slowly bend one knee.

- Dropping the knee drops that hip ... which means the opposite hip must have 'see-sawed' upwards. Can you feel that being wedged in your test tube (as you are!), when your knee bends, and the opposite hip hikes up, your hand seems to slide down the side of that straight leg, shortening the waist on that side?
- If you then aim to keep your eyes horizontal and your nose vertical, do you notice your head tilts sideways towards your bending knee?
- Come back to standing straight, bend the other knee, feel for that hip dropping and the other hiking, and notice the opposite arm slide down the outside of your straight leg, shortening the waist on that side, whilst lengthening the neck.
- Keep swapping from one bent knee, opposite sliding arm/short waist/lengthened neck to the other bent knee, opposite sliding arm/short waist/lengthened neck ... feeling the 'I need a wee' jiggle? Maybe it's just me. Some have dubbed this 'The Test-Tube Jiggle' because those words work better for them. Have fun with it anyway - all great movement should feel enjoyable, otherwise what's the point?
- And the 'point' of this drill is ... the hike and drop of the pelvis ... working along the sides of your body ... *now* can you feel the jiggle?
- (This is a really good one to do in a tight queue ... and maybe when you really do need a wee ... or indeed, if you get stuck in a test-tube).

Run again and notice if there are any differences generated by the increased awareness along the sides of your body. If this has opened up some more space for you, use it regularly to build and embed the motor programme.

INTRODUCING THE TWIST

To Sagittal and Frontal Cogs, we - of course - complete our tri-planar joint rotation potential with the **Transverse Cog**.

 Anatomy Dog-Leg: For our purposes, just think of movement in the **transverse plane** as a **rotational or twisting movement.**

You'll be delighted to know that this is an easy one to get savvy with ... but *beware* ... 'transverse' equates to rotational movements which are considered neurologically the most demanding, and physically the most challenging. How many folk do you know who collapsed in a heap when they reached round to pick the magazine up off the floor? With detail added, it was a *twist and a bend* that 'did it'. Similarly, the stories of backs 'going' just by reaching from the passenger seat to the back seat ... already bent through sitting this time, followed up by the *twist* ...

Anatomy Dog-Leg: We slithered out of the water as fish; several eons later, we were totally over the restriction of only being able to move laterally to generate forward motion and had discovered propulsion in the up and down oscillatory plane (think galloping chimps); and by the time we'd made it to Homo sapiens (latin for "wise man" by the way!) - evolved in the 'rotational plane of motion' - we became the most efficient mammals on the planet because we no longer had to fight gravity ... we were finally 'at one' with it. In fact, we depend on it - not just for the apples falling off the trees, but for the pressure holding bodily fluids in our vessels for transporting around our now vertical body. Gravity? Fabulous! We'll twist inside your field and stay grounded, thank you.

So whilst *rotation* seems to be our genetic winning streak, many bodies have become somewhat 'stuck' or 'twisted' in one direction, creating rotational asymmetry. It is no accident that we started the pyramid with upright first (sagittal plane), then weight shift (frontal plane - think 'along the tennis court's baseline') and we bring in rotations last (transverse plane). Remember the simple test showing the importance of the order of play:

Head Alignment For Maximum Rotational Potential: vimeo.com/244976667

- Stand, out of alignment, with a forward lean (sorry - it'll only be brief).

- Look to your left and right - as far as you can comfortably - note the limits of your visionary field (and whilst you're there, using your increased self-awareness, how much tension are you holding, just to stand still? *Everything is tense, right? Everything except the abdominals ... innards are now on their way out - and no, we didn't cue James to stick his out ... they did that all by themselves!*).

- Now stand upright and tripod your weight evenly between heels, ball of foot and base of little toes; toes are making ground contact but are relaxed (now, can you feel those abs fired up? And just about everything else has relaxed? *Phew, innards are back where they should be, safely held in place*).

- Look again to your left and right - as far as you can comfortably - note the limits of your visionary field ... bigger panorama, isn't it? Optimising your DNA-driven rotations entirely depends on your body *owning* its vertical.

It's so important for you to be able to notice where you are in terms of alignment whilst in motion; a brief spell of running whilst turning your head on top of a relaxed neck "this way and that way" will give you another 'flavour' of vertical to taste ... and concrete the benefits of working on your sagittal plane stacking.

Necks can only be relaxed if heads are perched beautifully on the top of their spines. Move your head only within a comfortable range of motion - and not too fast to avoid getting dizzy ... you might find you can rotate better in one direction than the other and so have 'work to do' on your spine rotations. Today might be Day One of your rotational journey - no need to rush - plenty of time ...

So, you've Sagittally Cogged, Walked, Run, Frontally Cogged, Turned your Head, Run again.

Now to investigate even more rotational prowess whilst in motion. As usual, comparing running 'passes' along the length of your venue - before and after new movement patterns - helps you identify changes in restrictions or tensions in your running bodies.

Rotations Safety Note: Whilst this move is very simple, don't be fooled. This is a VERY strong movement which should be first performed *well within your comfort levels;* explore what your body can manage quite easily before you challenge yourself closer to your limits. Whilst it's unfeasible to think that improvements can be made if we all remain well within our comfort zones, there is often only a fine line between nudging the boundaries of our ranges of motion and poking holes through them.

THIS IS WHERE SLOW SPEEDS AND PAYING ATTENTION VIA INTERNAL 'SENSING' - AKA 'NOTICING STUFF' - ARE CRITICAL.

You might not know where your inner 'snags' are, because your body might not have moved in this way for as long as you can remember! Work with your body thoughtfully and respectfully. If you notice a significant discrepancy between opposing rotational directions, consider seeking help from Anatomy in Motion bodyworkers who specialise in movement patterns.

Transverse Cog:
"I Can See Clearly Now ... !": vimeo.com/244974045

- Stand, feet hip distance apart, the outside of each little toe lined up with the outer ankle bone (this might make you feel as if you're 'toeing-in' - and that's fine, and indeed common - but we want the rotation to start from as anatomically-neutral a position as possible; if your leg is in its habitually 'turned out' position to start with, what rotational possibilities will you be able to explore?)

- Find vertical before you do anything else:
  - abs ✔
  - relaxed neck ✔
  - length at the back of the neck ✔
  - 'wobbly head' with no tension required to hang onto it ✔
  - weight balanced between heels and base of toes ✔
  - tripod foot ✔
  - 'open' and relaxed ankle ✔

Relax in this position - rest your bones one on top of the other, and let THEIR rigidity hold your body up inside the field of gravity; if muscle tension is holding you up, how are you going to rotate with evolutionary ease?

- Shift your weight over, towards one leg.

- Keeping a 'tripod' contact with your weighted foot (heel, base of big toe, base of little toe), bring your opposite arm across the body, to rotate the spine towards the weighted foot.

- The arm rotates the ribcage, which rotates the spine, which rotates the pelvis, which rotates the thigh bone, which rotates the shin bone, which rotates the ankle and foot.

- Aim to keep the weighted foot grounded with 3 points of contact as the weight moves strongly to the outside of the heel (your foot is fully supinating); the opposite foot has helped with the whole body rotation by coming up onto an internally swizzling forefoot (heel off the ground).

- When your arm and body can't rotate any further, keep turning your head.

- When your arm, body and head have reached the limit of their rotation, see if your eyeballs can keep going. Note your peripheral vision limits using the edge of your view as your marker.

- Come out of this rotation, and repeat to the opposite side.

- Now repeat the whole sequence again without any extra effort, just smooth rotations, and notice if your peripheral vision is the same or has expanded.

- Can you see 270 degrees round from where your eyes were looking at the beginning?

Given *Motion is Lotion* and this is a running map-book, once you've rotated twice to each side, run around your venue to see if anything tangible has changed in your body. Has running form changed? Is there more movement globally? Does it feel easier? Commonly after this movement pattern, folk report noticing the outside of their feet for the first time whilst running!

Practice makes Progress, so repeating the Cog-Run-Compare rhythm up to a handful of times will hone the drill form so you become familiar with the cog and give enough opportunity for tangible differences to be felt and objectively measured through your peripheral vision improvements. After the initial two rotations to each side, some prefer to only do one rotation to each side between 'comparison runs', especially when the outside air temperature is nippy. Listen to your body, and do what you need to stay warm and happy whilst you explore.

Common feedback *'sensings'* from the addition of the 3rd dimension of joint rotations often start with an exclamatory *"WOW!"* referring to the difference in the field of vision between the first and second cog. Following closely come comments along the lines of taller, straighter, freer, more relaxed, easier, more foot contact with the ground, more rotation, some rotation (where there was none!), more abs (additional 'newly-woken' oblique abdominal action), more of a sense of being 'held in the middle by a girdle', the upper body movement coupled with *The Lemni* feeling easier and more dynamic. All pretty encouraging given the small amount of input.

Anatomy Dog-Leg: The whole abdominal wall (transversus, rectus abdominus, internal and external obliques) 'wraps around' the front and sides of the torso, creating both movement, functional stability of the torso above the legs *and* a means of keeping the internal viscera in situ; our abs literally 'hold us in', without us having to 'hold ourselves in' - aren't we cleverly made?

Less desirable, less familiar but that crop up occasionally, are tales of woe where lower backs protest. A screwed-up face at the end range of motion means you're over-challenging your body by either moving too quickly and overcooking the rotation, and/or not applying the earlier highlighted message of starting the movement with *only that amount of muscle tension required to stand still!* (Page 189).

If you are self-observant, self-diligent and self-helpful you'll harness your energy and motivation and direct it towards movement that is healthful rather than injurious in nature. As the owner of your body, you've got this. You have control. Take it easy. The journey towards efficient movement in gait of all speeds is exactly that - a process. In terms of 'unwrapping', think onion rather than satsuma. Layers people ... you know how I love layers...

So - you're all 3D now - congratulations! You now hold tenure of your Evolutionary Rights.

Having ball-parked the first third of Level 4 as warm-up and revision of sagittal and frontal planes of motion (roughly minutes 1-25) and the second third as discovering the transverse plane of motion, then 50 minutes along the trail you should have joints that have an enriched idea of their 3D rotations, with the augmented reaction of the fascia and muscles to these joint rotations. Nice.

You're ready for the penultimate **Principle.**

WHAT DO WE NEED TO FEED OUR MUSCLES?

This is a good question, but given you're either reading or listening to this and I'm here writing it, it's somewhat rhetorical. You might have a fleeting thought on nutrition, it could spark a discussion with your running mate regarding sugar-burning versus fat-burning (another time!), but I'd stake my reputation on the fact that no-one will consider ... o-x-y-g-e-n. That invisible stuff which we can't live without - at least not for any longer than 3 minutes. That stuff which folk - with the exception of pro athletes who go to great lengths to deprive themselves of it either at high altitudes or in altitude tents - take for granted. That stuff which - once optimised in circulating blood - can increase your aerobic capacity by 10-20%.

Now that last statistic generally captures everyone's attention. Who wouldn't want to know how to achieve such an upgrade? Should you continually push the boundaries of the 'lactate threshold'? Ought you do more anaerobic work? (Folk don't normally see the irony of that sentence until after they've said it). You might be thinking that resistance work is the answer, or just harder training generally. Perhaps you think you should just factor in *more* training in your already packed schedule or simply be able to cope with more pain?

My answer comes in the form of another question: *"How do you breathe?"* And if I was with you, I'd brace myself for the full force of all the smart-alec quips that come with the territory of 'teaching' breathing form.

> "IN THEN OUT, REPEAT".
> "BEEN DOING IT ALL MY LIFE, COACH".
> "CAN DO IT IN MY SLEEP, BOSS".

Love it. Wonderful stuff - this *is* meant to be fun, after all!

A more accurate presentation of my question would be: *"What do you breathe WITH?"* (the hilarity continues ...)

Let's find out. Keeping yourself warm, run again around your field or up and down whatever venue you're occupying, mindful of your newly-generated 3D running form, and now additionally task yourself with the job of finding where you get your air from. How do you drive it into your muscles? What draws it in, drives it around and throws out what you've used?

Just a few minutes of running - always using every opportunity to sense the *principles* of what you've already discovered - might not give you the answers; but they'll come as soon as you stand still again. Be ready to capture the revealing next few seconds, and play 'detective'. As soon as you come to a stop, put one hand on your upper chest and one hand on your belly; as you breathe, which hand moves more? And what is your mouth doing?

The vast majority of you (there might be one or two that are 'in the know'!) will be standing there with your mouths open and chest pumping - literally 'catching your breath'. Which suggests your breathing accessory muscles are working hard, but your main breathing muscle, the diaphragm - and, dependent on how you measure, plausibly the second biggest muscle in the body and *easily* the most forgotten one - is performing as an accessory, if bothering much at all!

Anatomy Dog-Leg: MUSCLES OF RESPIRATION

The Primary Muscles of Inspiration (an active process) work to increase the volume of the thoracic cavity in 3D (top to bottom, front-to-back and across):

- Diaphragm - a sheet of internal skeletal muscle that extends right across the bottom of the thoracic cavity or ribcage and contracts to increase all of its 3 diameters
- Intercostals - muscles lying between the ribs.

Efficiently, 'quiet' expiration is a passive process achieved by the elastic recoil of the lungs, the relaxation of intercostal muscles and diaphragm and an increased abdominal wall tone, forcing the relaxing diaphragm back up.

Accessory Muscles involved in Forced Inspiration:

- scalene group of muscles along the neck (elevation of 1st & 2nd ribs)
- sternocleidomastoid muscles connecting the chest to each side of the head via the collarbones (elevation of clavicle)
- pectoralis major & minor and serratus anterior muscles, lying across the front and back of the ribcage respectively (elevation of 'rest of' ribcage)

Accessory Muscles involved in Forced Expiration:

- muscles of anterior abdominal wall
- quadratus lumborum muscles of the posterior abdominal wall (it's the deepest abdominal muscle and commonly referred to as a back muscle)
- latissimus dorsi muscles across the back
- serratus posterior inferior muscles at the junction of the ribcage and lower back.

If this is you, you're likely to be limiting your aerobic capacity simply through habitually poor breathing. The unbelievably good news is you can increase your aerobic capacity (by up to 20% the science indicates) simply by improving your breathing habits. How much monumental effort do you suspect you'd have to put in to gain these kinds of advantages through traditional practices? And, yes - I AM proposing you don't need to. I'm thrilled for you just writing this!

Now, I'm not suggesting for a moment you sit there and learn respiratory anatomy; the 'dog-leg boxes' simply provide a soupçon of the factual information easily available in medical texts and on-line to, hopefully, whet your appetite to discover more. Not through study, but by opening your mind and then exploring your body.

Anatomy Dog-Leg, continued: "When patients with respiratory problems struggle to breathe, they use their accessory respiratory muscles to assist the expansion of thoracic cavities. They lean on a table or put their hands on the knees to fix their scapulae and clavicles, so these muscles are able to act on their rib attachments and expand the thorax." [ring any bells, runners?]
Referenced from: Gray's Anatomy, K. L. Moore's Clinically Oriented Anatomy, R. Snell's Clinical Anatomy

Mosby's Medical Dictionary, 9th edition goes as far as to say that "often" [Often!!!] "elevated effort of breathing contributes to increased anterior-posterior diameter of the chest (barrel chest) over time. ... their use [the sternocleidomastoids, scalenes and pectorals minors for forceful inhalations, and the abdominals for forceful exhalations] represents an abnormal or laboured breathing pattern and is a sign of respiratory distress".

Did you know that chest breathing (apparently, the guaranteed modus operandi for stressed folk) is using the secondary muscles of respiration? And that belly breathing - or diaphragmatic breathing - uses the *actual, full monty, primary role* muscles of respiration? Babies and children breathe like this all the time ... until they grow up and discover 'stress'. Diaphragmatic breathing isn't the domain of yoga gurus after all ... it's simply the 'human zen' (chest breathing WILL climb your shoulders towards your ears, and that's never 'zen').

I found it astonishing when I discovered on my First Aid course that around 10% of A&E admittances are nothing more than 'breathing pattern disorders', but with breathing right at the top of the 'life totem pole', they are considered priority medical emergencies.

So, hands-up if you struggle with muscle fatigue, muscle cramping, endless trigger points ... and were breathing with your chest! Breathing is exquisitely sensitive to stress, and your diaphragm can become like any other muscle - stressed. If your shoulders are around your ears, the posture lifts your ribcage, which can pull on the diaphragm. If you become habitually stuck in that shape, it can feel difficult to catch your breath as the tension in the diaphragm muscle limits the contraction and expansion rhythm that is our life force. You might catch yourself 'deep sighing' at rest, as your body instinctively sucks in a great lungful of missing oxygen. Your brain may reflexively instigate a yawn or three if you don't start self-oxygenating! A stressed diaphragm affects breathing patterns, and poor breathing is stressful. It's a self-perpetuating cycle.

Anatomy Dog-Leg: 'Hyperventilation' actually refers to an accumulative imbalance of excess carbon dioxide over oxygen, rather than an excess of oxygen, and often results from taking in great mouthfuls of air but not exhaling properly; this causes distressing physical and mental symptoms that range from muscle spasms/pain (excess carbon dioxide creates acidosis) and extreme muscle fatigue all the way through to chest pain perfectly mimicking angina, pseudo-asthma symptoms, panic and the 999 call.

But of course the whole story of respiration isn't just about the *muscles* of breathing. What about that most wondrous of appendages we have - our nose? Next to *The Lemni*, your nose is the most effective self-coaching running tool you own. And it's free. And frankly, it deserves some love. After bottoms, it must be the most 'angsted-about' body part, much maligned for its rather fit-for-purpose sticking-out-ness.

Big Shout-Out to noses. You've gotta love them. My delightful husband says my feet are ugly and whilst he loves my nose, he also tells me its 'substantial'. I love my feet - they've run me to places I was told they couldn't; I love my nose - it's run me to places I was told it couldn't. Appreciate ALL your body bits - they all work together, and if you love them all, you'll be amazed at what they can achieve together. I'm well into my 50s now, and I'm no where *near* my limits!

Noses are fascinating.

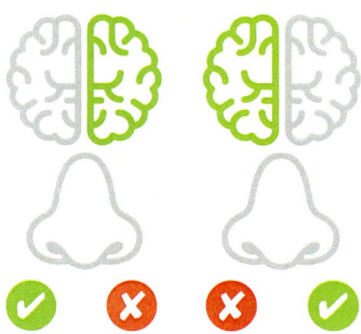

If you hold the left nostril closed and increase the airflow through the right nostril, you'll wake up the left brain to give you improved verbal performance. Close the right nostril and increase the airflow through the left nostril and the right brain gets a poke, offering enhanced spatial performance (Shannahoff-Kalsa, 1993).

Two openings, with each one innervated by 5 cranial nerves from the opposite side of the brain. Working both together and independently the nostrils function to filter, warm, moisturise, dehumidify and smell the air. Around a third of exhaled heat and moisture is retained when exhaling through our nose. Saliva build-up can keep you self-hydrated for hours. I've tested this extensively, and as I mentioned in *The Beginning*, I didn't need a drink until the aid station at around 35km during my nose-breathing marathon experiment in Amsterdam.

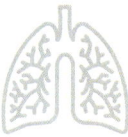

Breathing in and out through both your nostrils regularly has been shown to regain elasticity of the lungs (Cottle 1980) and improve overall lung volumes (Swift, Campbell, McKown, 1988). Counterintuitively, most of our oxygen is taken up during the exhale if performed through the nose rather than through the mouth. The nostrils, being smaller orifices than (most!) mouths, create a slower escape of exhaled air and significant back pressure into the lungs. This gives the lungs more time to extract the oxygen. So more oxygen is extracted. The science - old and newer (Cottle, 1972; Rohrer, 1915) - says 10-20% more! Huzzah!

Your day-time breathing habits have been found to carry over into your sleep. Day-to-day mouth breathing (on the inhale as well as the exhale) predisposes you to mouth breathing when you're asleep ... and nocturnal mouth breathing is a BIG cause of loud snoring. Take that to the next level and you've got sleep apnea, with apnea being a precursor to heart attacks and dying in your sleep (there's that Totem Pole of Life again, with Your Breath right at the top).

Breathing is the only vital function under voluntary and involuntary control. Next time you're out and about, notice how many slack-jawed, rather gormless-looking walkers and runners surround you ... if they're moving they're certainly breathing, but are they optimally oxygenating their whole beings, and are they as glum as they look? Clever scientists have confirmed what intuitive body workers have always known ... that there is an unbreakable bond between the biomechanics of the breath and the state of mind ... *and we have more control than we think.* Finding the subject of breathing irresistible now?

> **"WHEN YOU OWN YOUR BREATH, NOBODY CAN STEAL YOUR PEACE."**
> **- ANON**

▲ ▲ ▲

NOSE-BREATHING YOUR RUN

Trot 'out and back' again, mouth closed unless you have a cold (in which case, why on earth are you running?), are recovering from a previous sinus infection (very messy) or if you have a deviated septum (very tricky - sadly, if this is you, you're unlikely to be able to benefit from nose-breathing training. Dropping your jaw to mouth breathe is your instinctive and appropriate response to limited air intake through the nostrils).

When you stop (mouth remains closed), pop your hands straight onto chest and belly, and this time you should notice your belly swelling out against your waistband, and your belly moving more than your chest. If you didn't 'get it' immediately, repeat a couple of times - there are no downsides to a thorough introduction to the mostly-forgotten, very substantial and hugely important DIAPHRAGM muscle.

The rest of your run is all about your internal voice guiding and encouraging global participation of all your body parts in order to run with more space, more movement, more mastery. You're seeking to *make best friends with your new mate Sensory Feedback*. You're discovering the combined brilliance of weight shift, rotation, the rolling lemniscate-motion of one chuck of a *Hot Potato* effortlessly gifting the next stride and the next (your very own in-built Newton's Cradle - more about this at Level 8) ... with the drawing in and driving down of great nostril-loads of oxygen into your lungs for effortless transportation around your upright body, which has all its tubes stacked in their rightful place ... for efficiency.

B-e-a-u-t-i-f-u-l.

Except you might already be noticing a peculiar aspect of nose-breathing running. Having unwittingly dried out your mucus membranes with however many years of open-mouthed exercise, its sudden closure appears to cause over-activity of said membranes with seemingly endless amounts of snot being produced. Hence the advice to carry tissues. By regularly practising nose-breathing running, the over-production *caused* by the endless drying effect of mouth-breathing, starts to balance itself and eventually everything just remains moist instead of dripping. Where *n=1*, in my marathon experiment I took a whole pack of tissues, just in case; I blew my nose once, just as Tarne was taking the picture ...

Apart from the obvious benefits that nose-breathing running brings of looking more elegant, relaxed and intelligent, a useful biomechanical aspect is that of fine-tuning the orientation of the thoracic curve. In runners' attempts to be upright, a few thrust their ribs upwards but with less of a tilt of bones backwards and more of a muscular squeeze between the shoulder blades. If you try it, you'll feel that the general tension around the shoulder girdle makes swelling the belly (diaphragmatic breathing) much more difficult.

" ... the swelling of the belly ...?"

Excellent, you've been listening and I can hear you from here; something along the lines of "I thought you said the abs were tight when we're upright - how can they be tight if I'm allowing my belly to swell?" On the surface, things can look and/or feel counter-intuitive, until you delve deeper. The viscera 'stays in', held nicely through the lengthened loading of our anterior abdominal wall which is there as a result of our vertical stature.

Anatomy Dog-Leg: There's an important 'forward motion' element here too. Put very simply: when upright, our 'extensor chain' muscles along the back of our body, both hold us up as well as push us forward, but they are SO strong, SO powerful, that if our abdominals didn't wake up, we'd get pulled into a backward arch like a human roadrunner - meep meep!

When we breathe in using our main (rather than our accessory) respiratory muscles, the diaphragm's contraction pulls it from a dome-up shape beneath the lungs, to a flattened, taut 'drum-top' offering increased space for the lungs to fill with air, and compressing the space that the viscera sits in. The belly wall 'gives' a little under the pressure in the abdominal cavity because it's elastic, and because we're not holding it in tight (which would make it really difficult to breathe with anything *other* than our accessory muscles!). So in the context of upright and breathing well, the belly is 'taut' but not locked tight.

So let's just review that. You have a rhythmical flattening of the huge diaphragm muscle on top of the viscera. There is pressure of the viscera against the taut (and elastic) abdominal wall with each inhale, followed by a reduction in pressure with the exhale ...

effectively massaging the internal organs of the abdominal cavity - which is pretty much everything bar the lungs and heart!!

YOU ARE AN INCREDIBLE, SELF-MASSAGING, SELF-OXYGENATING, SELF-HEALING, SELF-REGENERATING, SELF-PUMPING, SELF-ORGANISING, SELF-ELIMINATING DREAM MACHINE.

When you encourage great 'system functionality' through great structural action you gain so much more than improved 10km times.

- ✔ A romp through the previous two dimensions of joint rotations.
- ✔ A swerve into the final movement dimension of rotation.
  - You'll delve into oppositional counter-rotation in the next lesson. For now, applaud burgeoning rotation of any description where movement was previously limited or suppressed!
- ✔ And a nose-dive (sorry - couldn't help myself) into breathing mechanics.

LEVEL FOUR CLOCK-IN/ CLOCK OUT ▲

With breathing at the top of the living totem pole, it would be logical to question why nose-breathing and the respiration muscles weren't addressed at Level 1. In organising the most efficient route, I decided Level 4 of the pyramid was most appropriate, in the absolute conviction that encouraging great breathing before one has opened up bodies that might be 'stiff, leaning Tower of Pisa's, following thin black lines with excessive or no rotation' is nigh on impossible.

One great step at a time … with a pack of Kleenex at the ready.

After the technical challenges of the first three levels, which generally require more time spent cruising their courses, the fourth seems a swift traverse by comparison. The reality is, your *progression* is what makes this level enjoyably uncomplicated. It's *because* you've been consistently tuning into your senses, your joint mechanics and your sagittal and frontal plane alignment, that adding rotation and a fuller lungful of air feels like child's-play. You are building your skills as you build the levels of your pyramid, and just like you, the whole becomes greater than the sum of its parts.

That said, rushing upwards to Level 5 is neither the goal, nor appropriate. You'll discover in the next pages that a higher TTF is required for the next stage of the trail. So relax and knock around here for a while here; breathe in its beautiful simplicity as you build resilience into both your soft tissue and your movement habits. Enjoy feeling your body *enjoying* its running. That view over your shoulder just gets better as your body unravels its restrictions and mindless, unhelpful habits.

Who better to tell us about the benefits of persistence but Kevin, who we met earlier, hinged 50° at the hips. He arrived glued to his asthma inhalers and whilst he still carried a puffer with him, he rarely used it once his 'pipes' lost their kinks and his lungs had easy access to 'enough':

"I came to you in early August after losing around 5 stone since May as I wanted to do a small Tri. As you know I had a number of issues: I was unfit, I was still over-weight and I had two opinions from different surgeons saying I needed hip replacements straight away. Not forgetting I had a motorcycle accident which lead to a shattered knee with all ligaments

snapped, a broken shoulder and two dislocated shoulders, and a broken wrist. This lead to over 10 operations and the thought of new hips when I was on the road to getting healthy had just about knocked me over and made me want to stop and give up.

> "PERSISTENCE GUARANTEES THAT RESULTS ARE INEVITABLE"
> - PARAMAHANSA YOGANANDA, INDIAN YOGI AND GURU

You then accepted the challenge of looking at my running which I knew was terrible. We went out and had our first session and it's fair to say my running was right up there with the terrible and even you couldn't hide how bad it was, as kind as you are Helen. Nevertheless, you started at the beginning and got me upright and week by week it got better; as I now know, it's all about form, form and just a bit more form. I got fitter and now I feel like whilst I am not the quickest I can run completely pain-free and run distances that I never thought possible with the weight and the injuries. As you know we ran a 5 mile run together without stopping and I can honestly say that the furthest I could go at the start of this was 50 metres without stopping. I do regular 10k now and I love running now, I am doing a half marathon in February this year which I can't believe - another dream that meeting you has made a reality, and I now know the limits are endless."

Kevin is now an Ironman.

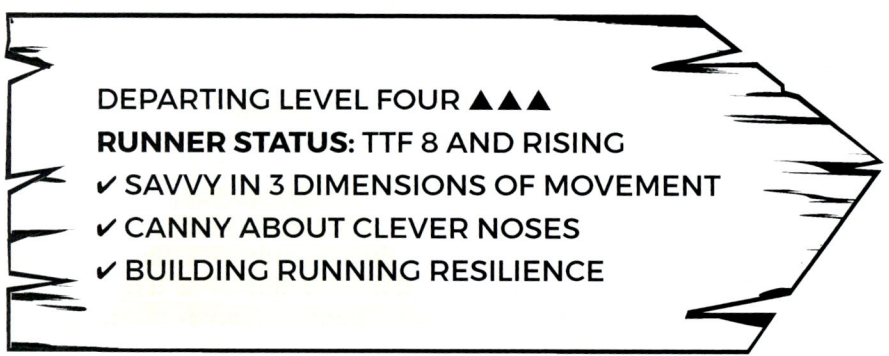

DEPARTING LEVEL FOUR ▲▲▲
RUNNER STATUS: TTF 8 AND RISING
✔ SAVVY IN 3 DIMENSIONS OF MOVEMENT
✔ CANNY ABOUT CLEVER NOSES
✔ BUILDING RUNNING RESILIENCE

LEVEL FIVE
THE STRIDE IS BE-HIND YOUUUU, HELPED BY WUJWUMS

LEVEL FIVE CONTENTS

Did someone mention speed?	207
Checkpoint Five	208
Introducing The WujWum	209
Speed Games	220
Brain Power	230
Checkpoint Five Noticeboards:	
Checkpoint Five Summary	235
Leaving Level Five	236

PRINCIPLE 5: HIP EXTENSION WITH BIG DADDY HALLUX

Are you OK ... until you try upping the pace? Do things start to break as soon as you go faster? Let's start unravelling that here.

 Introducing the WujWum, and discovering the recoil benefits of hip and big toe extension for effortless speed.

DID SOMEONE MENTION SPEED?

Many runners come to me champing at the bit to get off their speed 'plateau', talking the talk about running efficiency, but the message between the lines is "I want more speed for no more effort and no more injury ... umm, now". And that's all entirely possible, apart from the 'now' bit. First, the work. It's illogical to expect more speed for no more effort, or minimal risk of injury, without all areas of your body talking to each other well, co-operating and exchanging energy.

So staying awhile with all the explorations at Levels 1 to 4 can only be a good thing. You'll get to 'own' that great vertical stacking, which when combined with space between each footfall, *generates* the full 3D rotations in joint mechanics almost effortlessly. These are the basic ingredients for your innate efficiency to grow *into* its potential.

Time spent developing aerobic capacity through the simple strategy of keeping your mouth closed when possible, driving the majority of the respiratory load to the enormous muscle designed for the task, creates both bell-bottomed lungs and oxygenated muscle tissue within which the joint rotations can then awaken an effective response.

Having said all that, pottering around slowly and/or with short strides, no matter how upright you are, isn't efficient either. So, the PRINCIPLE of where we get speed *from* needs to be introduced as soon as it's going to be *safely* productive. The big question is 'when?'

Speed is a form of 'intensity', which is a red flag word; ergo, stay alert to your tissue tolerance factor. Speed is a big one, so you need a TTF of 8 or more for this.

 TTF 8 You notice the restriction only when active on rough terrain.

If you're tempted to launch with TTF 6, because you barely notice your pain anymore, or TTF 7, because you only notice your niggle the day after a run, the likelihood is the opening of the stride with the addition of effort will overtax that which is still healing. You might even regress a couple of TTF stages, which would be so frustrating. Accidents happen, but application of the TTF table is entirely down to your control. If you need an outlet for your energy, master Level 3 - the incline tempers the stride, so only the intensity of effort is a factor for consideration.

Whilst you're patiently allowing your body the time to strengthen to its TTF of 8, keep your running practice and drills loose, free and relaxed ... and intelligent-looking. You have been practising with your mouth closed, haven't you? And by the way, have you clocked how many slack-jawed folk are *trotting*? I mean, if you're working hard you *will* open your mouth, but if you're trotting at a conversational pace and there's no-one to chat to ... just saying.

No slopes are needed for this session, in fact, the flattest section of the quietest road you can find is ideal. You'll need your and you'll be using some markers, in the form of foliage of some description, but you can pick those up once you're at your chosen venue. Oh, and not forgetting 'layers' ... your TTF is influenced negatively by chilling-off prematurely!

CHECKPOINT FIVE
NOTICEBOARD

TERRAIN: FENCE OR WALL OPTIONAL, FLAT GROUND
RUNNER STATUS: TTF 8
KIT LIST: LAYERS, COMFORTABLE FOOTWEAR, GROUND MARKERS, YOUR LEMNI

INTRODUCING THE WUJWUM

Right at the beginning of this section of the trail is a runners' cache. All that's needed to open the treasure chest of know-how is:
- the understanding that three planes of joint rotations are ours by the design of nature,
- that exchange of soft tissue information flows through the joints and from the joints,
- that optimising joint movement improves how easily we move, and
- that sensory awareness is the key to using joints safely and constructively.

It's hidden here because by the time you reach it, you have all this intuitive knowledge. At Level 5, you're holding the key.

With your growing confidence in making good decisions for yourself based on your body's feedback, coupled with an expanding sense of each part of your moving body, I invite you to consider what I alluded to on page 90; revamping your pre-run routine with the reserve of running riches that is a '**Wa**ke **U**p **J**oints to **Wa**ke **U**p **M**uscles' sequence. A WujWum … first a new metric, now a new acronym. Change is Good. Change is Flow. Change is Life. And a WujWum series before a run has passed with flying colours in testing. As Russ wrote: *"WujWums are the best running preparation I've ever done. Everything feels lovely after doing them. It's amazing how many running-related niggles they help prevent".*

WujWum [wuj-wum]
Plural: WujWums
Acronym: Wake Up Joints (to) Wake Up Muscles
Noun: a detailed drill moving joints to safe 'end-range', finding space and effecting soft tissue recoil reactions.
Verb: to WujWum (used with and without object)
I WujWumed, he is WujWuming, we WujWumed in the Sagittal plane.

Third only to bringing folk back to the *joy* of running and ridding the world of glum running faces, my wholehearted desire is to see WujWums everywhere. In the parks, at the track, at the start-line, on doorsteps; at check-points, alongside aid stations, on football pitches, at athletic arenas; the potential places to unleash possibly dormant soft tissue through lack of joint space is limited only by our imaginations. I dream big: *"dream no small dreams for they have no power to move the hearts of men"* said Johann Wolfgang von Goethe.

WujWums. See? You're rolling that around your tongue already, aren't you?

 With the intention of making sure you're set up for success, let's remind ourselves of a few key criteria regarding movement:

1. We're going to be our full height through bones stacking on top of each other, rather than 'pulling ourselves to our full height' with excessive muscle tension; put another way, you're going to let your structure be shaped by being a balanced bag of bones. Think 'Jenga'. Even reading that might help you feel more relaxed!

2. Recall that if bones don't move, joints can't act and muscles can't react! (one of Gary Ward's Big 5 Rules in *What The Foot?*). You already know that if you want to 'work' the glute you've got to move *all* the bones it's attached to; you haven't finished the job if you only move your leg bones!

3. You've always known that the bones you're getting ready to move aren't bendy; it's the joints that bend and the muscles crossing the joints get stretched under load, which is an eccentric contraction. This is the aspect of efficiency in gait that's so easily illustrated with the thought of *catapults*. It's the spring-back, elastic recoil of the eccentric contraction that gifts us almost 'free' movement in terms of energy expenditure. "Muscles lengthen before they contract" is number one of *Gary's Big 5*.

With that refresher in mind, let's start our WujWums by revisiting The Cogs with specific attention to that moment at the 'end range of motion' which sets us up for soft tissue recoil:

The Sagittal WujWum: vimeo.com/244974539

- Head, mid-back and bum against a wall if you have one handy, outside of feet parallel to each other (if you remember this alignment from Level 4, you'll probably feel as if you're 'toe-ing in'; that's OK - alignment often feels 'odd' initially. It just shows you're making changes).

- Inhale, softening the belly, allowing the pubic bone and base of your chest bone/sternum to separate.
- Feel your legs internally rotate to access the inside of the heel, without losing your 2 points of contact - base of big toe and base of little toe - across the forefoot.
- Your pelvis tilts forward; pubic bone drops down and tail-bone lifts up.
- Ribcage tilts back as the base of the chest bone lifts.
- Skull tilts forward (without losing wall contact, if it's there); nose and chin are following pubic bone.
- Arms *externally* rotate, and
  - shoulder blades retract towards the spine, pulling
  - arms backwards and shoulders down.
- Most at this point will strain, and in the effort of the drill, will extend their elbows *and* their wrists. Let's all do this the first time - so your arms are straight and pulled behind you as far as they'll go if the wall is in the way, with your wrists bent backwards, palms facing the ground.
- **Now flex the wrists and bend the fingers at the knuckles so they point upwards ...** *did you notice your arms travelling further back, as your shoulder blades came closer to the spine, as the chest lifted more and the chin dropped more? Your pelvis probably tipped forwards a bit more too!*

- When no further travel in that direction is possible, your joints have reached their end range of motion and the soft tissue is fully stretched with torque, through non-linear movement.
- There is a pregnant pause ... a defining moment of zero motion ... before travel can start in the opposite direction ... let's make the first few centimetres of that travel *completely free* ... the sum total of a stretched catapult being released ... you're not going to move all the way to the opposing position on the recoil, but you can start the journey there carried on the wave of high velocity spring-back. It appears that the central nervous system loves high velocity - it gets very excited by it, and *remembers* it!
- Your movement will have slowed within nano-moments, allowing you to relax into the exhale.
- Your pubic bone is now travelling *towards* the sternum.
- Feel your legs externally rotate to access the outside of the heel without losing your 2 points of contact - base of big toe and base of little toe - across the forefoot.
- Your pelvis tilts backwards; pubic bone lifting and tail-bone dropping.
- Your ribcage tilts forward and the base of the chest bone sinks towards the rising pubic bone. If you feel you're doing a standing abdominal crunch, BRAVO!

- Your skull tilts backwards (without losing wall contact) with your nose and chin once again following the direction of the pubic bone.
- Arms *internally* rotate, and
  - shoulder blades protract away from the spine, pulling
  - arms forward and bending elbows, both heading into flexion.
- Just as an exploration, let's play first with bending the wrists and fingers forwards into flexion. Move slowly until you feel you can't travel any further.
- **Now extend the wrists and fingers backwards ...** did you notice your arms travelling further forward, as your shoulder blades separated more, as the chest caved more and the chin lifted more? Your pelvis might have tipped backwards more too!
- When no further travel in that direction is possible, your joints have reached their end range of motion and the soft tissue is fully 'loaded'.

- There is a pregnant pause ... a defining moment of zero motion ... before travel can start in the opposite direction ...
- After a few breath cycles, step away from the wall by a few steps ... can you feel a difference in your body from your usual reaction to the same 'cog'?
- You just might feel more 'energised' ... right to the tips of your fingers.

I love this one ... *everyone* **seems to love this one!**

- *The Frontal WujWum: vimeo.com/244975049*
  with a view to accessing **'end range of motion high velocity recoil'**:

- Feet under hips, aligned so the outside edges are parallel to each other.
- Breathe in and then side bend on an exhale, using just the weight of a hanging arm to take you there.
- Side bend further on your next inhale as you breath into - and swell - the ribs.
- Side bend further by pushing sideways into the outside hip, so that it sits *outside* your base of support.
- Side bend further by turning the dangling arm into a reaching one, pointing in the opposite direction to the travelling hip, with the awareness travelling right through to the extending fingertips.

- Bodyweight + gravity tilts the heels, whilst you're mindful about not *losing contact with the full breadth of the forefoot*
- Pull your head to upright, with nose vertical.
- When no further travel in any direction is possible, your joints have reached their end range of motion and the soft tissue is fully 'loaded'.
- *There is a pregnant pause ... a defining moment of zero motion ... before travel can start in the opposite direction ...*
- Repeat a few times to each side.

Recognise *I'm a Little Teapot?* With additional zing? This is the one that invokes noises such as "aahhhhgghhhh, that's good", and if it's only on one side, then the question is 'why?' Does that side need more space, or a rest? Not knowing gives you an opportunity to investigate. Do it in front of a mirror; does the 'aahhhhgghhhh' come from a bigger movement which might suggest the other side is less mobile and needs careful attention? Noticing stuff is endlessly interesting. Stay relaxed about it and avoid self-criticism; just be amazed at what your body can do now and give it every opportunity to improve.

- ***The Transverse WujWum:*** vimeo.com/245612911
  ooooooo ... with "end range of motion, high velocity recoil"? Be careful with this one!

- Remember, the "I don't know how I did it Doc, I was just grabbing my kitbag to go pump some iron, and it just 'went'" scenario? You can seek a greater range of motion safely, by *travelling very slowly when you sense yourself close to your end range*. The central nervous system will relax if it doesn't feel threatened by quick movement as you get towards end-range. I invite you to embrace **caution** as a common-sense default here because of the neurological demands innate in a 'twist' action.

Given this is only the second time I've mentioned this movement cog, let's revisit the guidelines:

- Feet under hips, aligned so the outside edges are parallel to each other, body stacked vertically with minimal muscular tension holding you there.

- Is your head perched effortlessly on the top of your head? A tiny adjustment might be all you need ... think 'float your head'. If that changed anything, you might have just released some muscle work - well done!
- Slightly shift your weight towards one leg.
- Following the movement direction with your eyes, allow a rotation to start from your arm crossing your chest and continue into the ribcage, and then via the spine to the pelvis, turning the thigh bone, trickling down through the shin bones to finally reach the heel and forefoot.
- Your weighted foot is a tripod with 3 points of contact - outside heel, base of big toe, base of little toe; your opposite foot is a toe-down/heel-up (plantarflexed ankle) swizzling assistant.
- Your arm/body rotation will stop before the head rotation, which will stop before the eyeballs have reached their peripheral vision limits.
- Another way of sensing this: when your arm and body reach their rotational limits, continue with your head; when your head reaches its rotational limits, continue with your eyeballs.
- Once at end-range, make sure you have full extension of the arm through the 'reach and splay of each finger and thumb'.
- Note what you can see at your end-range of vision.

- Engaging a sense of quietly 'releasing this rotation' having met the resistance at end-range slowly, will be the safest way of accessing recoil in this plane.
- Repeat in the opposite direction.
- Repeat the whole WujWum to each side once more, noting the new vision panorama. See how assertive I was there? Drawing on the experiences of ALL my clients, whether running or in clinic, *everyone* sees further ...

This is the one that creates waves in folks' senses; *"I could see **so much** further!!"* I've got a soft spot for this one.

Having completed a handful of sagittal, frontal and transverse global WujWums, what about specific attention to your feet? After all, between them they house 25% of the bones in your body, and with 66 joints on the move, that's a lot of potential soft tissue helpful reaction as they touch down with each stride:

The Foot WujWum: *Talus Turning vimeo.com/244973880*

- Stand, with feet your 'Goldilocks' distance apart.
- Given this WujWum is all about *feet*, make it your goal to have the entire forefoot of each foot in contact with the ground throughout; from the base of the big toe to the base of the little toe. It's easy to have 'some' forefoot in contact with the ground; your intention for this drill is to feel *ALL* of it.
- Hold the image of each front of your ankle in mind - that space between your ankle bones. This space represents your talus bone.
- Thinking only of the talus bones (or tali), slowly turn them to face 10 o'clock. Don't help with your body, but allow your body to follow the result of what's happening down at ground level.
- Can you feel your left foot is on the outer edge of its heel, with its arch higher and your right foot is on the inner edge of its heel with its arch flatter? Your left foot has supinated, and your right foot has pronated.
- Notice that your left leg (the one you've turned towards) is straight, and the right knee has softened.
- *Work to maintain full breadth of forefoot contact at all times on both feet - base of big toe through to base of little toe.*

- When you can't turn your 'tali' any further - or if you could you would lose some of the breadth of the forefoot, so you won't - let go of the WujWum and allow your feet and body to settle at 'centre'.
- Repeat to the other side, turning your talus bones to face 2 o'clock.
- Work to achieve a tripod, 3-point contact on both the left pronating foot and the right supinating foot.
- You'll notice that now the left knee has softened, and the right knee has straightened as you rotated towards it.
- With luxurious slowness as you rotate (it's hard to do this fast unless you're cheating by turning your body), squidge the flesh of your soles as you roll in one direction and then the other, being intent on moving all the feet bones inside your skin.
- Repeat a few times; it's actually quite hard work so you don't need many reps to know you've worked!

So, perhaps for the first time, you have systemically woken up every joint in your body, and therefore animated to varying degrees every soft tissue sinew. How do you feel as you walk away from your last WujWum?

Common observations are taller, fizzy, more relaxed, ready to go, full of energy, amazing ankles, happier, taller, looser, freer, calmer, more open, BIGGER FEET, did I mention taller? And we haven't even started running yet ...

If you happen to be running in a group, the general ambience after a WujWum warm-up is likely to be relaxed yet energised, folk chatting to each other and exchanging feedback. Wonderful - and exactly what you want from a social run. You could help each other too - add 'eyes' to each other's senses. I love it when I hear runners help each other feel 'stuff'. No rules, just awareness.

Walk briskly to continue your warm-up and notice the difference in your walk now you've WujWumed. Always be on a quest for more detail in your self-exploration.

Incorporate *The Lemni* to help to you sense the roll of your shoulders and the movement of your torso - it should feel a bit like shrugging on the strap of an empty backpack, or when someone helps you on with a jacket from behind. You're not actually lifting your shoulders, they 'get lifted' by the gentle side flexion of the spine. You'll see folk 'twisting' as they run, but as you'll discover very shortly, it doesn't seem to be ideal from an efficiency perspective; it might look like a rotation, but - amongst other things - it isn't a 3D movement. Imagining being *Rocky Balboa* 'air-boxing' as you run in the dawn mist gives many a good feel for the benefits of the three-dimensional essence of the movement. You might remember Mat's reference to Ali, when we first introduced *The Lemni*.

The wrists stay relaxed so that they can be involved in the weight shift too. If you compare using *The Lemni*. with a deliberate flick of the wrist sideways like the 'return' of an old-fashioned typewriter versus the 'up, over and down' movement of playing 'Snap', flipping Scotch Pancakes, hoola dancing or tossing hot potatoes from one hand to the other, you'll layer more positive reinforcement for helical movement in 3D rather than in lines. Together, the flow of the rolling shoulder girdle and wrist, generate a 'hand to opposite foot' action. When senses are struggling, *always* exaggerate a movement to feel it, then relax to allow a more natural, fluid motion. In time, you might become aware of 'gliding shoulder blades'.

Trotting along the coast road in Lanzarote, I will never forget when all Alan's pennies came hurtling down and he suddenly exclaimed: *"You mean ALL I HAVE TO DO is let things go?!"* To offer that context, it had taken his senses a couple of years to peel down to that particular layer of the onion.

It's often difficult to see things as they truly are. We see things as WE are. 'We' are the filter. So if 'tension is holding you together', your sensory feedback can get filtered accordingly. Even those well along their efficient running journey can suddenly recognise they're still 'hanging onto some body-part or other'.

"It's the most obvious which is so difficult to see most of the time. People say "It's as plain as the nose on your face". But how much of the nose on your face can you see, unless someone holds a mirror up to you?" - Isaac Asimov, American author and biochemist

Smooth, relaxed, effortlessly brisk walking will happen when global 3D motion is simply 'enabled'. Invariably, better movement is about switching *off* muscle tension, rather than adding any of it!

Remember **Progress NOT Perfection.**

Adding intensity in the form of speed on this session means that the warm-up run needs to be thorough, just as it was when you covered Hills at Level 3. A rough guide would be brisk, non-stop movement of increasing speed (walk to trot to run) of roughly 30 minutes or so, whilst staying relaxed and focused on what information your body is feeding you internally. Please remember that if you're in a group, the warm-up needs to be at the speed of the slowest! By now, better general body alignment and ease of movement from one foot to the other using the whole body rather than disjointed bits of it, should be feeling 'yours'.

SPEED GAMES

You've arrived at your venue with its flat 'running runway', long enough to be able to run for up to 10 seconds in a straight line at a sprint; give yourself a little leeway in length to prevent feeling as if you're going to run out of space - possibly literally!

Much like Level 3, there is so much going on during this session that spelling it out as more of a list, rather than penning a story, is practical. So once again, the bullet points are for clarity not laziness on my writing behalf.

This is The Speed Game:

- You identify a start point for your 'sprint'.

- You identify the difference between a run and a sprint. The big give-away is that a sprint gait is forefoot only - the heel descends (otherwise how are you going to load the Achilles tendon - the biggest tendon in the human body) but doesn't make it to the ground. If your heels touch the ground you're probably not accelerating hard enough to use your power fibres!

- You trot to your identified start point with whatever form thoughts you're going to be using during the 'sprint'.

- You run as fast as you can whilst holding said form, and you drop one of your markers at stride 22 (that's 2 for a rolling start and 20 'big ones').

- Once you've dropped your first marker, slow to a walk to begin your recovery.

- Full recovery - which means breathing rates have returned to normal - should take no longer than 2-3 minutes.

- In that recovery time, you'll be performing the next drill. There's no stopping as such, because even though you're stationary you're working on more exploratory movement patterns. The goal is to 'keep the kettle boiling' and so not cool-off prematurely.

- After the 2nd sprint, you pick up the marker closest to the start, so the marker left on the ground is always showing the fastest sprint.

- A maximum of 10 sprints are completed, so the interval section of the session should last a maximum of 30 minutes.
- If you start flagging after for instance sprint 6 or 7, then you can still perform the drills, but just enjoy running them rather than sprinting them.

The following is a VERY BASIC, pared-down explanation of muscle fibre activity and their energy sources. I've kept it as simple as possible and feel it's not possible to say less and still get enough of a message across to enable you to work your way through this level safely and productively. Full commentary is not what this book is about, but if you're really interested, there's plenty of established science on this to be found on the internet and in many texts; I'll reference all mine at the end of this map book.

Why 20 sprint strides (with the rolling 2 to start)?

Sprinting is alactic (meaning there is no production of lactic acid), type IIB muscle fibre work, with the energy source being creatine phosphate. The 'life' of a type IIB muscle fibre before it fatigues is 70-150 seconds, depending on how conditioned the athlete is. Through trial and error, 20 sprint strides (with the rolling 2 to start) seems to both come in at around 9 seconds for most non-elite athletes (read: 'normal' folk) AND be the number that most can count and sprint to before serious flagging occurs. 10 x 9 seconds = 90 seconds, building in a buffer for human errors in counting and stopping.
So it's simply an easy way of eliminating the danger of over-running. And faffing around with a timing device when you're on your own doesn't work at all!

What happens if you continue longer than 150 seconds?

If you're still running as fast as you possibly can after 150 seconds, no *matter how conditioned* you are, you're no longer running using the type IIB muscle fibres; they have done their job and have 'downed-tools'. Expired, if you will. Adios - mañana (literally - they'll be ready again tomorrow, but for today, they're 'done').

And of course, if you're still putting in the same effort levels (as fast as you can) you'll be going slower, because you can no longer sprint. Your explosive 'sprint fibres' are exhausted. Honestly, you're kidding yourself if you think you're still sprinting. But if you ARE still at it - if your type IIB fibres have crawled into an exhausted corner and aren't helping - your type IIA fibres <u>must</u> be taking up the slack. These are anaerobic and use glycogen as their primary fuel source, and take <u>from 48 hours and up to a week</u>, depending on the person, to recover. So if you're still running hard, your recovery time is at least twice as long as the type IIB fibres. Which is fine, unless you happen to add intensity before they're recovered. It's very easy to over-train ... and it's very easy not to! Just keep an eye on those accumulating seconds.

 What's happening if I'm 'going backwards' after only 6 or 7 sprints?

Generally, this simply reflects the process of conditioning. You might not be conditioned enough (yet!) to fulfil the POTENTIAL of your type IIB fibres. Nothing to worry about and now you'll be able to objectively watch your progress; monitoring how many sessions it takes to achieve 10 sprints before fatigue sets in, is a clean and honest measurement of progress.

If you ARE a conditioned runner, then did tension creep in? You're all familiar with the TV commentators cry of: "He/she's 'tying up'"?

... tension <u>restricts</u> the fluid, flowing motion of running, and when folk try too hard, they actually disable their innate efficiencies, and speed drops!

With the format of 'sense-drill-compare' hopefully well-entrenched in your mind and body, your route today will unearth hip extension and big toe action. Did you know that the 'hallux' refers to your 'big toe'? Even the word sounds *mighty*, doesn't it? We'll learn more about its true clout further along the trail, but for now - still in 'principles mode' - this section focuses on the treasure of **more speed for no more effort.**

With such a bold statement, we need a control - an objective measure of improvement. Grab two markers - sticks and stones work well; leaves can to a certain extent, provided it's not windy.

The Game's 'rounds' are as follows:

Sprint 1: The Control
Post warm-up; running as fast as you can whilst still holding basic form (upright, tracking width, letting bones move, etc). First marker goes down.

Drill 1:
Jiggling the Nerve Chassis: *https://vimeo.com/245650444*
- Jump up and down on the spot for 1 minute.
- Your feet leave the floor, but only just.
- Everything is relaxed enough for lungs to emit a soft 'huhh-huhh-huhh-huhh' noise through a slightly open mouth.
- It's very hard not to smile during this drill; James failed to keep a straight face! Given no tension is allowed, let the grins come!
- Let your arms dangle by your sides, above your head, anywhere you fancy, and let your wrists and hands jiggle too.
- You might get burning calves before the minute is up - if you do, switch to alternating feet to ease the eccentric loading of the calves, but return to low jumping as soon as your calves allow (very soon your calves should tolerate the full time, and the gazillion reps this drill generates).
- On stopping when the minute is up, you will probably find your whole body is 'fizzing' with circulation and energy ... (the video shows how much Leyton enjoyed it!)

Sprint 2:

After 'Jiggling The Nerve Chassis' complete your second sprint. Did combining a shot of excitement to the central nervous system with a lot of calf-conditioning reps and lovely movement through the feet in the sagittal plane (toe-heel-toe) make you any faster? If you have run further, the first marker, nearest to the start gets picked up. If this is 'slower' then you leave the furthest marker (the first) in place (you get the picture, don't you?!).

Drill 2:

Is There Poo On My Shoe? *vimeo.com/244973570*

- Remember this movement pattern from Level 2? Now it's combined with the Frontal Cog to enhance its effect.
- Standing upright, with feet under hips, aligned so the outside edges are parallel to each other.
- Side bend on the exhale using the weight of the hanging arm, then belly breathe in, swelling the ribcage and adding to the side bend.
- Then shift the entire weight onto the outside leg as you lift the same side foot as the hanging arm, knee falling inwards, working the ankle as hard as possible to view the sole from the little toe side (eversion of foot) - *Is there poo on my shoe?*
- Come to standing again and repeat, but this time shift the weight onto the *inside leg* by lifting the outside foot, allowing the knee to fall *outwards,* and working the ankle as hard as possible to view the sole from the big toe side (inversion of the other foot).
- Repeat with the side bend in the opposite direction.
- Dependent on how long it's taken you to walk back to start the next drill, you can repeat the sequence once more (remember you've only got 3 minutes or so before you start cooling off too much).

Sprint 3:

After 'Is There Poo On My Shoe?' complete your third sprint. Having thoroughly checked both soles from both directions, resetting the frontal plane and opening the foot joints from side to side, are you any faster?

Drill 3:

Codpieces and Nipples - Differentiated: *vimeo.com/244975528*
Having established the transverse plane of motion at Level 4 of the pyramid, we're now exploring its opposition between the spine and the pelvis; although it would seem at first glance to be 'Detail', it is the beginnings of the *Principle* of Hip Extension and the Stride Being Be-Hind Youuuuu:

- Split stance, feet hip distance apart, toes pointing forward, both heels down. Let's start this with your right foot forward.
- Rotate everything left, allowing the movement to travel from the torso into the pelvis, down the leg and into to the ankle and foot. Nipples and 'codpiece' are now pointing towards 10 o'clock (I NEVER need to say more) with toes pointing straight ahead.

- Keeping the rotation in place, lean your weight into your front leg so the rear heel peels up off the ground; your rear leg stays straight, with the foot supinating and making ground contact base of big toe to base of little toe; your forward leg bends and the foot pronates, arches flattening and foot spreading.
- Keeping your 'codpiece' at 10 o'clock, pick up your arms into 'running position' and rotate your nipples to 12 o'clock. Left foot remains supinated, right foot pronated ... and doesn't that feel ... easy? Balanced? Strong? ...
- Did you notice the change and increase in tension through your left hip flexor and across the whole of your abdominal wall, including your obliques and waist muscles?
- Now, without restricting your pelvic position, take your nipples further round to 2 o'clock and notice the extra twist of the torso bringing your codpiece around to 12 o'clock.
- Did you also notice how the tension through your left hip flexor and across your midriff decreased? *If the torso over-rotates, it will drag the pelvis back around from its lovely hip-extending position. The only way you can access massive upper body rotation and full hip extension is if you twist yourself through the middle to the extent you 'wind' yourself. Over-rotated, you might also have felt less stable: instead of one open knee and one locked one, you've now got two 'open' (bent) knees balancing on a rear big toe and only the outside edge of the front foot. No tripods, no full breadth of forefoot anywhere.*

For great spine/pelvis functional opposition, gifting great hip extension and productive action in BOTH feet, *Differentiate your Codpieces and Nipples* folks! *The upper body does rotate, but relative - and counter - to the dominant pelvic rotation:*

- If codpiece is at 10, for simplicity we say nipples are at 12; they're probably at half past 12 but it's too much of a mouthful to say or think on the hoof.
- If codpiece is at 2, nipples are at 12; again, probably more like half past 11, but that spoils my lovely mantra!

So the drill is actually very simple and very quick:

- Split stance
- Rotate whole body towards rear leg; codpiece will be at 2 o'clock if left foot is forward and at 10 o'clock if right foot is forward.
- Front foot is always soft, open and pronating, tripod contact; rear foot is always locked, closed and supinating, only full breadth of forefoot contact.

- Counter-rotate nipples to 12 o'clock noticing the natural holding 'girdle' of fully-loaded abs, and a lengthening load through the trail leg hip flexor.
- Swap legs and repeat in the opposite direction.
- 3-5 differentiations each side can be done quickly and easily.

The more you do this drill, the better your feel becomes of how much *your* body can rotate its upper body against the rotation of the pelvis, before the torso counter-rotation becomes the undesirable dominant force. You're opening your hips to the world of extension, and getting a strong sense of the eccentric loading of the midriff. For a great visual of this, google Jessica Ennis running and watch the diagonal creases in her skin from lower ribs to opposite hip.

Sprint 4:
After Codpieces and Nipples complete your fourth sprint: with rotations newly-differentiated, and rotations in the feet joints considered, were you any faster without *trying* to be? Did you feel more 'midriff torsion'? Did you become more aware of what happens when a 'busy' upper body rotation 'quietens' the pelvis? And were you able to sense when the pelvis held 'command' over the rest of your rotations?

Drill 4:

Oh! Mr Darcy *swoon!/yawn* (a huge favourite - and not just of mine!) *vimeo.com/244975824*

- Stand in split-stance, weight in the front foot - same side arm bent with hand and elbow at shoulder level; rear heel up - same side arm by side.
- Turn your head towards your bent arm, placing the forward cheek on the back of your waiting hand, as if ready to look over your shoulder.
- Staying long in your skeleton *(float your head off your neck)*, breathe in deeply into your belly so that it swells softly, lengthening the space between the base of the sternum and the pubic bone, extending the spine.
- As you inhale, push down through the side of the pelvis you've turned away from into the rear toes, pushing them into the ground.
- Simultaneously, squeeze the shoulder blade of the shoulder you're looking over, as if to pull it towards the opposite hip.
- You have *Swooned*
- Or more exactly, you've created a magnificent oppositional twist with the spine rotating with the ribcage, and the pelvis heading off in the opposite direction.

- Pushing down through the straight knee and open ankle into the ground, helps to drive you upwards into your full height and avoids over-arching which would over-load your lower back.
- Encourage the movement to come via the breath; think more about creating the feeling of an 'extended yawn' rather than actively arching backwards, which would be too aggressive.

Anatomy Dog-Leg: As you 'swooned', you were contracting the 'posterior oblique sling' (latissimus dorsi to opposite glutes - a big X across your back) and eccentrically loading the 'anterior oblique sling' (pectorals, external obliques, transverse abdominals to opposite adductors - a big X across your front) as a way of accessing the largest, propulsive muscles. If you're familiar with Thomas Myers' pioneering work described in his book "Anatomy Trains", you were opening the 'front line' in order to get access to more 'back line'. There'll be more about this at level 8 of the pyramid.

- It *definitely* works to imagine yourself swooning into Mr Darcy's arms ... even for the chaps!
- Repeat a couple of times to each side.

Sprint 5:
After 'Oh! Mr Darcy', enjoy your fifth sprint. Apart from the fun of embarrassing yourself in public, did this assist speed? For many, this drill carries great value in terms of 'bang for your buck', and even though runners may roll their eyes at the 'ridiculousness of swooning', I watch them return to it willingly, because of the effortless gains it brought them. They hadn't trained harder to go faster than three minutes previously and they hadn't tried harder (they were already running as fast as they could!). They had simply accessed more reaction from soft tissue responding to joint movement.

BRAIN POWER

From half-way through the session, we start to tap further into the power of the brain. Whilst we know that an action requires brain output, a 'thought' also produces a measurable 'output' (all proper science; a great resource if you're interested in how brains work is the Neuro Orthopaedic Institute, NOI at *noigroup.com*). So, from 'woken-up bodies' we start to supplement with brain-power.

> OUR BRAIN IS THE INVISIBLE WIZARD, WITH THE STRUCTURAL ARCHITECTURE OF OUR BODY PRODUCING THE VISIBLE EVIDENCE OF THE MAGIC … WHEN WE START PLUGGING INTO BRAIN-POWER, LIMITATIONS START DISAPPEARING.

The consistent caveat in the second half of The Speed Game - repeating the drills and adding a thought to the sprint - is 'fatigue'. As more fully explained in the earlier anatomy section, if you notice yourself flagging during a sprint, make that your last one for the session. You can still perform the drills as part of the process of mastery and joint rotation optimisation, and you can still run afterwards practising adding the brain power, just don't sprint; keep the run at a comfortable effort level. As your running resilience and fitness improves, you'll be able to execute more sprints (up to a maximum of ten) before fatigue arrives.

Drill 5:
Repeat 'Jiggling The Nerve Chassis'.

Sprint 6:
Harness the effects of Jiggling the Nerve Chassis by adding the 'thought':

> ENERGY <u>RISES</u> THROUGH BONES <u>FALLING</u> WITH GRAVITY …

Noting that it's very cool that bones are the strongest conduits of energy - both literally and figuratively. Remember, you're not *doing* anything, you're letting *"whatever wants to happen with the thought"* do it all. Does anything change?

Dog-Leg: Credit for the concept lies with a Tai Ji teacher from Australia, called Adam Mizner, who after a long session of standing practice, came up with a fabulous kinaesthetic metaphor to the help his students 'get it': "Feel as if the bones are rising up through the melting flesh".

For our running purposes, the words had to be tweaked, but I feel we're still 'talking the same language'.

<u>*Drill 6:*</u>
Repeat **'Is There Poo On My Shoe?'**

<u>*Sprint 7:*</u>
To the body/brain effects of 'Is There Poo On My Shoe?' and continuing rising energy/falling bones, add the 'thought':

TWO POINTS OF CONTACT ...

Base of big toe to base of little toe is what we lever off to access full breadth of foot. Any differences?

Important! Big Toe Alert: big toes seem to come in all shapes and sizes ... and angles. Does yours point straight? Does it seem to want to pull over to your other foot? Or does it want to say hello to the little toe, interfering with your second toe in the process? Is it bent? *Can it bend?* Given the subject of efficient running and a principle being big toe extension, can it lift? We're looking for 60° of big toe extension, *whilst the ball of the foot stays in contact with the ground.* Does one big toe move or point differently to the other?

Your answers will help your journey; awareness of ground contact is the beginning of change, but as mentioned before, this book is not designed to 'fix' you. If either of your big toes looks like it could use some help, please find it; Anatomy in Motion practitioners can unravel the story of how your big toes arrived in their present state and figure out interventions to help. **Your running life can transform when Big Daddy Hallux becomes alive to its potential.**

Drill 7:
Repeat **'Codpieces and Nipples - Differentiated'**

Sprint 8:
To the body/brain effects of 'Codpieces and Nipples', rising energy/falling bones and two points of contact, add the 'thought':

TRAIL LEG

Drill 8:
Repeat **Oh! Mr Darcy! *swoon!/yawn***

Sprint 9:
To the body/brain effects of 'Oh! Mr Darcy', rising energy/falling bones, two points of contact and trail leg, add the 'thought':

LEAVE THE PELVIS BEHIND YOUUUUU!

This penultimate sprint brings us to the fullest potential of hip extension via:
- extension of the thigh bone in the hip socket (trail leg - sagittal plane)
- pelvic drop (falling bones - frontal plane)
- pelvic rotation (leaving the pelvis behind - transverse plane).

The combination of all three planes at the hip, gifts the ideal ground contact from which to harness rising energy for the next stride: two points of forefoot contact in a supinated foot.

 Which brings us to the fulfillment of the Intention Marker: the recoil benefits of hip and big toe extension for effortless speed.

Drill 9:
Free-style!
Choose the drill you feel had the most impact on your body - this stimulates self-discovery and internal sensing through reward!

Sprint 10:
Provided you're conditioned enough to still be sprinting (if you don't know what this statement means, you've missed an important-for-you caveat; nip back to the beginning of Brain Power or the basic anatomy sections of page 221 & 222 for self-preservational clarity) this is the culmination of everything that has gone on before. Your two 'thoughts' are:

space for all toes - you have spent over an hour opening up your body and building more space to access the entire breadth of your foot which generates great potential for ...

recoil ... expansive striding through the free energy of fully loaded elastic tissue recoiling - only possible through the trail foot's grounded, charged contact ... Big Daddy Hallux all the way through to Pinky.

Space ... and Recoil ...

> "MIND IS THE MASTER POWER THAT MOULDS AND MAKES,
> AND MAN IS MIND, AND EVERMORE HE TAKES
> THE TOOL OF THOUGHT, AND, SHAPING WHAT HE WILLS,
> BRINGS FORTH A THOUSAND JOYS, A THOUSAND ILLS:
> HE THINKS IN SECRET, AND IT COMES TO PASS:
> ENVIRONMENT IS BUT HIS LOOKING-GLASS."
> - JAMES ALLEN, 'AS A MAN THINKETH'

For so many, these simple words inspire great movement patterns. Many are surprised to find themselves fastest on their last sprint, when they'd expect to be tiring. Having reached sprint number ten, they may well be tired, but they're also more open and technically more efficient through the physical drills and the mental processes. Their body can occupy more space without effort, and their soft tissue can effortlessly recoil because their movements are freely expansive. It's an exciting, and often revelatory session.

With the WujWum sequence before the walk-into-longer-run warm-up, followed by The Speed Game, a good 60-75 minutes will have passed by now. Give yourself another 15 minutes or so for a gentle recovery trot-to-walk back to base.

LEVEL FIVE SUMMARY CHECK LIST ▲

- Introducing The WujWum and a sequence of sagittal, frontal and transverse and feet pronation/supination end-range of motion WujWums as a prequel to the usual walking warm-up.
- A lovely, long, lubricating, running prelude to the intensive drills.
- The Speed Game:

✔ 'Control' Sprint.
✔ 4 drills to highlight sagittal, frontal and transverse plane joint rotations and the activity of the Posterior Oblique Sling/Back Functional Line:
  - Jiggling The Nerve Chassis
  - Is There Poo On My Shoe?
  - Codpiece and Nipples - Differentiated
  - Oh! Mr Darcy *swoon!/yawn*
  with '9ish second' sprints (22 strides) after each one.
✔ Repeat of each drill, followed by a sprint with a thought:
  - energy <u>rises</u> through bones <u>falling</u> with gravity
  - 2 points of contact
  - trail leg
  - leave the pelvis behind youuuuuu ...
✔ Final drill is 'freestyle'; whichever you felt had the best effect in you body.
✔ Final sprint uses 'space' and 'recoil' as primary thoughts to pull together the now-effective hip extension with an ever-present Big Toe.
✔ 15 minute recovery trot into a final walk back to base.

CONGRATULATIONS!!

All the Principles have now been covered, and what I see as 'The Essentials for Running Efficiency' are in place. You've been building a solid and broad base for your pyramid, and The Detail to come in Part Two will enhance your current understanding, improve your movement proficiency and upgrade your ability to make savvy training schedule decisions. Plenty to look forward to.

With all the Principles now in place, there is often a reactive 'rush' to climb further up the slopes of the pyramid, when what's really needed is a reactive 'pause' to consolidate, *and* enjoy mastering both the drills and the skills of somatic awareness. The process of building running resilience so that the joy of running is there for the taking, requires embedment of movement patterns, of soft tissue strengthening and of acuity in terms of 'reading' your sensory feedback. Think of it as 'never running alone', with these three with you on each running outing: your brain, your body and your sensory awareness. Each one needs attention in order to develop and be capable of layering Detail on top.

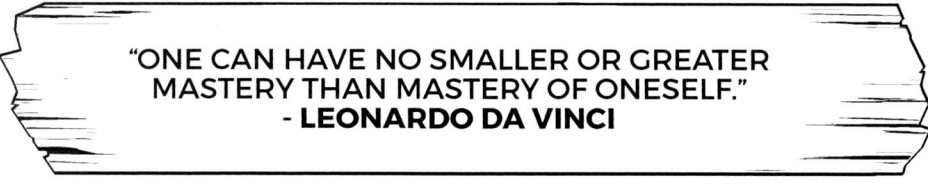

"ONE CAN HAVE NO SMALLER OR GREATER MASTERY THAN MASTERY OF ONESELF."
- **LEONARDO DA VINCI**

As the American motivational speaker Jim Bouchard succinctly put it:

"THE BRIDGE BETWEEN KNOWLEDGE AND SKILL IS PRACTICE. THE BRIDGE BETWEEN SKILL AND MASTERY IS TIME".

Returning to practise this particular level - as for the Hills at Level 3 - the intensity factor of speed requires being mindful about first allowing full recovery of challenged muscle fibres and soft tissue connections. In fact, the first few times you perform this session, I'd suggest not running the next day whilst you give your body a chance to tell you about any areas that may have become over-stressed in the excitement of it all. Once you're conditioned to the added intensity, it's perfectly acceptable to run the next day if you want to, avoiding excesses of either volume or resistance as a sensible precaution.

When planning your running, include sessions to open up your stride regularly - whether up a hill or on the flat - provided your TTF is high enough; in early stages of conditioning either the hill session *or* the speed session once a week can be very productive. For those well-conditioned, one of each every week is quality training.

In addition to enhancing your run training, using the drills you've learned in Part One during everyday life is a wonderful way to improve your general mobility; they are a movement practice you can incorporate into your day easily. Starting the day with **Coffee & Cogs**, or **Waking up with WujWums** would be a great habit to develop, and no-one can stay glum for long if they Jiggle their Nerve Chassis every once in a while. Mix it up and enjoy opening your body in as many directions as it has available. Seek out those invisible lines of tension and erase them regularly and thoroughly; not only will you feel more mobile, but your running will continue to improve in its fluid, relaxed, enjoyability.

efficiently
elegantly upright
endlessly relaxed
effortlessly mobile
elongated into 'space'
emerging with potential for freedom of motion

Liz - a 'coffee and cogs' kind-of-a-girl - reminds us of the benefits of practice and progress:

"Well, the duathlon was a success!! I managed a 1.35 and was aiming for a 1.40 so I was super chuffed!! Also, if I had been in the veteran category (too young by 6 mths) I would have come 4th in my age range. So I'm calling it a resounding success.

I did 'brazen hussy' [aka codpiece & nipples - differentiated] on both runs and see-sawed in the cycle.

I might just have to do another one ...
Thank you :)"

As you continue your running journey and revisit the principles and drills you feel help you most, give yourself goals. Before each run, you should know what you want to get from it; it doesn't need to be big or complicated, and it can be as simple as *noticing more*. It could be to come back feeling energised, having breathed better than last time, to have enjoyed hill efforts ... the list is endless. Clear purpose and greater awareness line the path to running efficiency; and wouldn't it feel great to keep achieving what you set out to, each time you step out?

> "INTENTION DEFINES AND SEPARATES ALL
> OUTCOMES OF MOVEMENT"
> **CHRIS SRITHARAN**

DEPARTING LEVEL FIVE ▲▲▲
RUNNER STATUS: TTF 8 AND RISING
✔ CONFIDENT IN BODY
✔ MINDFULLY CONNECTED
✔ BEST FRIENDS WITH SENSORY FEEDBACK
✔ WUJWUMING ROUTINELY
✔ STRONGER, FITTER, READY FOR DETAIL

THE PYRAMID CLIMB
TO EFFICIENT & JOYOUS RUNNING

CURRENT ALTITUDE: HALF-WAY UP
TERRAIN AHEAD: TASTY

PART TWO
BUILDING DETAIL ABOVE THE MONUMENTAL BASE OF NOW DEEPLY-ROOTED PRINCIPLES

Here you are! Midway, and about to set off on the second half of the trail up the running pyramid. It took as long as it needed to, and - as if I was with you - let's enjoy the view together for a while, review the progress you've made since you started and muse on the *monumental* groundwork you've completed. Did you take the direct route here, or did you take a few unexpected detours?

Maybe you were in a great place to start with, and counted yourself as a curious runner, a budding one or simply one seeking more joy from your running? Let's say you brought an uninjured 'self' to the base of the pyramid, you discovered you could sense stuff straight-away once you applied yourself to the task, you challenged your mind and your body but didn't overcook anything and arrived here having suffered no other setbacks in your life, whether in work, love or health. Marvellous, lucky you!

After a couple of weeks playing with sagittal and then adding frontal plane movement, you probably arrived at hill drills a month after you started, without your calves even squeaking. You added rotations the following week and sneaked in a speed session six weeks after you first put your head on right. Then you relaxed and enjoyed yourself for a while, mastering movement using all three planes of motion both globally and at each joint (apart from the knee and the ankle, which *should* only move in two and a single plane respectively!), strengthening and opening your body out with either a hill session or a speed session each week, reacquainting your nostrils with some vortex-level suction and appreciating that four WujWums a day keeps stiffness at bay.

Today *can* be three months from when you launched your efficiency project, but it probably shouldn't be earlier. You need a sense of being able to *add* detail to the 'big picture' you've been evolving internally, without losing the integrity of the foundations.

On the flip side, there's a good chance you bought this map book *because* of a cycle of injuries, repetitive strains or simply 'not getting anywhere' with your running. Your starting TTF might even have been as low as 1, so let's use that as an example.

Back then, you couldn't even walk without feeling your pain or restriction, so you spent a week just walking and 'topping and tailing' - getting your head on right and waking up ankles you had *no idea* were so immobile. You felt better as the day wore on, but you could still feel the problem as soon as you got out of bed the following day. You added just the drills of Level 2 and brought some weight shift to your movement patterns. After another week of sagittal *and* frontal plane mobility, your walking and waking states improved enough that you felt safe complementing them with the transverse cog of Level 5. You were now enjoying the walking time you'd spent running prior to your injuries, and were noticing how good your internal radar was becoming. You'd made friends with your mate, Sensory Feedback, and felt ready to add some strengthening and larger movements; on a step at home and when you came across hills on your walks you played with the glute loads of Level 3. Your body really enjoyed absorbing the effects of these, and as a way of testing your body's resilience to the landing loads of running, you added Jiggling the Nerve Chassis (Level 5) to your daily drills the following week. Initially, you could only manage a few seconds before your calves screamed for mercy (thank goodness you hadn't tried a run yet!), but by persisting - little and often through each day - you were soon able to perform the drill with no ill effect for the full minute with both feet jumping at the same time.

Over a period of six weeks, you'd introduced your body to all three planes of motion, bedded them in over miles of walking, improved your somatic awareness, strengthened those muscles you would be using for running later and had taken control. When you attempted the full session of Level 1 at the beginning of the seventh week, the pain you remembered didn't happen. Huzzah. You had started your own healing journey and were now off and running, literally.

Aware that 'Route A' - from the first Principle to the first Detail - would probably take three months, you had a hunch to take it more slowly than that, and listened patiently to exactly what your body was telling you each day, acting on the information accordingly. Confident in your sensing, you took your daily cogs to WujWum level so that your body could begin feeling for the elastic recoil that would assist running efficiency in due course.

You covered Hills with triumphant success three months after the start of your journey, and with human nature being what it is, totally abandoned the TTF table in your eagerness to get to Speed. You'd done so well with Hills that you felt quite sure your body was up to a bit of sprinting a fortnight later. You felt 'something dodgy' on Sprint 4 when you were *'trying to push your pelvis back'*; you ignored Sensory Feedback, failed to ease off before disaster struck and instead, pushed for not one but *two more sprints* before your body then stopped you. Oh no!

With emotions running high, you threw all your toys out of the cot, drank a few beers, expended the energy surrounding your frustrations with some serious venting to whoever would listen, and wallowed in a puddle of misery for a while. 14 weeks into your pyramid, you felt you'd blown it. You hadn't of course; it was a 'just' a setback and all part of the journey of self-discovery.

Once you'd dusted yourself off, you sat down with the trail guide and re-read *The Beginning*. With hindsight and the benefit of a new day, you could see the reasons for the upset soft tissue were its TTF of 6 which simply couldn't cope with the opening of the stride at that intensity, *and* not realising that you'd fallen into the use of old, unhelpful, *'doing'* vocabulary.

Back on track, brain re-engaged, you guided yourself to where you were last comfortable, *and stayed there awhile.* As it turned out, re-tracing your steps didn't take as long as the first time, and six months after you first began taking control (read: relying on yourself) you were ready for the challenge of Speed. This time you *knew* you were TTF 8 and you let things happen within your body. It was a magical session, parked for posterity in your memory banks as a Personal Success.

What took one person six weeks to achieve might take another six months and *it doesn't matter.* In fact, not only does it not matter, *of course* the timelines are so disparate! Life is *messy*. Running is *messy*. Messy *is* Life and Life is Good so even if you don't think that

"THE FULLNESS OF LIFE IS INCUBATED IN ITS MESSY PLACES"
- AMY DICKINSON, AMERICAN COLUMNIST

Messy is Good, it is what it is and Messy is Everywhere. Deal with it by *"making more use of the feedback provided by your senses ..."* (I wonder if the amazing Mr Doidge needs a running session ...?).

In addition to completing the first five pyramid levels, you need time to amortise all the physical challenges and mental connections of Part One. There's every scenario possible between Route A and B and there'd even be a Route C if I laboured the point, so to avoid that, let's say you're likely to be ready for the first 'Detail' somewhere between 3 and 9 months into your efficient running journey. If it seems to be taking longer, you probably need to seek help either in a clinic environment, or with one of our PFM coaches. Now that we have global communication at our finger-tips, you could even just ask me if you have a question about your progress. *Helpful* is my middle name ...

You've been building and developing your running efficiency at your own pace and it looks and feels Absolutely Right for you. You've applied consideration to where your body parts are in space as you move, where you feel free and where you don't, what feels better and what doesn't. You've connected your Big Toes to your Little Toes, your feet to your skull and your brain to everything, including what may or may not be on your feet. You've taken control and you're mixing up your sessions so you avoid the pitfalls of 'same stride, same terrain, same efforts'. You don't yet know what's at the top, but with the journey so far having been productive and enjoyable because *you're* holding the reins - regardless of any frustrating hiccups along the way - you're keen to continue exploring. Anticipation is in the air ... let's trot on, and recce the lay of the land immediately surrounding this vantage point.

"MASTERY IS IN THE REACHING, NOT IN THE ARRIVING".
SARAH LEWIS, AUTHOR

So what *is* this 'detail' that keeps getting mentioned? Happily, it's not 'detail' as in 'the nitty-gritty of form inefficiencies', since that sounds quite tiresome, and could even come across as rather more dictatorial than is healthy in discussions relating to human movement.

Anatomy Dog-Leg: 'keto', or ketogenic diet, is a very low-carb diet, designed specifically to result in ketosis. It's similar to other strict low-carb regimes like the Atkins diet or LCHF (low carb, high fat). On a keto diet your body switches its fuel supply to run almost entirely on the nigh-on unlimited supplies of fat.
'Carbs' or carbohydrates are foods full of sugar and starch, and include foods like bread, pasta, rice and potatoes. Traditionally, 'carb-loading' has been considered ideal pre-event nutrition for runners to increase glucose levels. The nutrition world seems to be changing ...

This detail is more the layering of relish on a lettuce leaf if you eat 'keto', or maybe in a club sandwich if you're into carbs. You've got the basics - say some baked ham and cheese - but what about some tomato next? We need some moisture to keep the flow going, and some crunch to get our teeth into - cucumber, anyone? My mouth is watering because I know what's coming. It might be the quietest one, but the first Detail is a show-stopper of a level.

If you haven't scanned back through the pages for a while, ideal preparation before launching further along the trail, is a quick glance through Levels 1-5, to remind yourself of all the aspects of movement you've been consolidating in your body - sagittal, frontal and transverse plane - how to find them, self-cue them and sense them. And watch the WujWum video drills again. I commonly find runners doing 'made-up' drills; they're doing what 'they think' it was, but what they remember as the drill is nothing like what they were originally shown!

REMEMBER THAT WHEN MOVEMENTS ARE **RE**AWAKENED IN THE BODY, **RE**INFORCEMENT IS **RE**QUIRED FOR THEM TO **RE**MAIN THERE. **RE**PETITION IS THE MASTER OF **RE**TAINMENT.

LEVEL SIX
THE SILENT, NON-SOGGY CUPPA

LEVEL SIX CONTENTS

Tasty Detail 1: Cadence 247
Checkpoint Six 251
Tasty Detail 2: Are you a soggy runner? 258
Tasty Detail 3: Discovering your Non-Soggy Paces 263
Tasty Detail 4: Collecting data with a MAFA 267
Checkpoint Six Noticeboards:
    Checkpoint Six Summary 272
    Your Energy Bucket 273